A History of the Townships

of Rock County, Wisconsin

Clark Kidder

Volume Six

Townships of Rock, Spring Valley, Turtle, and Union

Pleasant Journeys,

Clark Kidder

First Edition

Updated June 22, 2015

© 2014-2015 by Clark Kidder

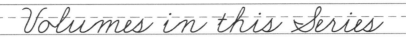

Volumes in this Series

Your Help is Requested!

This book is a work in progress. If you have any Rock County rural school photographs (interior or exterior) or any histories, memories, items (bells, etc.) I would be interested in receiving copies (scans, prints) to include in future editions of this book.

Even if you have a better quality version of a photo already used in this book I'd be interested as several photos were scanned from newspapers or photocopies and are not as clear as they could be. Scanning photos at 300 dpi in JPEG is usually sufficient. Please contact me via email at cokidder@hotmail.com.

Dedication

I'm dedicating this book to two teachers that had a tremendous impact on my life:

Mildred F. (Kidder) Yahnke

Mildred was my aunt and resided in Milton, WI. After teaching at Kidder, Oakdale, and North Milton one-rooms schools and Wilson School in Janesville, she became Rock County Supervising Teacher from 1954-1964. She and her husband Walter had no children of their own, but enjoyed spending time with their many nieces, nephews, and the countless kids that filled the classrooms where she taught.

Mildred encouraged me to start compiling our family's genealogy when I was yet a teenager – a natural extension of my early fascination with research and writing. She and Walter took my brother and I on day trips to places like Circus World Museum in Baraboo, WI, among others.

Geraldine "Gerry" B. Anderson

Gerry Anderson was my kindergarten teacher at Milton West Elementary School. She used to bring her students on field trips to our farm in Milton Township. Gerry was my mentor. She and I remained friends and spoke often until her passing. She was such a kind woman, always full of childlike enthusiasm.

Table of Contents

Preface

I grew up on a farm adjacent to the Rock River one-room school in Milton Township. My grandfather, Earl Kidder, sold the school board an acre of land for the creation of a ball diamond. The school closed before I was old enough to attend it, but as a youngster I often climbed the wooden style that was built over the wire fence surrounding the ball diamond and would go visit the Loren Moore family that purchased the school building after it closed and made it their home. This, and the fact that my aunt, Mildred (Kidder) Yahnke would often reminisce about her days of teaching in the Kidder, Oakdale, and North Milton one-room schools is the reason I have always had an interest in the subject.

When I decided to write the history of Rock County's rural schools I had no idea there was once nearly 160 of them! Despite the immense task of gathering material on all these schools, the process of the process of doing so has been a very enjoyable one. I have had the pleasure of meeting and interviewing former one-room school teachers and pupils, paging through ancient record books kept by the schools, etc.

I've arranged each township in Rock County alphabetically and each school alphabetically within each township. A Rock County School District map dated June 1938 was utilized and overlayed on a 1917 Rock County Atlas and appears at the beginning of each township chapter. Each school is lettered A-Z on these maps based on the order they fell in geographically from North to South.

Acknowledgments

A book such as this would not be possible without the assistance of others. I would like to thank the Rock County Historical Society in Janesville, WI; the Luther Valley Historical Society in Footville, WI; the Milton Historical Society in Milton, WI; the Clinton Community Historical Society in Clinton, WI; the Beloit Historical Society in Beloit, WI; the Irvin L. Young Memorial Library in Whitewater, WI; the staff (especially Nancy Mulhern) at the Wisconsin Historical Society in Madison. Special thanks to Chad Dudzek for all his hard work proofreading the book as well as formatting it for both the Kindle and print editions. Many thanks as well to the countless individuals that took the time to share their memories and photos.

Introduction

Provisions for a school system in what would later become the State of Wisconsin were first made under the Ordinance of 1787, which stated that religion, morality, and knowledge being necessary to good government and happiness of mankind, schools and the means of education shall forever be encouraged. The Ordinance stated that section number sixteen of every township should be reserved for the maintenance of public schools within the said township. As early as 1803, when applications for land grants were made for schools, Congress usually granted them this "School Section" as it came to be known. In 1825 Congress passed a law granting the sixteenth section of each township for school purposes. This was later adopted as a part of the Wisconsin State Constitution in 1848.

The land that was to later become Rock County, Wisconsin was then located in Michigan Territory. The Territory law stipulated that each township should have the responsibility of examining teachers and visiting schools. The cost of building the school was to come from district taxes on property, but it could be paid in labor or materials in lieu of money. If other monies were insufficient, a rate-bill tax could be levied on the parents in proportion to the number of children they had in school. Parents were required to contribute wood for fuel, again based on the number of children in school. The cost of teaching indigent children was to come from general property tax.

As soon as twenty electors would reside in a surveyed township, they would elect a board of three commissioners, holding office three years, to establish districts, to apply the proceeds of the leases of school lands (from Section 16 of each township) to the payment of teachers wants and to call school meetings. In 1839 the law was revised and read, ". . . there shall be elected annually at the town meeting five persons to be inspectors of the common schools in the town. They shall appoint the teachers and visit the several schools in their respective towns quarterly or oftener, if by them deemed expedient." It also provided each district should elect three school trustees (a director, clerk and treasurer), holding office one year, to locate a school house, hire teachers for at least three months in a year and levy taxes for the support of the school. Thus while the town was the unit of civil administration, the school district became the unit for control of the school – the board consisting of members of families that resided in each school's district. The districts were essentially not public school districts, but private.

It was not until 1875 that women were allowed to hold any of these positions. Wisconsin Statute (Section 513) read, "Every woman of twenty-one years of age and upward may be elected or appointed as director, treasurer or clerk of a school district, director or secretary of a town board under the township system; member of a board of education in cities, or county superintendent." Regardless, women did not begin holding such positions until many, many years later. For instance, in District #4 of Johnstown Township in Rock County it was not until July 9, 1934 that Mrs. Mary Pitt was elected clerk.

Each district was often no larger than four square miles, with the school located in the center of the district. The reason for the small size of the district was so no child would have to walk farther than two miles to school. There were, of course, exceptions to this rule.

The earliest schools in Rock County were constructed of log or stone in the 1830's by the hardy pioneers that made their way into our area from cities and states to the east. These early schools did not have a curriculum they adhered to. In fact, instruction was often given in farm homes – not in an official schoolhouse. The length of the school year in the early years often consisted of just a three-month winter term. Later, spring and fall terms were added, but it was not until 1885 that the state of Wisconsin mandated that school be held for at least six months of the year, and that children between the ages of seven and fifteen attend school for at least twelve weeks. Anyone between the ages of 4 and 20 could attend school, regardless of race, gender, or nationality.

During the 1850's the log schools began to be replaced by frame structures, many in the neoclassical style of architecture. Brick was occasionally used in the construction of schools, but most were frame structures.

It was customary for a man to teach during the winter months as many of the students were large and older (often unruly) males kept home to work on the family farm during the spring and summer months. Parents assumed (even as late as the mid twentieth century) that their sons would take over the family farm or establish one of their own – that daughters would become farm wives and would not go on to college; therefore there was no need for 'book learnin.'

Women taught the summer terms as they consisted of smaller more ruly (mostly female) children not kept home to help on the farm.

It was common for teachers to board with the various families in the district their school was located in and the cost of boarding was most often incorporated into their teacher's contract for each school. They would stay for a week or two and then move on to a new family. This practice was customary until automobiles became popular and teachers could make a timely trip to school from their homes in nearby cities.

A law was passed in 1848 creating a town superintendent position; however, the superintendents often lacked in qualification for performing their duties, such as selecting suitable teachers and supervising classrooms. A movement began in 1855 to abolish the town superintendent position and create a county superintendent position. As a result on April 11, 1861, an act to create the office of County Superintendent of Schools was passed:

> "The People of the State of Wisconsin, represented in Senate and Assembly, do enact as follows:
>
> SECTION 1. There shall be chosen at the general election held on the Tuesday next succeeding the first Monday in November, of the year 1861, and biennially thereafter, a county superintendent of schools for each county of the state."

By January, 1862, fifty-four county superintendents were elected by the people of Wisconsin. The superintendent's salary was set at a minimum of $400.00 per year. Rock County created two county school districts, with the west half being District #1 and the east half being District #2. Each half had its own County Superintendent.

O. D. ANTISDEL
County Supt. of Schools.

Orley D. Antisdel. He served as Rock County Superintendent of Schools from 1903-1923. Source: 1917 Rock County Atlas/Library of Congress

The County Superintendents were to examine and certify teachers, perform general inspections of the schools (condemning any deemed unfit), arrange for the construction of new schoolhouses when required, oversee the formation of teachers' associations, organize and conduct at least one institute annually (introducing the best methods of instruction in the schools, and advise school boards on various legal matters such as ventilation of school buildings. The position was held by men in Wisconsin until 1875.

After the county superintendent position was established the power for certification of teachers was transferred from the township superintendents to the county superintendent. Three grades of certificates were created and examinations were to be given on moral character, learning and ability to teach. The lowest, or third grade certificate, required passing grades in orthoepy, orthography, reading, penmanship, intellectual and written arithmetic, primary grammar, and geography; for a second grade certificate grammatical analysis, physiology, physical geography, elementary algebra, United States history, and theory and practice of teaching. The top, or first grade certificate, added to these higher algebra, geometry, and natural philosophy.

A third or second grade certificate was good for one year and a first grade for two years. All were limited to the county in which the certificate was issued.

In 1868 a state board of examiners was created with power to issue certificates good in any county. Eventually this form of certificate was extended to five years, and the highest was good for the life of the holder.

By 1915 a County Supervising Teacher position was established as it became impossible for the County Superintendent to adequately visit and administer at the 100 plus rural schools in each county. The supervising teacher could show up unannounced at the schools. They were also responsible for working with school boards and providing support in general for the teachers.

State legislators passed a bill in 1857 to create a system of Normal Schools to train teachers at. Many Rock County teachers, including this author's aunt Mildred (Kidder) Yahnke, were trained at the Normal School in Whitewater, Wisconsin. It opened in September, 1868 and was the second such school to open in the state (the first was in Platteville in 1866).

In 1899 the legislature passed an act which "declared that the county board in any county in which a state normal school is not located was authorized to appropriate money for the organization, equipment, and maintenance of a county training school for teachers of the common schools." Just such a school was begun in Janesville on September 11, 1911 and operated until 1933.

MISS SADIE CLAPP
County Supt. Assistant.

Miss Sadie Clapp. She was Deputy Superintendent of Schools in Rock County in 1913 and in 1915 became the first Rock County Supervising Teacher. Source: 1917 Rock County Atlas/Library of Congress

In 1913, the legislature passed a law authorizing any school board with responsibility for a high school, and in a county where there was no normal school, to offer a teacher training course. By 1924, twenty-nine high schools offered organized teacher training courses.

By the 1960's, all of Wisconsin's county normal schools closed when elementary school teachers were required to have four years of preparation rather than the two years previously required in normal schools. Because of this, many one-room school teachers with only two years' preparation attended summer schools at four-year colleges and universities to complete their bachelor's degrees in order to meet the four years of preparation requirement.

A Teacher's Third Grade Certificate presented to Jennie E. Kidder in Milton on March 31, 1881 and signed by William Jones, Rock County Superintendent of Schools, Dist. No. 2. Jennie was a great-great aunt of the author. Courtesy of the author.

Many Rock County teachers attended this Normal School in Whitewater, Wisconsin for teacher training. It opened in September, 1868. Courtesy of the author.

Many teachers began teaching when only nineteen years old. It was common for them to teach their younger siblings if they secured a job at the school in their district after graduation. Many of the boys in the class would tower over the heads of their young teachers.

It was uncommon for a female teacher to teach more than a couple years for a variety of reasons. The profession was considered to be a temporary one due to the prevailing belief that a woman's place was in the home and should she not continue teaching after marriage. Sarah May (Waite) Hartshorn taught school for a short time in 1903 at Belding School in Rock County. When she taught school it wasn't proper for young women to make a living for themselves if they didn't have to, so her father decided it was best to collect her teacher's pay and returned it to her when she was married.

Teachers were sometimes let go after disputes with board members, parents, or because of their inability to keep the children under control.

In 1907 the state legislature enacted a new compulsory attendance law. This stated that children between the ages of 7 and 14 must attend some public, parochial or private school for six months if in town and villages, and eight months if in cities. All children between the ages of 14 and 16 must attend at the same time, unless granted a permit to work by some judge, factory inspector, etc. They must attend regularly twenty days each school month, with an exception to be made in the case of physical or mental deficiency.

The uneven distribution of our rural school children according to land valuation throughout the state made the educational facilities quite unsatisfactory. Section 5 of state law stated that money raised for school purposes should be distributed to the towns and cities of the state according to the number of children between the ages of four and twenty years.

In 1927 an equalization law was passed which attempted to correct this fault. Districts not having a valuation of $250,000 according to the law would receive aid from the state while those having $250,000 or over would receive only the $250 per teacher from the state and $250 per teacher from county.

The discrepancy in pay between male and female teachers was prevalent from the earliest years until well into the 20th Century. It was presumed that a man needed the higher pay to support his family whereas the woman was simply working for herself until she was married.

The development of school libraries was very slow, especially in rural schools. All laws for libraries were repealed at the time of the Civil War. In 1921 the sum of $20.00 per pupil was made available for school libraries. The first organized movement to develop reading circles in the state was started about this time. In 1923-1924 more than 190,000 children and 8,500 teachers were given recognition for their reading circle work. A Traveling Library System and supplementary texts was made available to schools of Rock County for a minimal fee.

It was not until 1919 that all school districts were asked to name each school at the request of O. D. Antisdel – Rock County Superintendent of Schools. Prior to this the schools were simply given the name of the district they were in, i.e. District #4 School, etc.

Poor lighting was often an issue in the early schools. Teachers would often stand by a window while reading aloud to the class and students would scoot their desks as close to a window as possible. As electricity made its way into the rural areas of Rock County in the 1930's, many (not all), of the rural schools upgraded from the natural light and the kerosene and gas lamps utilized for decades prior.

Further modernization of the schools occurred during the Great Depression of the 1930's as part of the Works Progress Administration (WPA) – established during President Roosevelt's term in office. People in the community were paid to put basements under many of Rock County's rural schools. This author's grandfather,

Earl D. Kidder, was part of a work crew that dug a basement under the Oakdale School in Milton Township during this time.

As the students made their way down dirt roads and across fields on their way to and from school it provided them a course in nature study that their counterparts in the city could only read about in textbooks.

There was bullying, much as there is today, but it was dealt with quickly. If a child acted up at school the teacher paid a visit to the child's parents almost immediately and the issue was swiftly dealt with. Because the teachers often boarded with families it afforded them the opportunity to get to know each family in their district intimately. The close interaction of the teacher with the parents and pupils in each district made it possible to achieve the goal of providing that exceptional education.

Children in all eight grades studied together and played together and in doing so developed a respect for each other and for their community that is so often lacking in larger schools. The children attending country schools developed a keen sense of place, of pride. The importance of a good education was instilled in them from an early age and they found a great security from the close-knit community of farm families that comprised each township school district.

Teachers genuinely cared about their students and poured their heart and soul into giving them the best education they possibly could. Children looked forward to, and indeed, considered it an honor, to be assigned the various duties that needed to be performed on a daily basis to maintain the school, such as starting the morning fire, carrying in wood for the stove, raising the flag, carrying buckets of water from a nearby farm or pump house, clapping the chalk out of erasers, and cleaning the chalkboard.

Two boys pumping water to bring back to their one-room school in Wisconsin circa 1935.
Used with permission of the State Historical Society of Wisconsin/Image 102617.

Many former pupils have both told me and have written about how their fondest memories of attending a rural school involved the yearly Christmas program. They would begin practicing just after Thanksgiving. Each child would have a speaking role and over the eight year period children attended their rural school they became comfortable at speaking in front of an audience because of it. This set the stage for them to excel in jobs many of them would have as adults that required them to speak to groups of people.

Many other fond memories involve the annual Play Days that were held in which students and parents alike all came together from schools located within each township to compete for ribbons in softball (Kitten ball), volleyball, horseshoes, etc. Champions from each township would then go on to compete at the annual county-wide Play Day held at a place such as the Rock County Fairgrounds. The very first Play Day was held in Magnolia Township in the spring of 1920.

These country schools were much more than just learning institutions, they were often the center of their community, indeed often defined their community. In the early days the school building often served as the meeting place for religious congregations until members could erect their own building. Other uses often included political meetings, elections, or club and lodge gatherings.

On June 10, 1964, an act to repeal all statues from 39.05 to 39.20 referring to the County Superintendent of Schools was passed in Wisconsin. The greatest impact on the Wisconsin school system occurred with the passage of a bill making it mandatory that all school districts become a part of a larger district operating a high school.

With the great number of small rural districts in the state, it was natural there would be some opposition to the new law. To comply with the law, county school committees were formed, hearings held and school consolidations affected. With improved roads and transportation, the one or two-room school was no longer needed to fulfill the educational needs of the community. This need was met by providing educational opportunities in large multi-roomed schools, with the best in heating, lighting and new equipment.

Play Day ribbons for Avon Township's Play Day on May 27, 1925. Courtesy of Brodhead Historical Society.

The American Association of School Administrators were in support of consolidation decades earlier, but seemed to acknowledge the important role the community played. In a 1939 document, they stated:

"Keep the schools and the government of the schools close to the people, so that the citizens generally, including the parents and taxpayers, may know what their schools are doing, and may have an effective voice in the school program . . . The relationship of the schools to the natural community and the closeness of the school to the people are of first-rate educational significance and are not to be sacrificed in the interest of 'efficiency.' If such a sacrifice is made to establish economical districts, we will find in a generation that something of deep significance which money cannot buy has been destroyed."

The 1964-1965 annual report on Rock County Public Schools sums it up well: "There was some unidentified togetherness that has not been captured by the new consolidated schools."

The one-room school, one of the most iconic symbols in America, quickly disappeared from Rock County's rural landscape. The youngest of the pupils that attended one are now in their sixties and just a handful of teachers that taught in them still survive.

Many of the school buildings themselves took on new lives as homes. Many were moved to nearby farms and used as a garage or granary. A couple of them, such as the Dougan School and Frances Wilder School, now serve as museums.

Their legacy lives on in the pupils and teachers still living that were fortunate enough to have attended them, and perhaps indirectly, in their descendants of these pupils and teachers as well.

Bibliography

Doudna, Edgar G. *The Making of Our Wisconsin Schools 1848-1948*, reprinted from the January, 1948 Wisconsin Journal of Education, 32 pgs.

Jorgenson, Lloyd P. *The Founding of Public Education in Wisconsin*. Madison, WI: State Historical Society of Wisconsin, 1956.

Patzer, Conrad E. *Public Education in Wisconsin*. Madison, WI. State Superintendent's Office, 1924.

Rye, Mrs. Theodore and Broege, Mrs. W. Charles, et al. *Bradford History*, 1976.

Smith, Alice E. *The History of Wisconsin: From Exploration to Statehood (Vol. 2)*. Madison: State Historical Society of Wisconsin, 1973.

Upson, Donald E. *Rock County Public Schools, 1964 – 1965*. Janesville, WI, 1965.

School Daze

Still sits the school-house by the road,
A ragged beggar sunning;
Around it still the sumacs grow,
And blackberry vines are running.

Within, the master's desk is seen,
Deep-scarred by raps official;
The warping floor, the battered seats,
The jack-knife's carved initial;

The charcoal frescoes on its wall;
Its door's worn sill, betraying
The feet that, creeping slow to school,
Went storming out to playing!

Long years ago a winter sun
Shone over it at setting;
Lit up its western window-panes,
And low eaves' icy fretting.

- John Greenleaf Whittier (1807-1892)

History and Graduates of the Rock County Rural Normal School

<u>1911 – 1933</u>

The Rock County Normal School was established in September 1911 on the third floor of Janesville's first free high school building, which opened to students in May 1859. It was located at Third (now Holmes) Street and Wisconsin in what is now Jefferson Park. When a new high school was built and opened in 1895, the old high school was renamed Jefferson School and served elementary grades.

" . . . Prior to this there had been no other institution in the county to train teachers for teaching positions in the 150 rural schools.

On May 11, 1911 the Van Pool Brothers received the contract from the Rock County Board of Supervisors to remodel the third floor of the old Jefferson School for the Rock County Teachers' Training School. In 1928 a survey of the building by the State Department of Public Instruction termed the building a fire hazard due to its dark corridors, wooden stairways, and inter-connected maze of rooms. So, during the Great Depression, with an oversupply of teachers, the increase in case of transportation, and the proximity to the Whitewater and Green County Normal Schools, the Rock County Rural Normal ceased to function.

The once proud structure stood bleak and empty after 1933, being used occasionally by Federal agencies during the depression and the war years. When razing started in January 1947 its only occupants were scores of pigeons. By early May the last stone had been trucked away. One lovely house, the Bliss home on Garfield Ave., was fashioned from the brick, with the balance of them being used for roadbeds and retaining walls along Rock River.

The graduating classes varied in numbers from 14 to 43. During the first approximately ten years, pupils with no high school or some high school experiences, took the two year course. High School graduates enrolled in the one year course. During the entire 22 years of existence about 585 graduated. Principal Frank J. Lowth and Miss Ella Jacobson served as the main instructors during this period. A so called, 'Model or Practice School' in the building was used as a training ground for the perspective teachers with an experienced teacher in charge. Names of teachers recalled who were on the teaching staff were: Florita Luce, Marie Dobson, Mrs. Lee, Beth Palmer, Mrs. Lola Webb, Emma Langworthy, Mrs. Fitzgerald, and Helen Simon. During the last few years the students walked to the Y.M.C.A. located on the third floor of the old Gazette building for their physical education instruction.

Each prospective graduate spent one or two weeks gaining teaching experience by being assigned to a rural school under the guidance of the regular teacher. Then, each fall Mr. Lowth and Miss Jacobson, first driving a horse and buggy, then later a car, visited each new graduate in his school in order to check his proficiency and to be able to recommend a third grade teaching certificate good for three years.

Some of the events of a more pleasing nature were the excursions to the School For The Blind, Janesville Gazette, the Parker Pen, Rock County Mental Institution and Poor Farm, and the State Capitol. Bird watching hikes proved enjoyable, also. There was always a picnic during the first week of school; the early classes going by street car to a site near the present Riverside Park, originally called the Chatauqua grounds. The students, in order to improve their culinary skills, served a dinner to members of the County Board in November.

On Friday afternoons when the Literary Society usually met, each student was required to answer roll call with an appropriate quotation. Programs consisted of debates, declamations, musical selections, and current events. A farewell party was held in the main room in late May; the rooms being gaily decorated with apple blossom boughs, lilacs, and gay streamers. Refreshments followed.

Graduation exercises for about the first ten years were held first in the old Christ Episcopal Church on Court Street, then the main room of the school, followed in later years at the Cargill Methodist Church on West Court Street. It was then that a dinner was held for the alumni which preceded the graduation exercises in the afternoon.

Since the closing of the schools the alumni reunions have met on the second Wednesday of June, usually in the evening, until 1970, when it was held at noon. To date all reunions have been held in Janesville with the following exceptions: Beloit, 1964; Edgerton, 1966; Evansville, 1970; Luther Valley, 1971.

Time marches on and the parade of progress has shown its effect in the educational field with the integration of school districts. Many parents and students have long forgotten what the one-room school was like, or they have never experience that early form of education.

After the closing of the Rural Normal School, the school's records were stored in a room of the old Court House. Later, a localized fire destroyed the records.

Here are the biographies of Mr. Lowth and Miss Jacobson:

Frank J. Lowth

Frank J. Lowth, educator and only principal of the Rock County Rural Normal School, was born January 2, 1872 in Lowell, Dodge County and died September 6, 1949. After serving as a rural and a grammar school teacher, Superintendent of Schools in Walworth, Clinton, and Evansville, he guided the Rock County Rural Normal School during its 22 years of existence. Among his better known textbooks were 'Everyday Problems of the Rural Teacher' and 'The Country Teacher at Work.' He married Maud Francis in 1901. They had three children: Geneva, Lowell, and Jean.

Miss Ella Jacobson

Miss Ella Jacobson, instructor and supervising teacher of the Rock County Rural Normal School for 22 years, was born May 22, 1878 in Sugar Creek Township, Walworth County. She died November 17, 1969 at the age of 91. For 53 years she served as an educator, mostly in Rock and Walworth Counties. The following memorial was read in her honor at our 58th annual reunion, June 10, 1970: 'Dedicated to her profession, to her church, to her family, and dedicated and loyal to us – her students and friends.' ''

(Source: Rock County Rural Normal 1912-1933 Directory-History; Revised Edition 1971. Courtesy of Clinton Community Historical Society.)

The ground that the former Jefferson School and Rock County Normal School occupied is now a neighborhood park called Jefferson Park. An historical marker was dedicated during a neighborhood ceremony at 9:30 am on Sunday, July 4, 2010.

THE JANESVILLE HIGH SCHOOL—JEFFERSON BUILDING.

The Rock County Rural Normal School occupied the third floor of the Jefferson Building Photo Source: Art Work of Rock County by W.H. Parish Publishing Co. 1893 Courtesy of Hedberg Library, Janesville, WI

Elida Hall posed for this photo on June 9, 1922 – the day she graduated from Rock County Normal School. In the autumn of 1922 she went to Marathon County, Wisconsin to take a position as teacher in a rural school, taking over for her sister Marjorie, who was recently married. Courtesy of Curtis Bochanyin.

RURAL NORMAL SCHOOLS OF WISCONSIN

WHY NOT TEACH IN THE OPEN COUNTRY?

Here you are **offered a chance** that can not be offered between the four walls of a room hemming in a city grade. In such a grade you get the glimpse of only one year of the child's life, but in the country school you have the first eight years of his school life in which to establish those **things that lie at the foundation of efficient living.** Country teaching when well done never narrows the teacher, for all the problems of a world lie before him for solution. The first eight years of a child's life in school under good teaching gives the flavor and quality to his after career. Many a successful man has said, "The things I have found most useful in gaining my success were learned in the first eight years of my school life." In the country school you meet the child who has grown up more or less conscious of a love for the brook, the field, the flower, the sky, and has seen the struggle of life at short range. Incidentally, he has been more or less impressed with the Creator's handiwork as shown in the elemental design of the open country life in its simple beauty born of the closer contact with natural law in its diviner ministrations to human life. The **efficient country teacher has the most wonderful chance** in the world to bring this home to the learning child in such a way that he is very loath to leave it for light and transient reasons. The country child is eager to learn under good teaching. He prizes knowledge and true culture when rightly presented to him as no other child in the world. Successful experience in the country school makes all subsequent phases of teaching in other kinds of school easier than without such experience.

The money returns for such service are constantly increasing so that by the time you are ready for the field you will not feel ashamed of your salary. In some sections even of our own country, they have more than trebled in the past five or six years. By the time you are prepared to enter the service of

6

The page above and the next are from a booklet titled Rural Normal Schools of Wisconsin, General Catalog, 1923-1924. Courtesy of Clinton Community Historical Society.

RURAL NORMAL SCHOOLS OF WISCONSIN

country teaching, the wages will be on a par with the high grade and dignity of the service rendered. The people all over are fast coming to see that investments in good teaching service are far better than money to support jails, court processes, and wars. The belief is rapidly growing everywhere that good teaching under right conditions is the surest remedy for those civic ills that seem ready to overwhelm us with revolutionary methods for the overthrow of our government. The country folk, like their city cousins, are fast looking to good schools as the only lasting remedy for civic diseases and the surest bulwark against the destructive tides of ignorance and false philosophy. They have come to know that the combination of the trained teacher and a good schoolhouse makes for peace as against strife, for thrift as against poverty, for happiness as against misery, and for better living as against the disappointed life.

"Planting Time"

7

The page above and the previous are from a booklet titled Rural Normal Schools of Wisconsin, General Catalog, 1923-1924. Courtesy of Clinton Community Historical Society.

Historical Marker dedicated July 4, 2010 at the site of the former Jefferson School – Rock County Normal School.
Photo by Clark Kidder.

List of Known Graduates of the Rock County Normal School

Class of 1912

Corrine Crandall (Mrs. Arthur Rohweder)
Rachel Ehrlinger
Juliette Finnane (Mrs. John Mulligan)
Sadie Finnane
Emma Foosberg
Elsie Gooch (Mrs. Orrin Cook)
Jennie Haugen (Mrs. Roy Hertzel)
Ruth Hemmingway
Florence McKinnon
Florence Nelson (Mrs. J. C. Johnson)
Ilene Sands (Mrs. V. E. Haberman)
Mabel Synstegard (Mrs. Selmar Thorson)
Cora Thorson (Mrs. Cora Bryant)
Alice Wilder (Mrs. John Willis)

Class of 1913

Esther J. Barnum (Mrs. Roy Arnold)
Harriet Connors
Mary Cullen (Mrs. Walter Saenger)
Irene Decker (Mrs. Jos. Kennedy)
Anna Forton (Mrs. C. Peterson)
Mabel Francis
Florence Bradford (Mrs. H. R. Hale)
Margaret Kelly (Mrs. Elmer Grytdal)
Alice Loofboro (Mrs. Philip Ling)
Edna Loomis
Nellie Maloy (Mrs. Leo Lay)
Florence McCabe (Mrs. Claude Babcock)
Nora McCarthy
Mamie McKewan (Mrs. Kenneth Smith)
Minnie Milbrandt (Mrs. Harold Arneson)
Flora Robinson (Mrs. Frank Heth)
Lydia Sommerfeldt (Mrs. Arthur Furseth)
Margaret Vickerman

Class of 1914

Margaret Arneson (Mrs. Jos. G. Ligman)
Josephine Barrett (Mrs. Reily)
Frances Byrne (Mrs. Andrew Houghton)
Marie Dobson (Mrs. Robt. Robson)
Nellie Hendrickson (Mrs. Nellie Heath)
Vera Irving (Mrs. Geo. L. Ryckman)

Zette Kealy (Sister Mary Aremelle Kealy)
Katherine Knight
Hazel Logan (Mrs. Palmer Gunderson)
Mary Madden
Arice Smith (Mrs. Harry Leng)
Pearle Tremblie (Mrs. Henry Hamilton)
Ruth Tremblie

Class of 1915

Gladys Anderson (Mrs. F. W. Hartman)
Alice Carroll (Mrs. Jos. Murphy)
Hazel Doyle (Mrs. Fred Kores)
Helen Flint (Mrs. Chas. Hackbarth)
Eleanor Fuller (Mrs. W. C. Carell)
Elizabeth Gower (Mrs. Frank Koebler)
Hazel Gower (Mrs. Robt. Kehoe)
Mary Hodge (Mrs. Arthur Martinson)
Florence Horne (Mrs. B. F. Arndt)
Bertha Knutson (Mrs. Jos. Johnson)
Ella Lien (Mrs. Bernie Ellickson)
Mary Agnes Malone
Isabelle Marshall (Mrs. Belle Schmacher)
Evelyn Merlet (Mrs. Geo. Hubert)
Martha Norum (Mrs. Olie Norby)
Lucy Putney (Mrs. Robt. Shumay)
Mamie Strang (Mrs. Stanley Wallace)
Marion Williams

Class of 1916

Grace Caldwall (Mrs. Glenn Barkley)
Marvel Cowdrey (Mrs. Merle Van Galder)
Alice Cullen (Mrs. Alice Finley)
Anna Ford (Mrs. Edw. Casey)
Margaret Donahue (Mrs. Floyd Flaherty)
Marie Fox (Mrs. Frank Farrington)
Myrtle Gower (Mrs. Jas. Stewart)
Marguerite Graham
Grace Gravedale
Mabel Hill (Mrs. Glenn Emerson)
Margaret Holden (Mrs. Russell Weary)
Olive Hupel (Mrs. Olive Hallenbeck)
Ann Kehoe (Mrs. Jas. Fanning)
Alma Kelhofer (Mrs. Samb)

Lydia Maloy (Mrs. John Batker)
Margaret O'Brien
Luella Robinson (Mrs. Paul Huie)
Marie Sullivan (Mrs. Ed. Daley)
Mabel Taylor (Mrs. John Wetmore)
Bertha Thorson (Mrs. Herbert Lee)
Dorothy Van Galder (Mrs. Fred Brummond)
Marie Vickerman (Mrs. A. A. McGinnity)
Ella Vigdahl

Class of 1917

Myrtle Apfel (Mrs. Chas. Clarke)
Mizpah Bennett (Mrs. J. F. Whitford)
Elva Benway (Mrs. Everett Goakey)
Elizabeth Berrett (Mrs. Quin J. Loomis)
Helen Bier (Mrs. Leo Roethle)
Francis Condon (Mrs. Frank Hantke)
Gertrude Condon (Mrs. Gert. Sweeney)
Orpha Coon (Mrs. Alex Hamilton)
Helen Cunningham
Ethel Davis (Mrs. Lewis Sisson)
Marguerite Fanning (Mrs. John Meely)
Rosalia Feirn (Mrs. Edwin Lueck)
Josephine Finnane (Mrs. Merwin Martin)
Susie Fjelsted (Mrs. Raymond Hamilton)
Margaret Ireland (Mrs. Donald Brady)
Genevieve Jacobs (Mrs. Lyle Beard)
Virginia Johnston
Genevieve Kealy (Mrs. Miles Fanning)
Nellie Logan (Mrs. Arthur Harris)
Beulah McCormick (Mrs. Matin Witt)
Agnes McIntyre
Ruth Milligan (Mrs. Bert McCoy)
Ella Rote (Mrs. Ernest Dunbar)
Josephine Sands (Mrs. August Lange)
Ruth Solverson (Mrs. Jas. Jorgenson)
Clara Sorenson (Mrs. Geo. Hood)
Beth Sullivan (Mrs. Duward Cass)
Alma Walters (Mrs. Floyd Chester)
Florence Westby (Mrs. Ralph Sommrud)

Class of 1918

Edna Barrett (Mrs. Wm. Perleberg)
Dora Conlon (Mrs. Bert Higgins)
Florence Conway
Harriet Donnelly (Mrs. Wm. E. Quinn)
Gladys Dunn (Mrs. R. H. Braukhof)
Iva Hollibush (Mrs. Walter Becker)
Irene Jones (Mrs. Leon Pratt)
Bertha Liston (Mrs. Albert Springstead)
Anna McQuire

Bessie Monahan
Erma Nelson (Mrs. Oscar Anderson)
Hannah Stuvengen (Mrs. Orrin Mason)
Orcelia West (Mrs. DeWitt Mac Duffies)
Helen Walters (Mrs. Francis Savage)
Mae White (Mrs. Vern Playter)

Class of 1919

Anna Bier (Mrs. Wm. Lannon)
Bessie Billings (Mrs. Clayton Honeysett)
Thelma Davis (Mrs. Jas. Scobie)
Julia Donahue (Mrs. Bert Wilson)
Myrtle Ehlenfeldt (Mrs. Clifford Vickors)
Josephine Fanning (Mrs. Jerry Easton)
Marie Hanson (Mrs. Clifford Rawlins)
Ida Julseth (Mrs. Harvey Brunsell)
Florence Kehoe (Mrs. E. W. Lueck)
Bertha Lapp (Mrs. Myron Burtness)
Jane Larkin (Mrs. Leo McKewan)
Aileen Manogue
Katherine Maston
Katherine Monahan
Hannah Onsgard (Mrs. Henry Anderson)
Delilah Pember
Ruth Sayre (Mrs. Leslie Bennett)
Harriet Shuman (Mrs. R. L. Anderson)
Helen Simon
Clara Sunby
Kiston Sunby
Mildred Waterman (Mrs. Robt. Gray)
Margaret Wieland (Mrs. David H. MacCulloch)

Class of 1920

Lillian Anderson (Mrs. Stephen C. Swann)
Hazel Behling (Mrs. Ben Green)
Grace Boyle (Mrs. Orville Lamb)
Jessie Crandall
Juliette Finnane
Clara Furseth (Mrs. Merlin Reese)
Marjorie Hefferman (Mrs. Clement Commons)
Hattie Hoag (Mrs. Dan McCarty)
Ella Jacobs (Mrs. Henry Ullman)
Jeanette Johnston
Alice Kelly
Ethel McArthur (Mrs. Morris Van Horn
Regina Mohr (Mrs. Albert Bitter)
Ethel Moore (Mrs. Rainie Danielson)
Mildred Peckham (Mrs. Carl Nelson)
Cecil Popanz (Mrs. Emil Schultz)
Ella Roen (Mrs. Alfred Mahlum)
Dorothy Stewart (Mrs. Russell Mathew)

Cecelia Ryan (Mrs. J. Sylvester Hoben)
Cora Stoney (mrs. Donald Gardner)
Cora Thompson (Mrs. Ray Roberts)
Theresa Trunkhill (Mrs. Thomas L. Spohn)
Loretta Vickerman (Mrs. R. W. McComb)

Class of 1921

Alice V. Bowen
Grace Caldo (Mrs. Howard Henke)
Lucy clark (Mrs. Gilbert Hudlow)
Ethel Cunningham (Mrs. James Feeney)
Florence Day (Mrs. Fred Pratt)
Alice Finnane (Mrs. Jos. Mullowney)
Elida Hall (Mrs. Jack K. Bochanyin)
Lulu D. Hamilton
Helen Henke (Mrs. Geo. Yates)
Burnette Knudson
Carrie Lee (Mrs. C. T. Dore)
Katherine Madden
Agnes Monaghan (Mrs. Hugh McCann)
Gladys Mulcahy (Mrs. Frank Meredith)
Corrine Murwin (Mrs. Lloyd Apfel)
Tessie Sisson (Mrs. Albert Woodstock)
Elsie Troon (Mrs. Harry Saevre)
Helen Van Glader (Mrs. F. H. Randall)
Inez Waters (Mrs. Jay Taylor)
Florence White (Mrs. Wm. Doering)

Class of 1922

Helen Abey (Mrs. Ross Stephenson)
Alma Babler (Mrs. Roy Fenn)
Louise Bartz (Mrs. George Kennedy)
Frances Bell
Mamie Bryant (Mrs. Harold Hunt)
Anna Carlson (Mrs. Lawrence Sterna)
Mary Doubleday (Mrs. Paul Robeson)
Virginia Dwyer
Ella Everill (Mrs. Albert Julian)
Lillian Gray (Mrs. Harry Tucker)
Eva Hamblett (Mrs. A. P. Penkert)
Eleanor Hemming (Mrs. Frank Buckley)
Genevieve Hyland (Mrs. Harold Asperheim)
Amy Johnson (Mrs. Phil Johnson)
Josephine Johnson (Mrs. Herbert Hanson)
Delia Kehoe (Mrs. John Koehl)
Pauline Kelly (Mrs. R. M. Hilgert)
Alice Knutson (Mrs. Andrew File)
Doris Latta (Mrs. Herbert Catlin)
Hazel Lawrence (Mrs. Charles Maloy)
Sarah Mansky
Marion Maxfield (Mrs. Robert Smith)

Frederica McBain (Mrs. C. D. Zdanowicz)
Mary McCann
Dorothy Merrifield (Mrs. Clarence Anderson)
Helen Miller (Mrs. Herman Smith)
Irene Mulcahy (Mrs. Otto Eggen)
Jospehine Nelson (Mrs. Otis Gunnelson)
Verna Schmeling
Lillian Schumacher (Mrs. Lawrence Hanan)
Hilda Simonsen (Mrs. Palmer Johnson)
Doris Sisson (Mrs. Walter Lange)
Ella Stetzel (Mrs. Charles Brown)
Ethel Vogel (Mrs. Lester Foreman)
Mabel Vogel (Mrs. George Smith)
Katherine Wieland (Mrs. Harold Russell)
Florence Wileman (Mrs. M. A. Kelly)
Alma Wobig
Helen Yates (Mrs. Fred Holland)

Class of 1923

Myrtle Anderson (Mrs. Brainard Trigg)
Margaret Bahr (Mrs. Victor G. Wolff)
Esther Bowen (Mrs. A. E. Natenshon)
Dorothea Blank (Mrs. Russell Gower)
Bernice Brigham (Mrs. Clarence Keehn)
Bernice Brown
Laura Bublitz (Mrs. Leonard Carlson)
Ethel Campbell
Ruth Canary (Mrs. Potter Palmer)
Flora Crandall (Mrs. Homer DeLong)
Margaret Davis
Mary Diederich (Mrs. Robert Peckham)
Lucille Gorrell (Mrs. Elmer Lembrich)
Dorothy Higgins (Mrs. Wlater Lentz)
Marie McCue
Ella Murwin (Mrs. Walter Bidwell)
Winifred Nelson (Mrs. Jacob Gempler)
Crystal Patriquen (Mrs. John Rosheisen)
Alice Peterson (Mrs. Alfred Larson)
Jane Ramey
Agnes Reilly
Lillian Roen (Mrs. Norris Slinde)
Mary Ryan
Eva Sharp (Mrs. W. Johannsen)
Cyril Sherwood
Ethel Walker (Mrs. Carl Becker)
Madge Winch (Mrs. Ellwood Shumway)

Class of 1924

Hildur Anderson (Mrs. Orville Worick)
Selma Berkland (Mrs. Paul Hattleback)
Wilma Bublitz

Anise Burchfield (Mrs. Hiram Rindy)
Esther Demrow
Margaret Drew (Mrs. Lee Collins)
Clara Duoss (Mrs. Ralph Rye)
Marguerite Graham
Ora Haas (Mrs. E. Alvin Hepler)
Evelyn Hawkins (Mrs. Glen Rogers)
Bessie Hughes (Mrs. Basil Kauffman)
Ruth James (Mrs. Ivan Whalen)
Elizabeth Lewis (Mrs. Wm. Kennedy)
Ruth Martin
Mildred Monaghan
Alice Nelen (Mrs. Chester Green)
Thelma Nelson (Mrs. Maxwell Gefke)
Winifred Oscar (Mrs. Gayle Hubbard)
Mary Pace (Mrs. Fred Everson)
Eva Parsons
Martina Pfeiffer
Marjorie Ridley (Mrs. W. R. Baker)
Mildred Schuler (Mrs. Stanley Alvstad)
Helen Tabor (Mrs. Harry Roberts)
Edna Trush (Mrs. William Condon)

Class of 1925

Mabel Behling (Mrs. LaVerne Klusmeyer)
Flora Belle Boynton (Mrs. Wm. DeLong)
Fannie Bryant
Carolyn Byers (Mrs. Glen Starr)
Bernice Clarke (Mrs. Orville Grenewalt)
Iolla Belle Cook (Mrs. Chalres Holbrook)
Catherine Fenlon
Mae Guernsey (Mrs. Herbert Jahnke)
Verona Holden (Mrs. Greydon Mabson)
Mabel Horton (Mrs. Wm. Burns)
Iva Mae Janes (Mrs. John Briggs)
Dorothy Knoll (Mrs. Herbert Hoopes)
Harold Knutson
Jeanette Langworthy (Mrs. Louis Kleimenhagen)
Winifred Lynch
Betty MacGowan (Mrs. Eugene Ackerman)
Janet MacGowan (Mrs. Elmer Rumpf)
Mary Montgomery (Mrs. John Burlake)
Carol Murphy (Mrs. Gordon M. Bly)
Thelma Nyman (Mrs. Harold Ronneburg)
Marie O'Leary (Mrs. George Nolan)
Bonnetta Pierce
Fay Stanton
Helen Schumacher (Mrs. Stanley Slagg)
Ann Stevens (Mrs. Ann Geach)
Mildred Storlie (Mrs. Clifford Halverson)
Beulah Wheeler (Mrs. Ollie Seigel)

Class of 1926

Marion Andrews (Mrs. Fred Drafahl)
Bertha Babler (Mrs. Lester Pratt)
Marie Bartz (Mrs. Walter Kutz)
Dorothey Bennett (Mrs. Walter Neils)
Mabel Capron (Mrs. Ivan Nance)
Catherine Carroll (Mrs. Clarence Peters)
Ivy Castater (Mrs. Theodore Miller)
Catherine Clark (Mrs. James Arnold)
Margaret Cutler
Mary Drew (Mrs. Sanford Saevre)
Thelma Garvin
Inez Heyerdahl (Mrs. Owen Gaarder
Agnes Jensen (Mrs. Wilbur Smout)
Ina Johnson (Mrs. Carroll Bly)
Raymond Krogh
Letha McCumber (Mrs. Croy Brewer)
Mary Ellen Masterson (Mrs. Leslie Knopes)
Olga Nielson (Mrs. Charles Curless)
Ann Reilly (Mrs. T. J. Sullivan)
Mabel Ryan
Sylvia Roen (Mrs. James Johnson)
Gladys Olson (Mrs. Wm. McCann)
Neleta Titus
Constance Trotter (Mrs. George Glass)
Ruth Truax (Mrs. John Large)
Edna Waller (Mrs. Ortha Hancock)
Alice Weaver (Mrs. Henry Blackwood)

Class of 1927

Dorothy Albrecht (Mrs. Lloyd Samp)
Dorothy Beeler (Mrs. Vincent Holden)
Evelyn Behling (Mrs. Roy Woodstock)
Harriet Clark
Helen Clark (Mrs. Stanley Fenrick)
Isabelle Crocker (Mrs. Winifed LeFevre)
Esther Duoss (Mrs. Russell Hall)
Evelyn Griffith (Mrs. Kenneth Barriage)
Nina Hanson (Mrs. Leo Dickenson)
Maxine Healy
Alfred Hensel
Edna Jones
Ruth Krause (Mrs. Harvey Welcher)
Beatrice Lamb
Edna Lorts (Mrs. Chester L. Dales)
Marguerite Mahlum (Mrs. Raymond Lindeman)
Lola McCaslin (Mrs. Frank Wilson)
Ralph Noyes
Bertha Odegard (Mrs. Jay Roe)
Gyda Pulson (Mrs. Joseph Mahlum)
Yvette Picus (Mrs. Sam Levy)

Evalyn Rathjen (Mrs. Roy F. Lichtfus)
Eileen Ryan (Mrs. Joseph O'Leary)
Beatrice Schloemer (Mrs. Earl Boylen)
Inez Taylor (Mrs. Maurice Reeder)
Martha Weir (Mrs. Martha Colbert)
Gladys Wiggins (Mrs. Grant Rossiter)

Class of 1928

Anna Abbey (Mrs. John Hall)
Laura Anderson (Mrs. Leslie Eaton)
Hazel Bass
Martha Bick (Mrs. Frank Osborne)
Kathryn Byrne (Mrs. Morris Burns)
Anastacia Finnane
Genevieve Gower (Mrs. Leon Geiger)
Ida Hadley (Mrs. Whilden Hughes)
Violet Hazeltine (Mrs. Russell Westby)
Hyla Jacobson (Mrs. James Kolman)
Margie Kuehn (Mrs. Sam J. Saltzgiver)
Clara Lange (Mrs. Carl Hantke)
Jean Lowth (Mrs. Frank Byers)
Isabel Meyer (Mrs. Chalres Kress)
Dorothy Millard (Mrs. Ralph Balch)
Mabel Mohns (Mrs. Ray Hazeltine)
Evelyn Murwin (Mrs. Harold Young)
Beulah Newman (Mrs. Alfred Schoenrock)
Veronica O'Leary (Mrs. Robert Condon)
Frances Popanz (Mrs. Merlin Francis)
Dorothy Rabyor (Mrs. R. Waite)
Lulu Reimer (Mrs. Arthur Howarth)
Lucille Staley (Mrs. Burgess Behnke)
Leila Simpson (Mrs. William Froh)
Joyce Spencer (Mrs. Donald Tucker)
Neva Stavn (Mrs. A. Hogue)
Florence Tess (Mrs. Richard Olds)
Elanor Tronnes (Mrs. Adolph Iverson)
Anne Young (Mrs. Harold Myrhe)

Class of 1929

Ruth Badger (Mrs. Orville Rowley)
Grace Burns
Nancy Clark (Mrs. Alvin Nelson)
Ruth Collins (Mrs. Ralph Maas)
Dorothy Decker (Mrs. Alvin Burtis)
Crystal Delsrud (Mrs. Clarence Olmstead)
Lillian Dybevik (Mrs. Elmer Tripke)
Mary Ford (Mrs. Alfred Johnson)
Ethel Gordon (Mrs. Harold Martin)
Lorraine Hannewell (Mrs. Herman Lovaas)
Corriene Haugen (Mrs. Emmett Arnold)
Ernest Heyerdahl

Evelyn Hoiberg (Mrs. Melvin Sveom)
Mabel Horan
Mildred Horkey (Mrs. George Rye)
Florence Jellyman (Mrs. Stanley Slightam)
Ella Kammerud (Mrs. Robert McCarville)
Edna Korban (Mrs. Roy Luety)
Frances Lay (Mrs. Wiliam Boudreau)
Gertrude Learn (Mrs. Glen Schindler)
Lorraine Linney
Lillian Lhotok (Mrs. Marvin Hansen)
Catherine McCarhtey (Mrs. Pete Kincaid)
Gladys McCumber (Mrs. A. R. Glick)
Lucille McDonnell (Mrs. Tom Ostby)
Sarah Fern Michael (Mrs. Clifford Hawkins)
Sylvia Olson (Mrs. Tilman Thoreson)
Alice Mitchell (Mrs. Hough)
Agnes Paulson (Mrs. Eugene Scott)
Gladys Roen (Mrs. Raymond Anderson)
Thelma Sisson (Mrs. Byrl Rowley)
Frances Tellifson (Mrs. Fances Patterson)
Gwenith Tim (Mrs. Robert Cullen)
Dorothy Wallin (Mrs. Davidson)
Helen Young (Mrs. Bert Benson)

Class of 1930

Adeline Bergerson (Mrs. Ray Fanning)
Hazel Caldo (Mrs. Othmar Weber)
Rosa Dary (Mrs. John Marks)
Florence Eddy (Mrs. Florence Mayberry)
Astrid Felland
Ruth Flock (Mrs. Leo Bier)
Alice Hannewell (Mrs. Harold Knudson)
Carolyn Hillison (Mrs. Harold Dooley)
Wanda Jensen (Mrs. Wanda Rime)
Alberta Kagel (Mrs. Bernard Perkins)
Bernice Kagel (Mrs. Bernice Collins)
Marion Lyke (Mrs. Ted Lander)
Ruth Mason (Mrs. A. E. Knauf)
Beth Miller (Mrs. Morris Woodworth)
Esther Pahl (Mrs. Marnon Olson)
Minnie Paulson (Mrs. Charles Arnold)
Mary Ryan
Alice Shade
Ruth Schultz (Mrs. Walter Desing)
Kathryn Tracy (Mrs. Ray Swingle)
Hazel Weber (Mrs. Kenton Fowler)
Ruth Young (Mrs. C. L. Asperheim)

Class of 1931

Luella Baars (Mrs. Fred Schultz)
Margaret Burns (Mrs. James Ford)

Vivien Burns (Mrs. Lawrence Krueger)
Chalotte Carmin (Mrs. Chester DeRemer)
Wanda Christiansen (Mrs. Edmund Litel)
Bernette Clark (Mrs. George Martin)
Jeanette Dahl (Mrs. Frank Stritof)
Mlidred Ethan (Mrs. Harry Hanson)
Elsie Felland
Ruth Franklin (Mrs. Lloyd George)
Mary Frusher (Mrs. Phillip DeReamer)
Grace Greenberg
Muriel Higgins (Mrs. Wm. H. Hillmer, Jr.)
Anita Johnson (Mrs. Leroy Finger)
Mildred Klingburg (Mrs. Arthur Olson)
Sophie Larson
Josephine Lipke (Mrs. Claude Darling)
Serene Lokken (Mrs. Robert Turner)
Mildred Marsden (Mrs. Mildred Poffinburger)
Rosalind McBeth (Mrs. T. T. Ramsey)
Agnes McIntyre (Mrs. Harold Falk)
Orpha McLaughlin (Mrs. Raymond Manion)
Doris Medler (Mrs. Floyd Roberts)
Margaret Meier
Ruth Michael (Mrs. Robert Douglas)
Inez Miller (Mrs. Einar Haakenson)
Alice Nelson (Mrs. Bennie Fosdahl)
Leona Nelson (Mrs. Leslie Brunsell)
Kathryn Nettum (Mrs. James Scott)
Bernice Richardson (Mrs. Herman Schultz)
Mabel Rognstad (Mrs. Thomas Tofte)
Helen Sanderman (Mrs. Douglas Haroldson)
Elda Schaffner (Mrs. Leslie Ehrlinger)
Mildred Siggelkow (Mrs. Elmer Fenrick)
Eleanor Spike (Mrs. Charles Carrier)
Avis St. John
Eleanor Stockment (Mrs. Russell Hebb)
Frances Taplin (Mrs. Dwight Clark)
Margaret Tierney (Mrs. James Drew)
Margaret Timm (Mrs. Charles Prieve)
Jeanette Walker (Mrs. Felix Rondeau)
Nina Williams
Letha Williamson (Mrs. Lawrence Warner)

Class of 1932

June Ames (Mrs. Eric Lescohier)
Mildred Anderson (Mrs. Arthur Showers)
Evelyn Ballard (Mrs. Earl Jensen)
Mabel Barnard (Mrs. Vernon Latzke)
Hazel Beck (Mrs. Carl Brehm)
Helen Bergerson (Mrs. Curtiss Hoff)
Doris Broughton (Mrs. Eric Moir)
Anna Brown (Mrs. Raymond Miller)

Sarah Bufton (Mrs. John Lee)
Dorothy Burrows (Mrs. Joseph Zigler)
B. E. Clarity
Gertrude Decker (Mrs. Dale Thompson)
Gladys Drevdahl
Isabel Duoss (Mrs. Edwin Meyers)
Vivian Erickson (Mrs. Henry Motzkau)
Luella Litch (Mrs. Arthur Ames)
Elizabeth Gordon (Mrs. Rodney Hart)
Rosalyn Hanson (Mrs. Donavan Wake)
Gerald Hill
Muriel Hillison (Mrs. Leon Bramble)
Ruth Holm (Mrs. Lawrence Finaness)
Evelyn Howard (Mrs. Walter Albrecht)
Mildred Hull (Mrs. James Hughes)
Edna Kaupanger (Mrs. Henry Sands)
Alice Kitelinger (Mrs. George Mackie)
Dorothy Larson (Mrs. Arthur Wobig)
Evelyn Marquardt (Mrs. Moore Maltpress)
Janette Otteson (Mrs. Halvor Kaupanger)
Olga Ottum
Dorothy Page (Mrs. Harold Hildebrand)
Winifred Priebe (Mrs. Grant Snyder)
Bernice Ransom (Mrs. Edward Hodge)
Anita Reich (Mrs. Gilbert Bentz)
Alice Reppen (Mrs. Olaf Hestness)
Alice Ryan
Irene Scherin (Mrs. Garnett Nobiensky)
Beatrice Smith (Mrs. Wayne Lipke)
Janette Snyder (Mrs. Harold Kohls)
Claire Thurman (Mrs. Andrew Peterson)
Wilva West (Mrs. Edward Henrickson)
Helen Wilke (Mrs. Henry Seward)
Joyce Winkley

Class of 1933

Ruth Allen (Mrs. Arthur Templeton)
Irene Anderson (Mrs. Edward Wallmow)
Olga Aslakson (Mrs. Ben Haakenson)
Colette Bach (Mrs. Matthew Corbett)
Marion Bjerke (Mrs. Marion Weston)
Patricia Brannon (Mrs. Harold Thompson)
Elmina Bumstead (Mrs. George Kelsey)
Irene Cole (Mrs. Maynard Smith)
Ethel Dockhorn (Mrs. Wm. Mullolly)
Virginia Finkh (Mrs. Waldemar Youngquist)
Charlotte Finley (Mrs. Edward Horkan)
Gladys Frank (Mrs. Floyd Frederick)
Carolyn Gesley
Ruth Gesley (Mrs. Ewald Selkurt)
Mary Havens (Mrs. Stuart Decker)

Helen Herbert (Mrs. Roy Baker)
Ethelyn Hield (Mrs. Clifford Roe)
Sarah Higgins (Mrs. Ernest Falk)
Eunice Helmbeck (Mrs. Arnold Ehle)
Margaret Hornburger (Mrs. George MacFarlane)
Eleanor Kaufman (Mrs. Alfred Vien)
Dorothy Kettle (Mrs. LaVerne Laird)
Virginia Kettle (Mrs. Vernon Miller)
Ruth Larson (Mrs. Clayton Thompson)
Karoline Lee (Mrs. Thomas Lawrence)
Carol Linderud (Mrs. Leroy Sundby)
Marion Long (Mrs. Orlin Holm)
Florence Mikkelson (Mrs. Fahs Nielson)
Alice McCarthy
Mary Niman (Mrs. John Reider)
Leona Norby (Mrs. Edward Zepka)
Helen Peterson (Mrs. E. A. Rowe)
Theodora Reenstead (Mrs. Leo Thorson)
Signe Sathre (Mrs. Neil Geske)
Cecelia Riege (Mrs. Clement Fagan)
Rachel Severson (Mrs. Harold Teubert)
Erma Simonson (Mrs. Howard Martinson)
Esther Snyder (Mrs. Neuman Bestul)
Alma Sundt (Mrs. Julian Sornson)
Viola Vigdahl (Mrs. Lee George)
Bernice Wallmer (Mrs. Orin Eidahl)
Mildred Wells (Mrs. Robert Robinson)

Recess Games

Children looked forward to recess time in the olden days as much as they do in modern times. The rural school lot and surrounding terrain often provided hills and streams for sledding or skating. Farm fields were covered with wild flowers, bird nests, and piles of leaves for the children to explore during recess. There were often teeter-totters and swings located on the school lot for the children to play on. In addition, many games were played in the schoolyard during recess, and a description of several of them is given below. When recess was over the teacher would ring the school bell to summon the children back to class. If the children were having an especially good time or didn't particularly care for a substitute teacher they would often purposefully not hear the bell ringing, much to the discontent of the teacher.

Anti-I-Over (Also called Annie-Over, Andy-Over, and Aunti-Over)

This game was played using a rubber ball, at least eight players (four for each side), and a building with a low roof. If the schoolhouse was too high then a garage, woodshed, or pumphoue located on the school lot sufficed.

A player from the "tossing team" throws the ball over the building, yelling "Anti-I-Over." The ball must be tossed in such a way that it bounces at least once on the opposite side of the building's roof. A player on the opposing side "catching team" tries to catch the ball. If the player is successful, the entire catching team runs around to the tossing team's side of the building. The person who caught the ball tries to tag members of the tossing team, either by touching them with the ball, or throwing the ball at them. If the ball touches a member of the tossing team, this person joins the catching team. The game continues with the catching team now becoming the tossing team. The purpose of the game is for one side to capture all the players from the other.

Dodge Ball

Players form two groups. One group forms a circle and the second group stands inside. Those players in the circle, using a basketball, or a rubber ball, throw the ball at players inside the circle. Those inside dodge as best they can. When players are hit, they join those in the outside circle. The last remaining player inside the circle is the winner.

Drop the Handkerchief

This was a popular game with younger children. A handkerchief or a chalkboard eraser was used for this game. At least eight players were needed to form a large circle. The person who is "It" runs around the outside of the circle and quietly drops the handkerchief behind one of the players – say player A. Player A chases after "It" and tries to catch "It" before "It" reaches A's place in the circle. If Player A does not catch "It," Player A becomes "It" for the next round of play.

Children playing Drop the Handkerchief at a school in rural Wisconsin circa. 1935.
Used with permission of the State Historical Society of Wisconsin/Image 101103.

Fox and Geese

This was a favorite winter game of the children and was best played after a fresh snowfall. A large circle would be tramped in the snow. Two cross paths were then made (much like spokes in a wheel) forming a hub, if you will, in the center of the circle. One pupil plays the fox and the others play the geese, until no geese are left. The center of the circle is safe, but only one player can be in the circle at a time. Everyone must stay either in the circle or on one of the spokes. The game continues until the fox has tagged all of the geese. The last person tagged becomes the fox.

Hide and Seek

In this game one player is selected to be "It." This person covers their eyes and counts to 100 and then tries to find the other children. "It" starts from home base and tries to locate the other children as they try to return to home base without being tagged by "It."

London Bridge

The game requires at least six children. Two children are chosen to be a bridge. They grasp each other's hands and raise their arms in the air so the other children can walk underneath. At the beginning of the game, the children form a line and march under the bridge singing:

London Bridge is falling down,
Falling down, falling down,
London Bridge is falling down,
My fair lady.

Upon singing the words "My fair lady," the children forming the bridge drop their arms and capture the child who is walking underneath. The captured child then replaces on of the children in the bridge. Another variation of the game is to take the prisoner to a corner of the room, singing "Off to prison you must go, you must go, off to prison you must go, my fair lady." In this version, the game continues until all of the children are caught.

Musical Chairs

The game was often played inside the school building on rainy days. A record player is needed, or someone to play the piano. Many schools had wind-up record players with a few records of march music which worked well for this game. Chairs are placed in a circle, one less than the number of children playing. Everyone marches around the chairs as the music plays. When the music stops, everyone quickly searches for a chair. The person who doesn't find a chair is out. Another chair is removed and the game continues until only one person is left marching and is declared the winner. This game works well with all ages; even parents enjoy it.

Pom-Pom-Pull-Away

One player is selected to be "It" and stands in the center of the field. All the other players gather back of a line drawn on the ground, about fifty feet away. A similar line is drawn on the opposite end of the playing field. The player who is "It" yells "Pom-pom-pull-away, come away or I'll pull you away." All of the players now run for the opposite end of the field, attempting to arrive safely behind the line. "It" tries to tag as many players as possible. Those who are tagged join "It" and the game continues, except this time everyone in the center tries to tag those who attempt to run across the field. The last person caught is "It" for the next game.

Red Rover

Parallel lines are drawn about fifty feet apart. One player is chosen to be "It" and stands in the center of the field. All the other players gather behind one of the lines. "It" calls out, "Red Rover, Red Rover, let (names a child) come over." This child then attempts to run to the opposite line without being tagged by "It." If tagged, this child then becomes "It's" assistant and helps to tag the next person called to come over. The last person tagged becomes "It" for the next game.

Ring Around the Rosy

Younger children especially enjoyed this game. At least four children were needed. The children walk or skip in a circle, holding hands and singing:

> Ring around the rosy,
> A pocketful of posies,
> Ashes, ashes,
> We all fall down.

And down on the ground they went. The game may be repeated indefinitely.

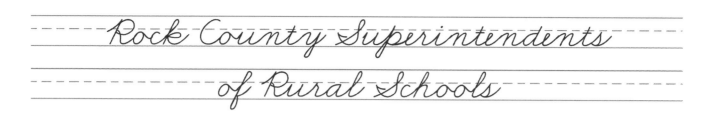

Rock County Superintendents
of Rural Schools

<u>1861-1964</u>

Information for this list came from the Wisconsin Blue Book and the Department of Public Instruction Annual Reports. In 1861 legislation created the elected position of County Superintendent of schools. In 1963 Chapter 565 of the Laws of Wisconsin established the Cooperative Educational Service Agency to replace the position of County Superintendent.

1861-1862 Rev. J. I. Foot

1863-1865 District 1: H.A. Richards
District 2: A.C. Whitford

1866-1868 District 1: C.M. Treat
District 2: J.I. Foot

1869 District 1: C.M. Treat
District 2: Rev. J. I. Foot

1870-1871 District 1: J.M. Harris
District 2: C.M. Treat

1872-1873 District 1: Edson A. Burdick
District 2: C.M. Treat

1874-1875 District 1: Edson A. Burdick
District 2: J.B. Tracy

1876-1879 District 1: Edson A. Burdick
District 2: J. B. Tracey

1880-1881 District 1: J. W. West
District 2: Wm. Jones

1882-1885 District 1: J. Boyd Jones
District 2: William Jones

1886-1889 District 1: J. Boyd Jones
District 2: J.C. Thom

1890-1901 District 1: Wm. Ross
District 2: David Throne

1902-1907 District 1: C. Hemmingway
District 2: O.D. Antisdel

*** 1909-1964 only 1 County Superintendent is listed with no district designation

1908-1910 O.D. Antisdel

1911-1920 Ashley Antisdel

1921-1923 Orley D. Antisdel

1924-1933 G.T. Longbotham

1934-1940 Mauree Applegate

1941-1943 Donald Upson

1943-1944 L.W. Porter (Acting Superintendent for Donald Upson during WWII as Upson was in the Navy)

1946-1964 Donald E. Upson

Rock County Supervising Teachers

<u>1915 - 1965</u>

1915-16 - No Supervising Teachers listed
1916-17 - Blanche Rice and Sadie Clapp
1917-1918 - Bill Harriet and Blanche Rice
1918-1919 - Jennie Dean and Bill Harriet
1919-1920 - Jennie Dean and Bill Harriet
1920-1921 - Maude Howarth and Martha Novaski
1921-1922 - Maude Howarth and Mary Rychwalski
1922-1923 - Louise Jacobson and Anna Olson
1923-1924 - Louise Jacobson and Anna Olson
1924-1925 - Anna Olson and Martha Johnson
1925-1926 - Anna Olson and Carrie Stewart
1926-1927 - Carrie Stewart and Ruth Hadley
1927-1928 - Ruth Hadley and Agnes Griffin
1928-1929 - Agnes Griffen and Ruth Longbotham
1929-1930 - Hattie Frederick and Agnes Griffin
1930-1931 - Hattie Frederick and Agnes Griffin
1931-1932 - Hattie Frederick and Mauree Applegate
1932-1933 - Hattie Frederick and Mauree Applegate
1933-1934 - Hattie Frederick and Mauree Applegate
1934-1935 - Hattie Frederick and Virginia Rowe
1935-1936 - Hattie Frederick and Virginia Rowe
1936-1937 - Hattie Frederick and Virginia Rowe
1937-1938 - Hattie Frederick and Virginia Rowe
1938-1939 - Hattie Frederick and Virginia Inman
1939-1940 - Hattie Frederick and Virginia Inman
1940-1941 - Hattie Frederick and Virginia Inman
1941-1942 - Hattie Frederick and Virginia Inman
1942-1943 - Hattie Frederick and Virginia Inman
1943-1944 - Hattie Frederick and Virginia Inman
1944-1945 - Hattie Frederick and Virginia Inman
1945-1946 - Hattie Frederick and Virginia Inman
1946-1947 - Hattie Frederick and Lloyd Porter
1947-1948 - Hattie Frederick and Lloyd Porter
1948-1949 - Hattie Frederick and Lloyd Porter
1949-1950 - Hattie Frederick and Lloyd Porter
1950-1951 - Hattie Frederick and Lloyd Porter
1951-1952 - Hattie Frederick and Lloyd Porter
1952-1953 - Hattie Frederick and Lloyd Porter
1953-1954 - Hattie Frederick and Lloyd Porter
1954-1955 - Hattie Frederick and Lawrence J. Anderson
1955-1956 - Lawrence Anderson, Charles Palmer, Harris Buros, Mildred Yahnke, and Frank Daniels (Did not separate the Supervisory Teachers from other professional staff)
1956-1957 - Mildred Yahnke and Harris Buros (listed as Supervisory Teachers)
1957-1958 - Mildred Yahnke and Harris Buros (listed as Supervisory Teachers)
1958-1959 - Mildred Yahnke and Harris Buros (listed as Supervisory Teachers)

1959-1960 - Mildred Yahnke and Harris Buros (listed as Supervisory Teachers)
1960-1961 - Mildred Yahnke and Lewis Loofboro (listed as Supervisory Teachers)
1961-1962 - Mildred Yahnke and Lewis Loofboro (listed as Supervisory Teachers)
1962-1963 - Mildred Yahnke and Lewis Loofboro (listed as Supervisory Teachers)
1963-1964 - Mildred Yahnke and Richard Skyles (listed as ESupv.)
1964-1965 - Mildred Yahnke (listed as E.Supv.)

Source: Information was obtained from the Official School Directory published by the Wisconsin Department of Instruction.

Eighth Grade Graduation Class Pictures

For Rock County Rural Schools

Eighth Grade graduates of Rock County rural Schools posed for this picture in 1947.
Courtesy of Elsie (Olmstead) Mathewson.

Likely Eighth Grade graduates of Rock County's Rural Schools in 1948. Courtesy of Richard and Joan Kidder.

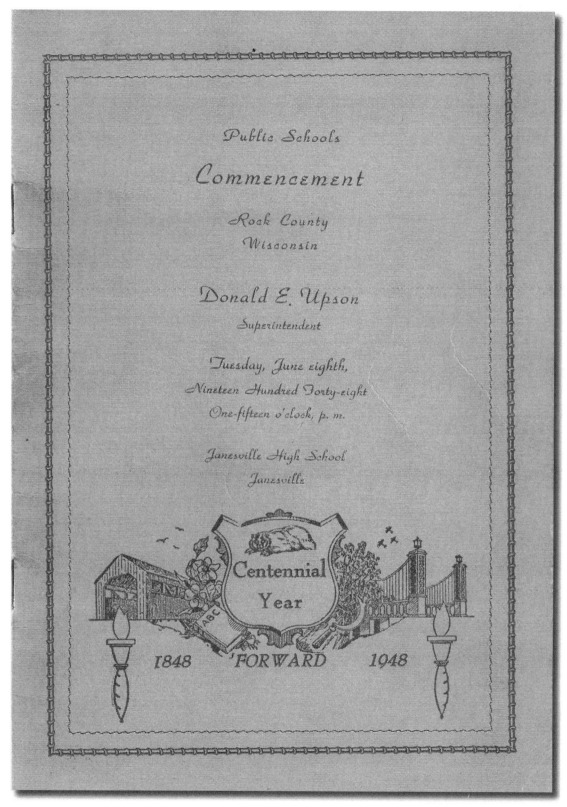

Public Schools

Commencement

Rock County
Wisconsin

Donald E. Upson
Superintendent

Tuesday, June eighth,
Nineteen Hundred Forty-eight
One-fifteen o'clock, p. m.

Janesville High School
Janesville

Centennial Year

1848 'FORWARD 1948

Cover of Rock County Rural Schools Commencement Program for June 8, 1948.
Courtesy of Richard and Joan Kidder.

Rock County Schools

Commencement Program

1948

Janesville High School 1:15 p. m.

Processional

Invocation .... Rev. J. S. Hubner

Singing .... 1948 Graduates

"On Wisconsin", "Wisconsin Hymn", "Want to be a Badger", " Glory to Rock County."

Director Mrs. Ellen Himle
Accompanist, Mrs. M. H. Hegge

Xylophonette Orchestra and chorus:

"Merrily, Merrily", "Lovely Evening", "Chop Sticks", "Now Is the Hour."

Schools:

Paul, Emerald Grove, Backhawk, Austin
Director .... Mr. Robert Muffley

Singing .... Footville Chorus

"Wisconsin Land of Beauty"................................ Monahan
"America the Beautiful"...Ward
Director ....Mrs. Edith Thorne

Singing Playlet .... Murray and Zilley Schools
"Little Dutch Kindergarten" .... In Costume
Diirector .... Mrs. Edith Thorne

Commencement Address .... Judge Harry Fox

Presentation of Diplomas .... Donald E. Upson
County Superintendent of Schools

Star Spangled Banner .... Audience

Benediction .... Rev. J. S. Hubner

Rehearsal Directors
Hattie Fredrick — Lloyd W. Porter

Inside cover of Rock County Rural Schools Commencement Program for June 8, 1948 shown on previous page. Courtesy of Richard and Joan Kidder.

ROCK COUNTY SCHOOLS—1951

Eighth Grade graduates of Rock County rural Schools posed for this picture in 1951. Held at the Janesville High School (now Marshall School) on South Main Street. Courtesy of Judy Cople.

Eighth Grade graduates of Rock County's rural Schools posed for this picture in 1952.
Courtesy of Clinton Community Historical Society.

Eighth Grade graduates of Rock County's rural Schools posed for this picture on May 23, 1953.
Courtesy of Mary Lou Schmidt.

1917 Township Map
of Rock County, Wisconsin

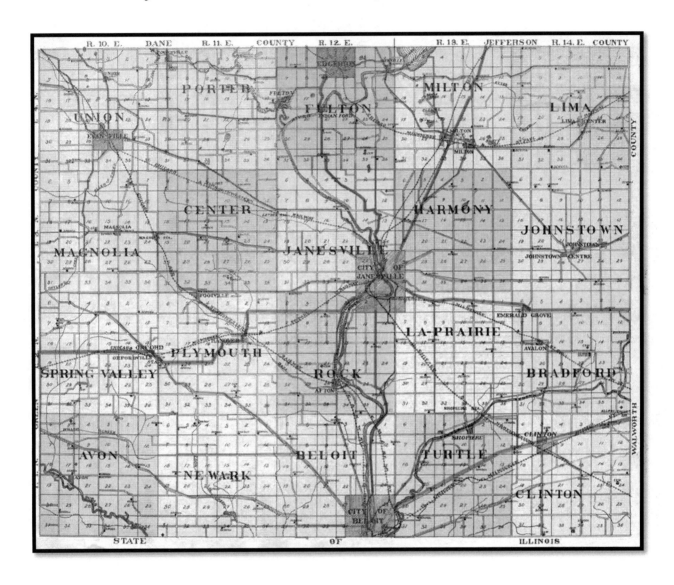

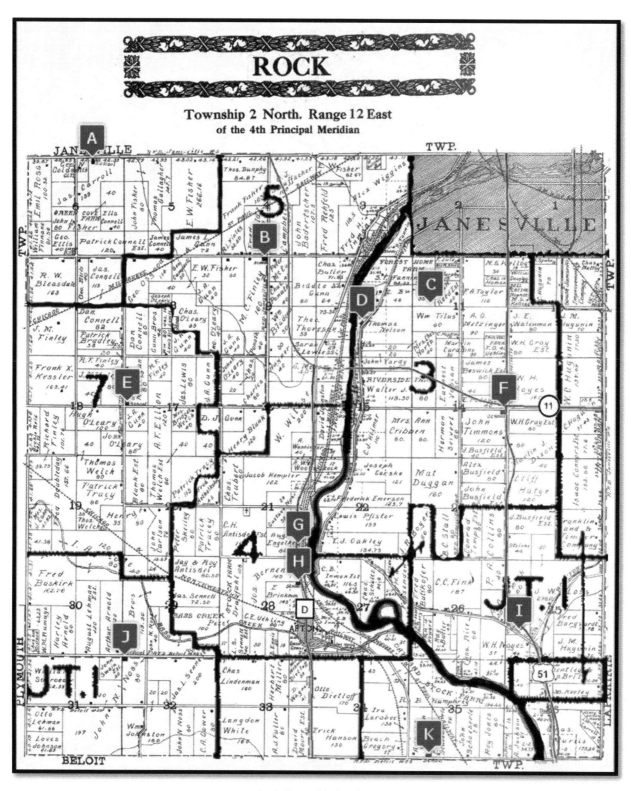

Rock Township in 1917

Map legend for facing page

- A. Willowdale School - *see page 97*
- B. Hayner School - *see page 83*
- C. River Valley School - *see page 91*
- D. Frances Willard (aka Willard) School - *see page 65*
- E. Bass Creek School - *see page 60*
- F. Frances Willard School (2nd location)
- G. Afton School - *see page 50* (1st location)
- H. Afton School (2nd location)
- I. Happy Hollow (aka Riverside) School - *see page 77*
- J. Pleasant Valley School - *see page 86*
- K. Town Line School - *see page 94*

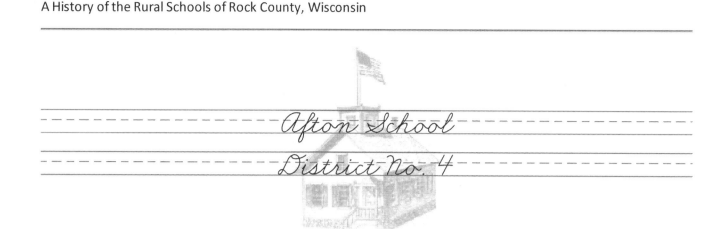

Afton School
District No. 4

Years of Operation

1847-1848 (Section 21) in Watts Hotel, one mile north of Afton

1848-1849 (Section 21) across the river from the prior school.

1849-1892 (Section 21) on Eau Claire Road west of County D – burned in February 1892. Baptist church here from 1850-1861.

1895-1959 (Section 28) a two room school on County D (Afton Road), a quarter mile south of previous school – just north of 7th Street, Afton.

Memories

"One noon hour after a warm spring shower and a muddy schoolyard, 'It's my turn to ring the bell!' came the strong voice of a sixth grade girl. I heard them all coming, laughing, talking, joking up the steps and into the entrance where the bell rope could barely be reached as it hung down through the ceiling from the heavy old steel bell. Then all at once, quiet – too, too quiet, except for the ringing of the bell! Going to see the reason for it, there they all stood string and open-mouthed at Marie's mud-spattered bright green bloomers, which were exposed every time she 'went up' with the knot at the end of the bell rope!

My best memories are of the friends and of their kindnesses. The generous way in which their good will was expressed at all times. The interest that the school board and parents took in the teachers and the school. The way in which we were welcomed to all meetings – Ladies Aid, 4-H, P.T.A., birthday parties, anniversaries, or any gathering. The expressed appreciation of anything we did for the children." – Harriet Quinn (teacher)

History

HISTORY OF AFTON SCHOOL
By Mrs. Bertha E. Stupfell, Teacher
Afton, Wisconsin
May 12, 1947

"Although the settlers were busy struggling to make a living they did not forget the fact that their children were to have an education. As early as 1847 a school was opened by Mr. Chas. Newton in the old Watts Hotel located a mile north of the village.

Here Mr. Newton taught school and after a year moved to a little building across Rock River where he also kept a school until 1849 when it then passed into Miss Kinney's hands.

The first residents in the neighborhood were Josiah Antisdel, Samuel Church, Harmon Daly, Simon and Clark Antisdel and Mr. Inman.

Early in 1849 a brick school house was erected across from the present gravel pit and about 40 rods west from the corner on the North Side of the road, which is about a quarter of a mile from the present school site.

Not much information is known about the school from then until 1872, except that school was kept during the winter months only and some of the pupils attended school until the age of 25.

In 1872 at the annual school meeting it was voted to have five months winter term and four months summer school term, a different teacher hired for each term. The School Board voted to raise $150 for a contingent fund.

A person desiring to teach school had to pass satisfactorily an examination each year, for which he, or she, would receive a third grade certificate. The standings were graded on a scale of ten, and the subjects were, Orthoephy, Orthography, Reading, Penmanship, Constitution, Mental and Written Arithmetic, and Theory of Teaching.

Marian Dunbar of the town of Center was hired to teach the Afton School at $25 a month for the five month term. The Board members were as follows; Timothy Lynch, clerk., W. H. Church, Treasurer, and Geo. Terwilliger as Director. Mr. C. M. Treat was county Supt. at that time.

In 1874 Mr. J. B. Tracy became County Supt. of Rock County.

The Treasurer's report for the 1874 was as follows:

Contingent Fund – $223.74

County School Money – 57.68

State School Money – 24.11

Dog Tax Money – 38.95

Total - $344.48

At the annual school meeting in 1874 it was voted to hire a man teacher for the winter term at a a salary of $140 and a lady teacher for the summer term at $112.

In 1875 Clara Moulton was hired at $27 per month for four months and she had an enrollment of 52 pupils.

In 1879 Alfred O'Brien of the town of Janesville was the first teacher holding a first grade certificate and was hired for $30 a month and the certificate was a two year license and the following subjects had been added to the requirement examination; Algebra, Geography, United States History, Natural History, Natural Philosopy, Geometry, and Civil Government.

In 1880 William Jones became County Supt. of Schools for Rock Co.

At the annual school meeting in 1880 it was voted to have four months winter term and four months summer term, the district expenses for that year, including teachers salary were $246.30.

In 1885 the voters of the district, seven in number, requested a special school meeting for the purpose of raising a district tax. The meeting was held in the Brick School house and they decided to raise $225 for expenses as they were short of funds.

On July 26, 1887, a special meeting was held for the purpose of building a new school house, but this motion was not carried. Then in August another meeting was called for the purpose of purchasing a site and building for a new school, but this too, was voted down.

The old Red Brick school was heated by a long heating stove which held sticks of cord wood 4 ft. long. The story is related that on the 17th of Feb. 1892 the children were huddled around the old stove as it was a cold winter day. Mr. Frank P. Starr, the teacher, was writing a lesson on the blackboard, when a couple of the big boys pulled a burning log out and laid it on the floor under the stove. A terrible smoke arose, so the boys quickly put the wood back in the stove before the teacher could find out the guilty ones.

That evening after school, these mischievous boys returned to the schoolhouse and finished the job of burning the building to the ground thus hoping this would be the end of the school term, however, they were greatly disappointed.

The School Board Members at that time were, Director A. R. Waite, Treasurer W. J. Miller and Clerk Wm. Brinkman. The board met at once and made arrangements with the members of the Baptist Church to hold school in the church basement until a new school could be built.

In 1893 Indian Mounds were discovered on the W. J. Miller property just south and west of the present school grounds which were heavily wooded at that time. A Mr. Skavelem, Professor at Beloit College, was given permission to dig up two of these mounds, but had to promise not to molest any more. Some of these Indian relics unearthed from these mounds can still be seen at the Beloit College Museum.

A number of meetings was [sic] held before a site for the new schoolhouse was chosen. The farmers wanted it built on the old location, but the village inhabitants wanted it nearer to the village of Afton. They finally compromised and agreed to the present location, and it was built there in 1895 on the Geo. Sims farm, and as the population had grown so speedily in these years, a two room schoolhouse was built.

In 1896-97 the school was made into a State Graded, the Board members being Director Peter Drafahl, Clerk Wm. Brinkman and Treas. W. J. Miller.

Mr. Frank P. Starr was re-hired at $400 a term to teach the upper grades with an enrollment of 30 pupils and Miss Elizabeth Stoddard, hired to teach the lower grades with an enrollment of 37 pupils.

At the turn of the Century their [sic] were 61 pupils with A. G. Hanry teaching the upper grades and Miss Ethel Soper the lower and David Throne was County Supt.

From 1905 to 1911 Miss Ethel E. Soper taught the lower grades and there were three different teachers for the upper grades during that time.

From 1911 to 1918 the enrollment decreased quite rapidly so that at the annual school meeting in 1918 they voted on a one room school again and to raise $1200 for expenses for the ensuing year.

In 1906 the following subjects were taught, Reading, Arithmetic, Language, Geography, Spelling, History, Physiology, and Penmanship.

In 1912 these subjects were added; Civil Government, Agriculture, Music and Drawing, and in 1939 Science was added to the curriculum.

The Afton P.T.A. organized in 1927 with Mrs. Harriet Quinn as teacher and the president of the first year was Mrs. Wm. Howland now living in Milton Jct. Wis.

The object was to enlist the co-operation of the home and school for the purpose of promoting the educational, civic and social development of the community, and to bring into closer relation the home, the school and the teacher. The P.T.A. is still an active organization in our school.

In 1931 a law was passed at the annual school meeting stating a child had to be six years old by the end of December in order to start school that fall.

On Sunday July 24th 1938 the first school reunion was held at Riverside Park in Janesville. The founders of this idea were Mrs. Cora Isaccs of Hollywood, Cal. and Otto Uehling of Afton. The purpose of these reunions was a general get together of former pupils, teachers and families who had ever attended the Afton school or lived in the village or school district from way back when to the present time and in this way old acquaintences would not be forgot. This reunion which was held on Sundays, consisted of programs of music and readings with a general address by some prominent citizen of the community, this speaker has been for the most times, former Sup't of School, David Throme of Beloit now in his 89th year. However during the last war these meetings were discontinued, but started again last year and are planning on one this year.

Our school enrollment has varied from 35 to 51 pupils during the last seven years. This spring we had the lowest attendance of 33 pupils.

We have tried to carry out the pupil-teacher plan in our school and found out the pupils take a greater interest in their work if they can help plan it. Most of our school activity business is carried on by the 'Loyal Brigade' Citizen League, a pupil organization.

In our school subjects we try to work them out in units wherever possible as we find it creates a greater interest.

The pupils of our school take part in the Rock Township Playday activities every year and for the last two years have entered the Mibs(?) Tournament sponsored by the Beloit Daily News each year. Our Champion Marble player is Miss Dolores Haase, who was last year also.

Every year we give a Christmas Program in the Rock Town Hall located in Afton and this program is an outgrowth of our reading and language work.

The P.T.A. sponsors a motion picture show in our school every month which is eagerly looked forward to by the pupils.

The School Board and the P.T.A. purchased black curtains for our school so we could view some of the pictures County Supt. Upson and Mr. L. Porter show in different schools in the daytime.

In 1940 the school board installed an oil burner which made more room in our schoolroom and less work and in 1941 they installed a running water system with the bubbler and sink placed in our cloak room and in our cloakroom we have movable coat racks.

The pupils and I, Mrs. Bertha Stupfell, feel we have one of the best school and school boards in Rock County and we are proud of both."

(Source: Area Research Center, Andersen Library, University of Wisconsin-Whitewater, Whitewater, WI; Rock 39, Box 3, Folder 16.)

Afton School was listed as a State Graded School in the 1952-53 directory and later became part of Rock Consolidated School. It was sold after closing and remodeled into a home. It was later torn down and a new home was built on the site.

List of Teachers

1847-48 – Mr. Charles Newton
1849 – Miss Kinney
1872 – Marian Dunbar of the town of Center (hired at $25 per month for a five month term)
1875 – Clara Moulton (hired at $27 per month for four months and taught 52 pupils)
1879 – Alfred O'Brien of Janesville (hired at $30 per month)
1892 – Frank P. Starr

1896-97 – Frank P. Starr (taught 30 pupils in the upper grades)
1896-97 – Miss Elizabeth Stoddard (taught 37 pupils in the lower grades)
About 1900 – A. G. Hanry (taught the upper grades)
About 1900 – Miss Ethel E. Soper (taught the lower grades)
1905-11 – Miss Ethel E. Soper (taught the lower grades) and three others taught the upper grades.
1927 – Harriet Donnelly (Quinn)
1938-40 – Jeanette Johnston
1940-50 – Mrs. Bertha E. (Bansemer) Stupfell of Afton, WI
1950-51 – Amelia Lauste
1951-56 – Mrs. Harriet Quinn of 1110 Lapham St., Janesville, WI (taught in Rock Consolidated
1952-53 – Mrs. Ida Misner of Afton, WI
1955-56 – Ida Misner of Afton, WI (later taught in Rock Consolidated)

List of Students

Haase, Dolores

Graduates in 1942

Busk, Carolyn Ann
Davies, Marlyn
Forrestal, Bill
McQuade, Mary Agnes
Schench, Delores
Sonnentag, James
Uehling, Louis
Weber, Fred
Worden, Donald
Worden, Richard

Graduates in 1944

Forrestal, Thomas
Green, Shirley
Marsh, Ronald
Telch, Richard
Teubert, Virginia
Weber, Carrie Mae

Students taught by Mrs. Bertha E. (Bansemer) Stupfell in 1945

Bradey, Janet
Bradie, Jackie
Empereur, Marilyn
Empereur, Marsha
Fradinburg, Steven
Garskey, Bernerd
Garskey, Dorothy
Garskie, Corel
Gasrude, Ronny
Gervice, Billy
Hases, Delores
Hases, Harlie
Hases, Maciel
Howdell, Leroy

Libby, Jack
Libby, Patricia
Libby, Roy
Libby, Shirley
Meyer, Jean
Meyer, Joyce
Meyer, Leroy
Milered, Billy
Milered, Freddie
Morteson, Delma
Neal, Joan
Nellpot, Everet
Pantell, Joan
Reeps, Elmer
Saldanas, Peter
Sherwood, Janet
Sherwood, Lee
Stark, Joan
Stark, Ronnie
Starks, Gladice
Starks, Mertle
Swien, Karen
Van Colter, Mansis
Van Colter, Ronnie
Weber, Frankie
Weber, Marie

Graduates in 1948

Brady, Janet
Haase, Marciel
Libby, Jack
Meyer, Jean
Meyer, Joyce
Weber, Marie

Board Members

Timothy Lynch (Clerk in 1872)
W. H. Church (Treasurer in 1872)
George Terwilliger (Director in 1872)
A. R. Waite (Director in 1892)
Peter Drafahl (Director in 1896-97)
William Brinkman (Clerk in 1892 and 1896-97)
W. J. Miller (Treasurer in 1892 and 1896-97)
Charles Martin (Director in 1952-53 and 1955-56)
Harry Robb (Treasurer in 1947, 1952-53, and 1955-56)
Walter P. Chapin (Clerk in 1947, 1952-53, and 1955-56)
Ray Meyer (Chairman in 1947)
T. Robb
William Busk
F. Kettlebone

Photographs

Afton School in 1945. Row One: Joan Stark, Patrica Libby, Billy Gervice, Jack Libby, Joan Pantell, Joyce Meyer, Marie Weber, Mrs. Bertha E. Stupfell (teacher), Janet Bradey. Row Two: Shirley Libby, Elmer Reeps, Jean Meyer, Dolores Hases, Leroy Meyer, Freddie Milered, Macial Hases, Frankie Weber, Everet Nellpot, Bernerd Garskey. Row Three: Peter Saldanas, Roy Libby, Janet Sherwood, Gladice Starks, Jackie Bradie, Mertle Starks, Harlie Hases, Lee Sherwood, Joan Neal, Ronny Gasrude, Mansis Van Colter. Row Four: Steven Fradinburg, _____ , Corel Garskie, Delma Morteson, Ronnie Stark, Marilyn Empereur, Ronnie Van Colter, Karen Swien, Dorothy Garskey, Marsha Empereur, Billy Milered, Leroy Howdell. Courtesy of Margaret Empereur.

Afton School during the 1947-48 school year. Courtesy of Rock County Historical Society.

Afton School in 1949. Courtesy of Margaret Empereur.

Afton School in 1951-52. Courtesy of Margaret Empereur.

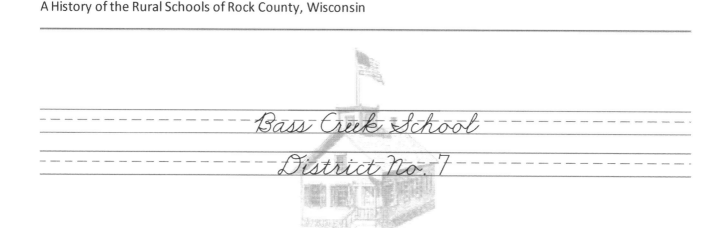

Years of Operation

Before 1858-1873 (Section 16) on Tripp Road, just east of Hayner Road

Before 1873-Before 1961 (Section 17) on Tripp Road at Murray Road (5546 Tripp Road), northeast corner of intersection.

Memories

"I recall the wonderful times we had during the winter months. Bass Creek schoolyard had a wonderful hillside for sledding and skiing. It was hard for all, even the teacher, to wait till recess or noontime to try the slope. How we did work to build our own ski jump! It turned out to be quite a successful project, too.

At Bass Creek, I had my first experience with sand burrs. Who would have thought that such little demons as sand burrs were hiding in that shady school yard. After the first softball game, I found out! It took the better part of the afternoon before everyone was comfortable again." – Jackie Scidmore (teacher)

History

Bass Creek School became part of Rock Consolidated School.

List of Teachers

Elizabeth (Lewis) Kennedy
Jackie Werfel (Scidmore)
1938-1950 – Mrs. Juliette (Finnane) Mulligan
1950-52 – Sadie Finnane
1952-53 – Jill Ritchart of 636 S. Garfield Ave., Janesville, WI
1955-56 – Jacqueline Werfal of Janesville, WI

List of Students

Graduates in 1942

Gunn, Biddle Francis
Carlson, Anna Marie

Graduates in 1944

Carlson, Marian Ellen
Gunn, Mary Eileen
Herbert, John F.

Graduates in 1948

Carlson, Edith

Risch, Ronald

Graduate in 1952

Finley, Cathaleen

Board Members

Clarence Scidmore (Clerk in 1952-53)

Mrs. Fred Risch

Mrs. Mae (Harold) Finley (Director in 1952-53 and 1955-56)

Mrs. Marie Kelsey (Treasurer in 1955-56)

Lester Kelsey (Treasurer in 1952-53)

Stella Murray

Mrs. Biddle Gunn

Howard Armfield (Clerk in 1955-56)

Frank Finley

Thomas Tracey

Photographs

Bass Creek School during the 1947-48 school year. Courtesy of Rock County Historical Society.

Bass Creek School in 1975. Courtesy of Wisconsin Historical Society, Reference Number 86724.

Bass Creek School in May 2015. Courtesy of the author.

Bass Creek School in May 2015. Courtesy of the author.

Frances Willard (aka Willard) School
District No. 3

Years of Operation

1853-1920 (Section 10) on South River Road and West State Street – later moved to the Rock County fairgrounds as a museum circa 1969.

1920-1936 (Section 14) on Center Avenue at Kellogg Avenue (a two story building).

1936-1963 (Section 14) on 3109 Oakhill Avenue at Kellogg Avenue. Called Frances Willard Trainable School.

Memories

"My first one room school was Frances Willard School (not the original) located on the corner of Avalon Road and Oakhill Road, in Janesville. At this time I lived four houses from the airport on Oakhill Road. It's funny, but the only recollections of Frances Willard School was of my couple friends, hitting a fellow student with my bike on the way home one day, and playing Red Rover at recess, so that must have been the highlight of my early education. I attended there from 1952 – 1953 at which time my parents moved to Center Township and I then went to Crall School, from 1954 to 1959." – Bonnie (Hill) Davis-Carroll of Milton, Wisconsin.

History

FRANCES WILLARD SCHOOL
By an unknown author

(Courtesy of Rock County Historical Society)

"The schoolhouse was constructed in 1853 by Josiah Willard and his neighbors to provide a place for the education of their children. An energetic progressive farmer, Willard settled in Rock Township in 1846. He helped found the Rock County Agricultural and Mechanics Association, which was a sponsor of the first State Fair of Wisconsin in 1851.

Frances Willard, the daughter of Josiah and Mary Thompson Willard, was born September 28, 1839, in Churchville, New York, but grew up on the family farm located on South River Road near Janesville. The original Willard house, Forest Home, was moved in the 19th century to 1842 South River Road from its original location at 1720 South River Road. The schoolhouse was located on a farm further south.

After leaving her Janesville home, Frances Willard studied at Milwaukee and in Evanston, Illinois. In 1858 she returned to her home in Janesville and taught at the schoolhouse where she had studied in 1853-54. Frances moved permanently to Illinois in 1859, where she continued her career as an educator.

In later years, Miss Willard became extremely active in the Woman's Christian Temperance Union, founding the World's W.C.T.U. She led the women of the nation, not only in a temperance crusade, but also towards the feminist ideal of equal rights, including the right to vote. Frances Willard, both before and after her death in 1898, was considered to be among the most distinctive American women of the nineteenth century. She is buried in Chicago.

The Frances Willard Schoolhouse stands today as a monument to early education in this country, and is listed on the National Register of Historic Places. It was closed as a district school in 1920, but the structure, and subsequently, the site were acquired as a memorial by the Rock County W.C.T.U. in 1921. In 1969, the W.C.T.U. donated the property to the Rock County Historical Society. The land was sold with covenants designating it as the Frances Willard Memorial site, to be used in a way compatible with the memory of Frances Willard, and the schoolhouse was moved to the Rock County 4-H Fairgrounds, to be used for educational exhibits. The historical society is currently completing a long-range restoration program for the building, and it now appears much as it did in 1853."

This school is listed as a State Graded School in the 1955-56 directory. Attached to the Janesville School District after closing. The earliest school building was moved to the Rock County Fairgrounds and is now a museum operated by the Rock County Historical Society. The fate of the two later school buildings is unknown.

List of Teachers

1858 – Frances Willard
1938-39 – June Ramsey
1940-42 – Vivian Parrish
1942-44 – Amy Benedict
1944 – Mrs. Ruth Knauf
1944-45 – Kathryn Tracy
1945-46 – Amy Benedict
1946-47 – David Lyons
1947-48 – Mrs. Evelyn E. Hatton
1948-49 – Jeanette Montgomery
1949-53 – Amy Benedict of Rte. 3, Janesville, WI
1951 – Mrs. Marie Nolan of Janesville, WI
1955-56 – Esther Johnson of Janesville, WI (Principal)
1955-56 – Mrs. Elinore Staffon of Footville
1961-62 – Robert Hedman of 1429 MacFar Lane, Janesville, WI (Grades 6-8)
1961-62 – Mrs. Helen Radtke of R. 2, Evansville, WI (Grades 3-5)
1961-62 – Mrs. Norma Carlson of 1525 Purvis, Janesville, WI (Grades 1-2)
1963-64 – Mrs. Marjorie R. Jones of Beloit, WI
1963-64 – Mrs. Joephine Darling of Edgerton, WI

List of Students

Clemans, Duane (attended from 1938-1946)

Graduates in 1942

Cribben, Bernadine
Duggan, Robert
Thierman, Wadena
Vobian, Maxine

Graduates in 1944

Thierman, Norman
Weberg, Beverly
Weberg, Juanita

Graduates in 1948

Mercier, Diane
Weberg, Audrey

Students attending in 1949

Longhenry, Susan (1st grade)

Students attending in 1952-53

Davis Carroll, Bonnie (Hill)

Graduates in 1962

Greb, Frederick
Grundahl, Mark
Osmond, Marie Annette
Pearson, Dan
Yeadon, David Lee

Board Members

Mrs. Rose Collier (Clerk in 1955-56 and 1961-62)
Mrs. Robert Hill (Director in 1955-56)
Mrs. Owen Clemans
John Cribben
John Lasse
Mrs. Dale Hergert
Mrs. William Mercier
Mrs. Wayne Day (Director in 1952-53)
Amos Grundahl (Clerk in 1952-53)
Elver Richardson (Treasurer in 1952-53 and 1955-56)
Roy K. Podewels (Director in 1961-62)
Walter N. Pfeiffer (Treasurer in 1961-62)
John Busfield

Handicapped Children's Board in 1963-64

Arthur Schrank
Gordon Hill
Wallace Hahn

Photographs

Frances Willard School. Post Card photo circa 1910. Courtesy of the author.

Frances Willard School on a Post Card mailed December 30, 1915. Courtesy of the author.

The Frances E. Willard School House, Situated One Mile from Forest Home on the Beautiful Rock River, near Janesville, Wis. Built in 1853.

Frances Willard School on an undated Post Card. Courtesy of the author.

Frances Willard School during the 1947-48 school year. Courtesy of Rock County Historical Society.

Frances Willard School in 1947-48. Teacher is Evelyn E. Hatton. Courtesy of Luther Valley Historical Society.

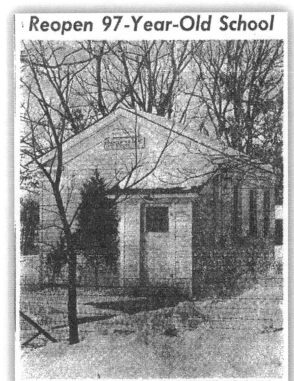

Reopen 97-Year-Old School

—Consolidated News Service photo

Frances Willard school, last used as a schoolhouse in 1920, will be reopened for classes Monday. The one-room school, named for the founder of the W.C.T.U., has been used by that organization as a memorial since 1930. Students of the Rock River Valley school district, near Janesville, Wis., will occupy the building.

Frances Willard Memorial School Will Be Reopened

(Consolidated News Service)

Janesville, Wis. — A 97-year-old rural Janesville W.C.T.U. memorial building, last used as a schoolhouse in 1920, will be reopened for classes Monday.

The one-room Frances Willard school will house students of the River Valley school district, where crowded conditions in the schools have forced board members to seek more classroom facilities. The building is named for the temperance crusader who attended school and taught there. It was last used 30 years ago, and since 1930 has been owned by the W.C.T.U. as a memorial to the founder of the organization.

Josiah Willard, father of the famed crusader, and his neighbors built the school in 1853. The W.C.T.U. has used the building in recent years as a youth hostel.

River Valley district, including the Fisher addition near the state school for the visually handicapped, now has an enrollment of 150 children. Board members say the enrollment is climbing. The school board has painted the old schoolhouse and installed a chimney and electric lights.

district is scheduled for Wednesday, for a vote on a proposed $10,000 fund to erect a two-room frame building on the same site as that occupied by the two-room brick school built in 1937.

The extra rooms may not accomodate enough pupils, however, and the old Willard building may continue in use even after the proposed building is erected. The local chapter of W.C.T.U., meeting with County Supt. Donald E. Upson and G. A. Korthals, R.R 3, clerk of the River Valley district, approved use of the memorial for school classes. Mrs. Grant Olin, 1047 S. Terrace st., is president of the local chapter.

The agreement, without expiration date, calls for maintenance of the school as a continuing memorial while it is used for classes. The River Valley school is now using two basement rooms as well as the original two schoolrooms, under a special state permit. There are five teachers in the building, two of them working in one room.

Frances Willard School is the subject of this 1951 article from an unidentified newspaper.
Courtesy of Area Research Center, Andersen Library, University of Wisconsin-Whitewater, Whitewater, WI.

BACK IN SERVICE — The Frances Willard school, where the famous temperance crusader attended classes and taught in 1858, will be used for school purposes again next month. It was last used nearly 30 years ago, and since 1930 has been owned by the W.C.T.U. as a memorial to the founder of the organization. Its use as a school in 1951 is due to crowded conditions in other schools of that area.

97-Year-Old School Will Reopen for Classes Jan. 8

Crowded schoolrooms in the River Valley school district, just south of Janesville in Rock township, will result in reopening of the 97-year-old Frances Willard school about Jan. 8.

The old building, erected by Josiah Willard, father of the famed founder of the W.C.T.U. and pioneer neighbors in 1853, was purchased in 1930 by the Rock County W.C.T.U. as a memorial, and in recent years has been used as a youth hostel.

River Valley district now has an enrollment of 150 children and the figure is constantly increasing. The area includes the suburban development in the Fisher addition, near the State School for the Visually Handicapped.

Voters Meet Jan. 10

A special meeting of the school district is called for Jan. 10 for a vote on a proposed $10,000 fund to erect a two-room building of wood construction on the same site as that occupied by the two-room brick school built in 1937. The extra rooms may not accommodate enough pupils, however, and the old Frances Willard building may continue in use even after that is finished.

Arrangements to use the old schoolhouse to meet the emergency housing situation were completed at a meeting held in the heatless building Tuesday evening. Attending were Mrs. Grant Olin, 1047 S. Terrace street, president of the W.C.T.U., Mrs. Ann Friis, 1127 Wheeler street, another of its officers, G. A. Korthals, route 3, clerk of the River Valley district, and County Supt. Donald E. Upson.

W.C.T.U. Co-operating

The W.C.T.U. gave full co-operation to school officials in the effort to provide improved school facilities. The school board will build a chimney, paint the old school and install electric lights. The agreement, without expiration date, calls for maintenance of the school as a continuing memorial while it is in use for classes.

Mrs. Marie Nolan, Janesville, a former teacher in the Hayner school, will take up her duties in the Frances Willard building when school reopens after the Christmas holidays. The modernization and clean-up work will be finished by that time.

The River Valley school is now using two basement rooms as well as the original two schoolrooms under a state special permit. There are five teachers there, two of them working in one room. The district has one of the worst problems of crowding in the county.

Frances Willard School is the subject of this 1951 article from an unidentified newspaper.
Courtesy of Area Research Center, Andersen Library, University of Wisconsin-Whitewater, Whitewater, WI.

Frances Willard School in 1975 at 3109 Oakhill Avenue.
Courtesy of Wisconsin Historical Society, Reference Number 73298.

Frances Willard School in 1975 after being moved to the Rock County Fairgrounds property.
Courtesy of Wisconsin Historical Society, Reference Number 49854.

Happy Hollow (aka Riverside) School
Joint District No. 1 with LaPrairie Township

Years of Operation

1858-1939? (Section 25)

___-1981 (Section 25) on Happy Hollow Road at Highway 51 (756 Happy Hollow Road), west side of intersection. Annexed to Janesville in 1962.

Memories

"It was a thrill for all the boys and girls at Happy Hollow School the day the Mothers' Club sponsored a trip to Wisconsin Dells. After eating our lunch in Rocky Arbor Park, we enjoyed the scenic boat trip on the Upper Dells, which made the day a memorable one for all." – Alice Pecor (teacher)

History

This school is listed as a State Graded School in the 1955-56 directory.

List of Teachers

1938-44 – Lucille McDonnell Ostby
1944 – Mrs. Alice Pecor
1944-47 – Ella Julian
1947-48 – Mrs. Ann Geach
1948-49 – Mildred Lippens and Alice Pecor
1949-56 – Mrs. Alice Pecor of 625 Sutherland Ave., Janesville, WI (Principal - to Happy Hollow Consolidated)
1955-56 – Mrs. Mavis Steiner
1961-62 – Mrs. Betty Vogel of 1649 S. Osborne, Janesville, WI (Grades 6-8)
1961-62 – Mrs. Ethel Hunt of R. 1, Janesville, WI; Principal; (Grades 1-2)
1961-62 – Mary Moyer of 115 S. Main St., Janesville, WI (Grades 3-5)

List of Students

Graduate in 1942
McClellan, Lulabelle

Graduates in 1944
Frye, John
Hildebrandt, Marvin
Marx, Patricia
Schulz, Leslie

Graduates in 1948

Kolberg, Harlan

Saunders, Russell

Weeks, Alice

Students attending in 1949

Longhenry, Susan

Graduates in 1952

Schrader, Patsy

Sutton, Robert

Graduates in 1962

Blank, Mary Pauline

Gallatin, Diane Lynn

Hendricks, Linda

Klick, Jane Elizabeth

Scott, Diane Lynn

Williams, Darline

Board Members

Mrs. Leontine Stoppielli (Clerk in 1952-53 and 1955-56)

Harold Weeks (Director in 1952-53 and 1955-56)

Arnold Klick (Treasurer in 1955-56)

Alfred Kolberg (Treasurer in 1952-53)

Mrs. Paul Frye

Fred F. Ritter (Clerk in 1961-62)

Marie Reeded

Oren Baxter (Director in 1961-62)

Daniel Shook (Treasurer in 1961-62)

Earl Tremblie

Photographs

Happy Hollow School in the 1947-48 school year. Courtesy of Rock County Historical Society.

Happy Hollow School in May 2015, looking northwest. Courtesy of the author.

Happy Hollow School in May 2015, looking north. Courtesy of the author.

Happy Hollow School in May 2015, looking northeast. Courtesy of the author.

Hayner School District No. 5

Years of Operation

Before 1858-1961 (Section 9) – on Hayner Road at Hanover Road, southwest corner of intersection. Moved to a farm just to the west at 4330 Hanover Road and used as the east addition to a farm house.

Memories

"The program was attended by most members of this district. Each pupil had a part. There were songs sung by different children and several one-act plays put on. The actors in one play used their own names. Its title was 'Why Phil Didn't Run Away.' It seemed that Phil was going to run away from home until Rick told him that Linda, the girl Phil secretly admired, was starting to show an interest in Gary. Phil decided that he could not let Gary outdo him, so he decided not to run away." – Alice Ryan (teacher)

History

Hayner School became part of Rock Consolidated School.

List of Teachers

1938-39 – Ella Julian
1940-41 – Alice Vickerman
1941-42 – Mabel Latzke
1942-43 – Frances Lauer
1943-44 – Mrs. Lillian E. Anderson
1944-45 – Evelyn Alderson
1946-50 – Mrs. Marie (O'Leary) Nolan
1950-56 – Alice Ryan of Rte. 5, Janesville, WI (then taught in Afton School until Rock Consolidated opened – then taught there)

List of Students

Alfred Lembrich (1940s)

Graduates in 1942

Borchert, Raymond
Gunn, Mary Beth
O'Leary, Tom

Graduates in 1944

Disch, Robert
O'Leary, Richard

Onsrud, Martelle
Schmidley, Allen
Skogen, Victor

Graduates in 1948

Jensen, Gerald K.
Lloyd, Raymond

Graduate in 1952

Rehfeld, Rita

Board Members

Webb McNall (Treasurer in 1952-53 and 1955-56)
Joe O'Leary (Clerk in 1952-53 and 1955-56)
Isaac Rebout (Director in 1955-56)
Fred Rehfeld (Director in 1952-53)
Elizabeth Gunn
John O'Leary
G.C. Schmidley

Photographs

Hayner School during the 1947-48 school year. Courtesy of Rock County Historical Society.

Hayner School in May 2015. School building is the right half of the house. Courtesy of the author.

Pleasant Valley School
Joint District No. 1 with Plymouth Township

Years of Operation

After 1858-____ (Section 25) on W. Plymouth Church Road, just west of Bakke Road. Joint with Plymouth.

1920s-Before 1961 (Section 32) at 5545 W. Plymouth Church Road, a red brick building. Joint with Plymouth.

Memories

"Several families of migrant workers moved into the community. Among them was Lewis – the fifteen year old who went home each noon with his brothers and sisters for lunch. As we glanced out of the window as he returned from lunch, it seemed that he was smoking. As soon as he reached the school yard, I called him in and asked, 'Lewis, do you have some cigarettes?' 'No, ma'am, but I got the makins.' Would you like some?' He thought I was asking him for a cigarette for myself!" – Helen Seward (teacher)

History

Pleasant Valley School became part of Rock Consolidated School.

List of Teachers

Josie (Finnane) Martin
Minerva Storlie (Bakke)
Mabel Klusmeyer
1917-18 – Genevieve Horkey
1928-45 – Eileen (Ryan) O'Leary
1945-49 – Sadie Finnane
1949-51 – Bernita Stluka Mathews
1951-56 – Helen Seward of Rte. 4, Janesville, WI
1956-__ - Alice Mackie (To Rock Consolidated)

List of Students

Graduates in 1942
Burrow, Ronald
Hass, Arnold
Miller, Donald
Noss, Sidney

Graduate in 1944
Burrow, Lorien

Graduates in 1948
Badertscher, Nancy
Nitz, William

Board Members

LaVerne Noss (Clerk in 1952-53 and 1955-56)
Clayton Arnold (Director in 1955-56)
Mrs. Merle Millard (Director in 1952-53)
Aloysius A. Wanninger (Treasurer in 1952-53 and 1955-56)
Howard Bakke
C.W. Burrow
Emily Tews
Clarence Horkey

Photographs

Pleasant Valley School during the 1947-48 school year. Courtesy of Rock County Historical Society.

Pleasant Valley School in 1975. Courtesy of Wisconsin Historical Society, Reference Number 83315.

Pleasant Valley School in May 2015. Courtesy of the author.

Pleasant Valley School in May 2015. Courtesy of the author.

River Valley School
District No. 1

Years of Operation

Before 1938-1958 (Section 11) on 2300 Kellogg Avenue at South Willard – northwest corner of intersection (now River Valley Park). Division of Frances Willard. It was within the Janesville city limits after 1954. It was a two-room school.

Memories

THE BRICK RIVER VALLEY ELEMENTARY
By Gail (Zebell) Lanza and Her Siblings, 2002

"The school was located on the northwest corner of Willard Avenue and Kellogg Avenue and the building is still standing. When I attended, only 1st through 4th grades were taught there. We were sent out of the area for 5th and 6th grades. My 5th grade was at Roosevelt and my 6th grade was at Washington. So I attended River Valley during the 1953/54 and 1954/55 school years. The school had two rooms – one to each side of the main entrance. The basement housed the milk machine, had a lunchroom of sorts and was used for summer activities and scout troop meetings.

Mrs. Nolan taught 3rd grade and Mrs. Maloney taught fourth. (Poor Mrs. Maloney; as kids will do, she had the nickname of Mrs. Baloney.) Another teacher was Miss Weaver. The principal was Mrs. Grace Knipp. Until 1954 River Valley School was outside the city limits of Janesville (in Rock Township). I don't know when the school was built.

There was another building separate from the original brick building. This housed the kindergarten through 3rd grade classes. This annexed building had a hall down the center with classrooms on both sides. It was parallel to Willard Avenue and is no longer in existence.

Some of the families who attended the River Valley Elementary School were Bell, Webb, Thompson, Splinter, Zebell. The rest I can no longer recall."

History

River Valley School is listed as a State Graded School in the 1952-53 directory. By 1951 the basement was being used to hold classes in in addition to the two upper rooms.

List of Teachers

1938-41 – Olive (Hupel) Hollenbeck
1941-42 – Melvin Swan and Mildred Johnson
1942-44 – Mrs. Hannah Anderson and Mildred Johnson
1944-53 – Mrs. Grace Knipp (to Lincoln School in Janesville)

1944-46 – Harriet Ehret – (Lower room)
1946-49 – Mildred Johnson – (Lower room)
1948-51 – Helen Henke (grades 4-5)
1950-51 – Gertrude Meyer
1948-49 – 3 teachers
1950-51 – 4 teachers
1951-53 – 6 teachers
1952-53 – Mrs. Grace Knipp (Principal) of 54 S. River St., Janesville, WI
1951-53 – Mrs. Mildred Whaley of 301 Randall Ave., Janesville, WI
1951-53 – Mrs. Jean Weaver of 1023 Bennett St., Janesville, WI (to Jefferson School in Janesville)
1951-53 – Mrs. Marie Nolan of 1012 Bennett St., Janesville, WI (to Lincoln School in Janesville)
1951-53 – Mrs. Helen Berkley of 1423 St. Mary's Ave., Janesville, WI (to Roosevelt School in Janesville)
1950-53 – Mrs. Frances Heffernan of 541 N. Pearl St., Janesville, WI

List of Students

Lanza, Gail (Zebell)

Graduates in 1944

Brooks, Harold
Brooks, Violette
Gosda, Donald
Hilt, Emanuel
Laurence, Delores
Matthews, Carol
Pell, Helen
Schaite, Richard

Graduates in 1948

Asplund, Fern
Brooks, Melvin
Fiedler, Donald
Gurney, Barbara
Henning, Ralph
Kessler, Donald
Morstadt, Carolee
Smith, Abram

Graduates in 1952

Bell, Buddy
Butler, Harriet
Campbell, Allan
Gurney, Robert
Helgeson, Judy
Henning, Annabelle
Milam, Edward
Milam, Norman
Morstadt, Frances
Pfeiffer, Chester
Robbins, Judy
Schroder, Dick
Willing, William

Board Members

Clarence Sutherland
G.A. Korthals
Orian Freeman
Harry Kath
Dr. A. J. Knilans
Mrs. E. J. Lamphier
A. H. Peterson
Paul Burfeind (Clerk in 1952-53)
Mrs. Hilmer Ambrose (Director in 1952-53)
Rollo Pfeiffer (Treasurer in 1952-53)

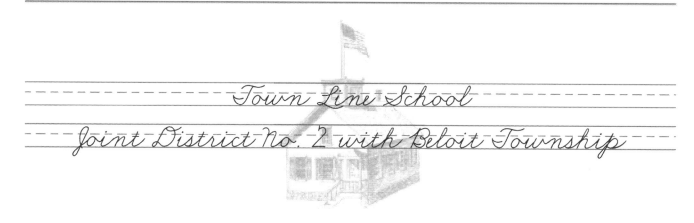

Town Line School

Joint District No. 2 with Beloit Township

Years of Operation

After 1873-Before 1961 (Section 35) – on Town Line Road.

History

Town Line School became part of Rock Consolidated School.

List of Teachers

1942 – Lucille Mayhew
1944 – Mrs. Mina Uehling
1948 – Mrs. Joyce Hurd
1952-53 – Mrs. Marian Everson of Rte. 3, Beloit, WI
1955-56 – Mrs. Margo Miller of Beloit, WI

List of Students

Graduates in 1942

Duggan, Betty
Von Brocklin, Alice
Peterson, Floy

Graduates in 1944

Behling, Allan
Dietz, Leroy
Stout, Lois

Graduates in 1948

Hansen, Verdelma
Behling, Elizabeth
Saga, Marilyn

Graduate in 1952

Meadows, Kathryn

Board Members

William Behling (Clerk in 1955-56)
Norman Haakenson (Clerk in 1952-53)
William Markley (Director in 1952-53 and 1955-56)
Frederick Neier (Treasurer in 1952-53 and 1955-56)

<u>Photographs</u>

Town Line School during the 1947-48 school year. Courtesy of Rock County Historical Society.

Town Line School in 1975. Courtesy of Wisconsin Historical Society, Reference Number 86570.

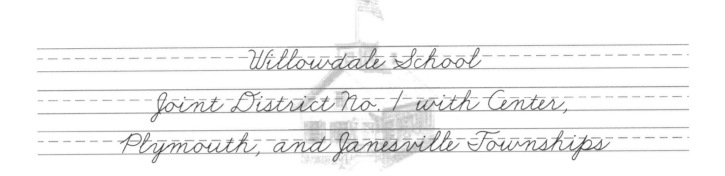

Willowdale School
Joint District No. 1 with Center,
Plymouth, and Janesville Townships

Years of Operation

Nov. 5, 1851-1908 (Section 6) a stone structure on Highway 11.

1908-1911 (Section 6) at same location. Destroyed by a tornado Nov. 11, 1911.

1912-1957 (Section 6) on Highway 11, just east of Kessler Road (5917 Highway 11).

Memories

"I shall never forget the day we were playing kickball at the Willowdale School. I had warned the children that if the ball ever went over the fence in into the road, I would get it. Under no circumstances were they ever to go into the road. Well, the inevitable happened! As the ball rolled into the road, a car was close at hand. I waited at the edge for the car to pass, while the children waited at the gate. We held our breath for fear the wheels would run over it, but to our surprise the car slowed up, the door opened, a hand reached out, scooped up the ball and instead of tossing it to our outstretched hands, tossed it into the back seat of the car and drove off. I shall never forget the look on the children's faces. Of course, I couldn't see my own, but I know that for the moment I think I lost my faith in humanity." – Mabel Klusmeyer (teacher)

"We used to get pails of water at the Willowdale tavern next door to the school. We got to climb a style [steps] that was built over the fence when we went." – Patricia Fleming

History

WILLOWDALE SCHOOL NEARING END OF 105-YEAR HISTORY
By Ruth Martin

(for the Janesville Daily Gazette, Nov. 21, 1956)

"Students of Willowdale School near Janesville expect to move out of their 44-year-old schoolhouse after the Christmas vacation and into the new West Janesville Consolidated School building on County Trunk A with pupils from Austin, Burdick and Riverside schools. The school is expected to be ready Jan. 1, 1957. It is located on the Magnolia Road west of the city.

Willowdale School district's history dates back 105 years and the present structure was erected in 1912 to replace the one destroyed in the tornado of Nov. 11, 1911. Willowdale School district is composed of parts of Rock, Plymouth, Janesville and Center townships. The school is located on Highway 11, 4 ½ miles west of Janesville at Willowdale.

First and eighth graders are being taught at Willowdale now. Mrs. Mildred Griffens is principal and Freda Siebel teaches. The second grade is at Austin with Mrs. Beulah Kloften the teacher. Riverside School housed the third and part of the fourth graders and Mrs. Marjorie Carey does the teaching. Part of the fourth grade and all of the fifth are located at Burdick School with Mrs. Helen Radtke the teacher. The sixth and seventh grades are also found at Burdick; Robert Demerow teaches the two grades. These teachers will handle the same classes in the new school.

An estimated 75 teachers have taught at Willowdale in the past 105 years. The district adopted the name 'Willowdale' for the school in 1919.

The first school was built Nov. 5, 1851, on the site of the present school. The land was given to district No. 1 by Dan Pepper and the school was built in a heavily wooded oak grove. Thirty-nine years later, in 1890, 10 of the oak trees died and were cut down for the small sum of $3.50. Seven more died in the next three years and in 1896 the present shade trees were planted by George Goldsmith. The trees cost only $6, school clerk records show.

The question of building a new school came up in 1893, 42 years after the school was built. It was voted against building a new school, so the old one was repaired. The question came up again in 1905 and again was defeated. But in 1908 the district voted to build a new school and let the contract to A. Summers, Janesville contractor, Aug. 6, 1908. George Goldsmith tore down the old building. James Mooney, George Schmidley and William Beyer were on the building committee.

During the 1896-97 school year flags became quite popular at schools and Willowdale voted to raise $25 for a flag and pole. Tom Ogden was paid $1.50 for raising the flag and George Goldsmith was paid $2 for digging the flag pole hole. The original pole was a tree but a metal flag pole was put up in 1918.

Wood was used to heat the Willowdale School building before 1909. Coal was first used in 1909 but the school now is heated by oil.

New desks were bought for the new school in 1909 but two years later the tornado destroyed the school. Classes were held in the Barnes Store building at Willowdale the rest of the year. Miss C. E. Clapp was teacher in 1911.

The district decided to build a new school in 1912 the same size and appearance as the one destroyed by the storm. J. H. Lentz, Hanover, was the contractor. This school has stood for 44 years with only a small fire in 1922 threatening its existence."

Willowdale School became part of Hillcrest School after consolidation.

List of Teachers

1908 – Lottie Skinner (last teacher at old school at school built in 1851)
1911 – Miss C. E. Clapp
1938-49 – Ella Vigdahl
1949-51 – Esther (Pahl) Olson
1952-54 – Mrs. Mabel (Behling) Klusmeyer of Footville, WI
1954-56 – Mrs. Mildred Griffens (Principal teacher) of Orfordville, WI (to Hillcrest Consolidated in 1955)
1956 – Freda Siebel

List of Students

Connell, William
Fleming, Patricia

Jeffris, T. M.
Severance, Janet (Simeth) (attended in 1941-3)

Graduate in 1942
Weis, Rosella

Graduates in 1944
Erdman, Donald
Horton, Donald
Morgan, Dennis

Graduate in 1948
Goodrich, Orville

Graduate in 1952
Lamb, Donald

Board Members

Mrs. Anne Lichtfuss (Clerk in 1952-53)
Ronald Bobzien (Director in 1952-53)
Joseph Weis (Treasurer in 1952-53)
George Schmidley
Charles O'Leary
Robert Connell
Frank Korn
Leonard Mooney

Photographs

Willowdale School during the 1947-48 school year. Courtesy of Rock County Historical Society.

Willowdale School in 1956. Courtesy of Luther Valley Historical Society.

Willowdale School in 1975. Courtesy of Wisconsin Historical Society, Reference Number 86493.

Willowdale School in May 2015. Courtesy of the author.

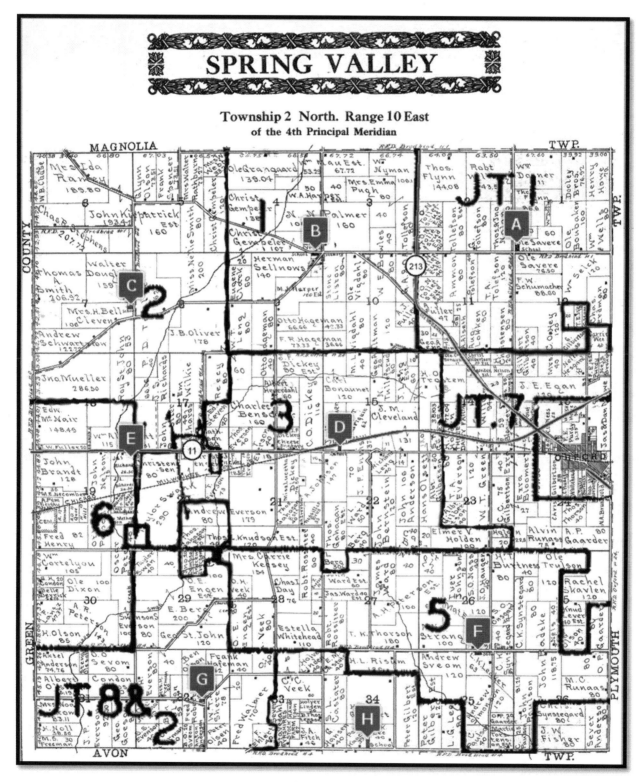

Spring Valley Township in 1917

Map legend for facing page

A. Beck School - *see page 106*
B. Spring Valley Corners School - *see page 167*
C. Scotch Hill School - *see page 140*
D. Spring Valley Center School - *see page 153*
E. Putnam School - *see page 120*
F. Rock Hill School - *see page 130*
G. Oak Hill School - *see page 111*
H. Randall (aka Taylor) School - *see page 121*

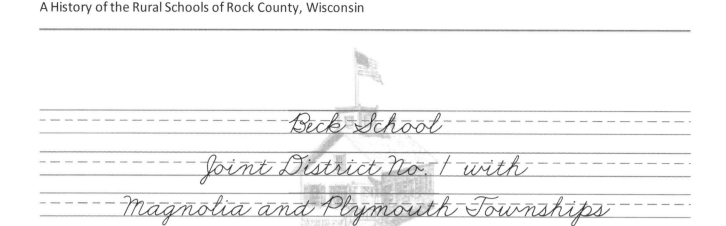

Beck School
Joint District No. 1 with
Magnolia and Plymouth Townships

Years of Operation

1858-____ (Section 12) Tollefson Road and Spring Valley Corners Road – southeast corner of intersection.

After 1878-About 1955 (Section 1) Tollefson Road and Spring Valley Corners Road – northeast corner of intersection. Located at 1311 S Tollefson Road. Students sent to Orfordville – Parkview after school closed.

Memories

"I'll always remember an experience I had during one of my first years at Beck School. I was playing ball with the children and an eighth grade boy, who was the pitcher, seemed to pitch the ball so fast that no one wanted to be the catcher. I volunteered to be the catcher and things went fine for a while. All of a sudden, a swift ball was thrown that I didn't stop. Instead, it went through my hands, striking me in the face and I fell to the ground. The frightened children came running and sobbing. One child remarked to the pitcher, 'Oh, you killed the teacher!'

Later I developed a severe headache and was told by the doctor that it was a result of being hit by the ball. He told me to remain in bed.

Now this was a busy time for the eighth grade students, because the following day was the date of final exams to be written at the Orfordville School. I told my four students that I wouldn't be able to be there, but if they had a question to ask someone in charge.

Late in the afternoon on the next day, I was surprised to see these four rather unhappy looking eighth grade students at my house. They had walked to my home to inform me that they knew they had all failed their exams because I was not there." – Gladys Drevdahl (teacher)

History

Beck School was consolidated with Orfordville Village School by 1955-56.

List of Teachers

1938-56 – Gladys Drevdahl of Rte. 1, Brodhead, WI

List of Students

Graduates in 1942
Randles, Lillian
Saevre, Richard
Willing, Virginia

Graduates in 1944

Flynn, William
Kopplin, Harold
Saevre, Donald

Graduates in 1948

Francis, Robert
Klusmeyer, William
Tollefson, Mary Ellen

Board Members

Mrs. Harry Saevre (Clerk in 1952-53)
Ray Roberts (Director in 1952-53)
Alvin Wells (Treasurer in 1952-53)
Mr. and Mrs. Ernest Tellefson
Carl Kjelland
O. O. Savre

Photographs

Beck School during the 1947-48 school year. Courtesy of Rock County Historical Society.

Beck School in 1975. Courtesy of Wisconsin Historical Society, Reference Number 87687.

Beck School in June 2015. Courtesy of the author.

Beck School in June 2015. Courtesy of the author.

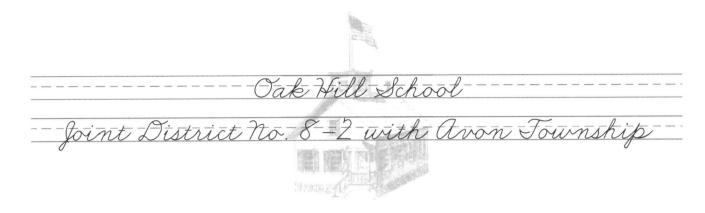

Oak Hill School
Joint District No. 8-2 with Avon Township

Years of Operation

1850s-Before 1961 (Section 32) on Hafeman and Avon Store Roads - northwest corner of intersection. Located at 16902 W Hafeman Road.

History

HISTORY OF OAK HILL SCHOOL
By Bonnie Wolter

"During 1933-1934 C.W.A. project included digging a basement under the school and other improvements. Vince Olson went to school there and remembers when the basement was dug out. He remembers different workers who had to dig the basement all by hand and having the farmers with their horses and wagons hauling the dirt away. Oak Hill was a stone building so they did not dig out the whole basement. Oak Hill closed and merged with Brodhead District in 1960. Seal Meligan bought it. Now it is used as a home.

One-room schools established an educational partnership and strong lines of communication between parents and teachers. Parents frequently stopped in to chat with the teacher before and after class. There was no need for formal parent/teacher conferences.

All in all, the one-room school provided many advantages: close relationships between school and home, small classes, the pride we gained by helping take care of the day-to-day needs of the school, respect for each other and ourselves, and many special memories. Sadly, it is now a lost educational experience, but an educational legacy that will never be forgotten."

Oak Hill School was attached to the Brodhead School District after closing. It was later sold to Seal Meligan in 1960 and used as a dwelling.

List of Teachers

1908 – Mattie Schoen
1938-39 – Viola Krueger
1940-45 – Mrs. Arice Leng
1948 – Betty Loudden
1945-49 – June Caldwell
1951-56 – Mrs. Josephine Neff of Sharon, WI

List of Students

Olson, Vince

Class of 1908

Anderson, Lewis
Anderson, Olive
Benjamin, Lula
Day, Flossie
Day, Tina
Everson, Albert
Everson, Oscar
Freeman, Adalf
Goeson, Edvin
Goeson, Lillian
Gravdale, Gertie
Gravdale, Grace
Gravdale, Telmer
Hegge, Oliver
Hegge, Tilmen
Huff, Agla
Huff, Malvin
Linden, Mary
Olson, Christina
Olson, Hervin
Olson, Oscar
Olson, Selmer
Rindy, Alma
Rindy, Gehard
Rindy, Silva
Stallen, Clara
Veek, Myron
Woodward, Dewitt

Graduate in 1942

Wilson, Lucille

Graduate in 1944

Olson, Wayne

Graduate in 1948

Ehlert, Rodney

Graduates in 1952

McCord, Lenore
Olsen, Gerald
Olsen, Robert

Board Members

Frank Hafeman (Clerk in 1908)
Peter Olson (Treasurer in 1908)
Joseph Everson (Director in 1908)

Harold McCord (Clerk in 1952-53)
Blanche Olson
Ralph Douglas (Treasurer in 1952-53 and 1955-56)
T. Rosebell Olson (Director in 1952-53)
Marvin Sveom
Roy Ehlert
Oscar Fry
Selmer Olson
Percy Whitehead
Mrs. Milla Olson
Perry Reavis (Clerk in 1955-56)
Mrs. Rosabel Olson (Director in 1955-56)
Elmer Caples
Tilman Amundson

Photographs

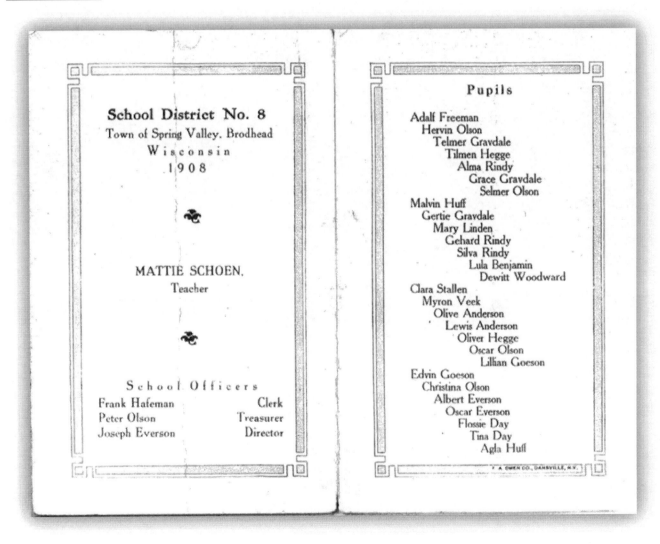

1908 Souvenir from Oak Hill School. Courtesy of Brodhead Historical Society.

Oak Hill School. No date, but circa 1900-1910. Courtesy of Luther Valley Historical Society.

Oak Hill School during the 1947-48 school year. Courtesy of Rock County Historical Society.

Oak Hill School in 1975. Courtesy of Wisconsin Historical Society, Reference Number 83273.

Oak Hill School in June 2015. Courtesy of the author.

Oak Hill School in June 2015. Courtesy of the author.

Outhouses behind the Oak Hill School in June 2015. Courtesy of the author.

Putnam School

Joint District No. 6 with Green County

Years of Operation

_____-1939? (Section 19) less than a half mile east of Highway 104 on the south side of Highway 11.

History

The following is from a handwritten note in the Rock County Historical Society archives states:
"Putnam School – Spring Valley Sec. 19. Import from Winnebago Co., ILL – built in 1850's – before moving to Spring Valley – S. side Hy 11 – ½ mi. E. of Brodhead – made into a home – owned by Raymond Anderson."

Putnam School was attached to the Brodhead School District after closing. It was sold to Seal Meligan in 1960 and used as a dwelling.

Board Members

John Brandt
Oscar Peterson (Director)
Fred Henry (Treasurer)
Donald Timm
Dr. G. M. Miller (Clerk)

Randall (aka Taylor) School
Joint District No. 2 with Avon Township

Years of Operation

Had "Taylor School" above the door at Randall School.

Before 1858-____ (Section 34) on Avon North Townline Road - between Nelson Road and Risum Road.

____-1956 (Section 34) on Avon North Townline Road one quarter mile farther east than previous school. Located at 15048 W Avon North Townline Road.

Memories

"Three of my happiest years in teaching were spent at Randall School. One thing in particular stands out among the memories of those years. At the end of the school year, the students always looked forward to Play Day. Neighboring schools took part in a day of contests in various athletic activities. No matter how other schools tried, they could never win over us in volleyball. The last year I taught at Randall, there were only ten students. But believe it or not, when Play Day ended we had our first place in volleyball! The students had set fine examples of teamwork and sportsmanship again." – Mrs. Vera DeVoe (teacher)

History

HISTORICAL NOTES ON THE RANDALL SCHOOL
By an unknown author

"The Randall school has always been known by its present name.

Captain A. N. Randall lived in the home directly across from the school. The Randall home and also the school were built of limestone; and are still in use.

Captain A. N. Randall was born in 1830 in New York. He was educated as a lawyer and in 1847 came to Wisconsin and settled in Avon township. He enlisted as a Captain of Company G, 13th Wisconsin volunteer infantry in the Civil War, on October 17, 1861 and served until mustered out in February, 1865. Henry Lee and two other brothers from Randall District served in the Civil War and were released at Vicksburg in August, 1865.

Captain Randall raised race horses and he had a half-mile race track on top of the hill west of the school. He served as a Wisconsin senator from this district in 1882 and at this same time Mr. John Huntly [sic], one of our earlier teachers in this school, served as our Assemblyman. This information was found in the Wisconsin Blue Book of 1882.

Most of the early settlers in our district came from New York in the 1840's and later the Norwegian immigrants came in the 1850's and 1860's.

The Lee Cheese factory, which is near our school was built in 1893 and was used until 1928 when it was closed. This was a community enterprise."

(Source: Area Research Center, Andersen Library, University of Wisconsin-Whitewater, Whitewater, WI; Rock 39, Box 3, Folder 17.)

HISTORY OF RANDALL SCHOOL
By Bonnie Wolter

"Randall School District, Section 34, received a land grant from the old Anderson farm north of Town Line Road, between east of Nelson Road and west of Lee Road. Randall School was recorded in the Platte Book 1873. The old stone school is still just west of Mark Marchant's fire number on the north side of the road. The wooded acres are still very hilly right through this area near the old school. The Randall District which is some 3,000 acres in Avon and Spring Valley Townships was split irregular on the north-south Town Line Road and the territory divided between Orfordville and Brodhead, giving the larger south part to Orfordville District and the remaining segments to Brodhead District. The northern sector, with 4 exceptions and comprising Spring Valley areas, goes to Brodhead.

In 1913 Clayton McNitt taught at Randall School. Clayton McNitt was their teacher for a year. Vera DeVoe was the last teacher at Randall School. She said that her best three years were spent at Randall School. No matter how other schools tried at play day, we had first place in volley ball every year!"

Randall School became part of Jt. School District No. 1, City of Brodhead through consolidation. It was purchased by Richard Taylor on November 3, 1964.

List of Teachers

1866-67 – Josephine Knowles (Taught from Nov. 19, 1866 to Feb. 19, 1867)
1867-68 – Celia A. Taylor (Taught May 20-Aug. 10, 1867 and Dec. 2, 1867 to Feb. 21, 1868)
1868 – T. S. Merrill (Taught from May 4 to July 2, 1868)
1868-69 – Sarah Mooney (Taught from Dec. 8, 1868 to Feb. 26, 1869)
1869 – Rogene R. Bodycoat (Taught from May 3 to July 31, 1869)
1869-70 – Sarah Mooney (Taught from Dec. 6, 1869 to Feb. 25, 1870)
1870-71 – Rogene R. Bodycoat (Taught from May 2 to July 22, 1870 and from Nov. 14 1870 to Feb. 7, 1871)
1871 – Dollie E. Springstead (Taught from May 8 to Aug. 5, 1871)
1871-72 – Sarah Springstead (Taught from Nov. 18, 1871 to Mar. 1, 1872)
1872 – Eliza D. Hamblett (Term began on May 6, 1872)
1872 – Rogene Bodycoat (Taught from June 26 until August, 1872)
1872-73 – Lenora L. Beals (Taught from Nov. 11, 1872 until Feb. 28, 1873)
1873-74 – Ellen E. Kennedy (Taught from May 5 to July 25, 1873 and from Nov. 10, 1873 to May 1, 1874)
1874-75 – John Huntley (Taught from Nov. 9, 1874 to Mar. 5, 1875)
1875-76 – Ada Randall (Taught from May-July, 1875 and from Nov. 8, 1875 to Feb. 25, 1876)
1876 – Betsy Gilbert (Taught from May 1 to July 21, 1876)
1877 – Helen Rathbun (Term began on May 7, 1877)
1877-78 – W. H. Randall (Taught from Nov. 19, 1877 to Feb. 19, 1878)
1878-81 – Mary J. Gilbert (Taught from May 13 to Aug. 2, 1878 and from Nov. 11, 1878 to Feb. 8, 1879)
1881-82 – Hattie E. Taylor

1882-84 – Fannie Partridge (Taught from Dec. 11, 1882 to May 1883 and again in December, 1883. Taught from March to June, 1884)
1884 – Lydia Dickey (Term began on July 11, 1884)
1885-86 – Cora Cox (Taught March to July, 1885 and January to March 1886)
1886 – Edna Smalley (Term began in June, 1886)
1913 – Clayton McNitt
1938-39 – Ivy Castator
1940-43 – Helen Henke (Yates)
1943-44 – Mrs. Mildred (Klingberg) Olson
1944-48 – Mrs. Viola Goeson
1948-50 – Thelma Olin
1950-53 – Barbara Lee of Rte. 3, Brodhead, WI
1954-56 – Mrs. Vera DeVoe of Brodhead, WI

List of Students

<u>Graduates in 1944</u>
Gilbert, Marjorie
Lee, Barbara

<u>Graduates in 1948</u>
Lee, Howard
McCaslin, Leonard

Board Members

Harold Nelson (Clerk in 1952-53 and 1955-56)
Robert Gessert (Director in 1955-56)
Paul Foss (Director in 1952-53)
Orville Lee (Treasurer in 1952-53 and 1955-56)
Oscar Gilbert
Harry Castator
Elmer Foss
Mrs. Robert Ames (Clerk)
Mrs. Davey Lee (Treasurer)

Records

The Luther Valley Historical Society has two ledgers. One covers a list of teachers and students taught for each term and covers the years 1866 to 1881. The other ledger covers minutes of meetings and expenditures (teacher's wages, repairs, etc.) and covers the years 1866 to about 1903).

Photographs

Visitor's Register for Randall School for 1869 and 1870. Courtesy of Luther Valley Historical Society.

Randall School during the 1947-48 school year. Courtesy of Rock County Historical Society.

Randall School Line Changed

Division Along Town Line Voted; Another Hearing Feb. 24

Prospects that Rock County's school reorganization would be virtually complete with the division of the Randall rural district in the far southwestern sector of the county were blasted at a hearing Wednesday in Orfordville.

About 3,000 acres in Avon and Spring Valley townships, comprising the Randall district, had been ordered cut on an irregular north-south line, and the territory divided between the Orfordville and Brodhead school districts. But at the hearing before Rock and Green county school committees at Orfordville, virtually unanimous objec-

Thursday, January 29, 1964
Janesville Daily Gazette

Following the hearing, the county committees met with the school boards, denied the resolution and drew up a new one dividing the district in accord with some of the recommendations made by electors. The committees were unanimous in approval of the new resolution, and set a hearing on this for 8 p.m. Monday, Feb. 24, in Orfordville High School.

Properties in Spring Valley, the Brodhead area, which were excepted and assigned to Orfordville are those of H. C. Risum, Percy Whitehead, Bell Gartland and Ruth Meisner, and Orville Lee. No exceptions were made in the Avon area assigned to Orfordville.

Jimmy Stewart Visits Madison

MADISON (AP)—Brig. Gen. James Stewart—Jimmy Stewart to his film fans—visited 325th Fighter Interceptor Squadron at Truax Field today as part of a tour of 30th Air Defense Command headquarters in Chicago and Madison.

tion was made and a wholly new dividing line drawn.

The new division, with a few exceptions, is on a north-south line on the Avon-Spring Valley border. Area to the south of the line, that is, in Avon Township, goes to Orfordville. The northern sector, with four exceptions, and comprising Spring Valley areas, goes to Brodhead under the new plan.

The Randall district is the last important district not already assigned to an operating high school district in accord with the state law in effect for the last couple of years.

The original decision of the Rock-Green county committees dividing the district into east and west sections was adopted Jan. 7. After hearing the objections at the hearings, this plan was scrapped, and the north-south division substituted. The original plan was that recommended by the Brodhead and Orfordville school boards in 1960.

Residents of the district proposed a division on an east-west line, the Townline Road, but including the Elmer Foss and Bert Murray farms to go to Brodhead. The committees refused to except the Foss and Murray properties, and they are retained in the Orfordville district. Their preference for Brodhead was based on prevailing bus route schedules.

This article regarding the division of districts, which included the Randall School district, appeared in the Janesville Daily Gazette in January 1964. Courtesy of Brodhead Historical Society and the Janesville Gazette.

Randall School in 1975. Courtesy of Wisconsin Historical Society, Reference Number 83274.

Randall School. No date. Courtesy of Brodhead Historical Society.

Randall School in May 2015. Courtesy of the author.

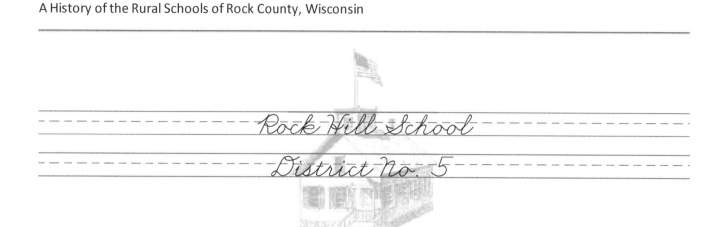

Rock Hill School
District No. 5

Years of Operation

Before 1873-1959 (Section 35) on Hafeman Road – just west of Holden Road. Located at 13919 W Hafeman Road.

History

Rock Hill School consolidated with Orfordville Village School. It was sold to Harold Johnson for $3,150.00 in 1960 and used as a home.

List of Teachers

1905-6 – Lou B. Robison
1910-11 – Genevieve Cavey (Horkey). Boarded at Matt Engelbreson's home.
1938-39 – Beulah Paulson
1940-41 – Persus Caldwell
1941-42 – Margaret Drew
1942-44 – Julia Detweiler
1944-46 – Naomi Jones
1946-48 – Mrs. Sue Rindy
1948-49 – Florence Doering
1949-51 – Nola Slaughter
1951-52 – June Caldwell
1952-53 – Mrs. June Mohns of Brodhead, WI
1955-56 – Mrs. Marie Wichelt of Brodhead, WI

List of Students

Piper, Irene

Class of 1905-1906

Burness, Irving
Burtness, Herman
Burtness, Mabel
Engelbretson, Sigda
Foslin, Carl
Gaarder, Frederick
Haugen, Geneva
Haugen, Jennie
Haugen, Maggie
Haugen, Oliver

Haugen, Oscar
Himle, Albert
Himle, Clara
Himle, Raynold
Himle, Rhoda
Horson, Bertha
Johnson, Julius
Johnson, Mabel
Johnson, Sigurd
Olson, Gullick
Olson, Olaus
Paulson, Albert
Paulson, Anna
Paulson, Elmer
Paulson, Peter
Runaas, Anga
Runaas, Melvin
Runaas, Minick
Saevre, Agnes
Saevre, Alfred
Saevre, Isaac
Saevre, Sanford
Simonson, Clara
Simonson, Josephine
Simonson, Sammie
Synstegard, Mabel
Thorson, Clarence
Thorson, Cora

Class of 1910-11 taught by Mrs. Alvin Runaas

Bement, Mabel
Braaten, Margaret
Burtness, Blanche
Burtness, Herman
Burtness, Lillian
Burtness, Mabel
Engelbretson, Oscar
Engelbretson, Sigde
Foslin, Carl
Foslin, Helmer
Haugen, Clara
Haugen, Geneva
Haugen, Jennie
Haugen, Oliver
Haugen, Oscar
Himle, Clara
Johnson, Julius
Johnson, Sigurd
Larmer, Maude
Ness, Orrion
Olson, Fern

Olson, Gullick
Olson, Olaus
Paulson, Albert
Paulson, Anna
Paulson, Elmer
Runaas, Agna
Runaas, Melvin
Runaas, Minnick
Saevre, Agnes
Saevre, Isaac
Saevre, Otis
Simonson, Clara
Simonson, Josie
Simonson, Melvin
Simonson, Sam
Synstegard, Mabel
Synstegard, Sophia
Thostenson, Helma
Thostenson, Ted
Worthington, Jessie

Graduates in 1942

Bryant, Oran
Paulson, Marian

Graduate in 1948

Burtness, Ann

Graduate in 1952

Stauffacher, Delores

Board Members

O. P. Gaarder (1905-6)
O. O. Saevre (1905-6)
Thomas Thorson (1905-6)
Matt Engelbretson
Sam Onsgard
Ted Haugen
Melvin Staven
Herbert Riaum
Vincent Burtness
Carl Stauffacher
Delbert Swarens
Herman and Mrs. Jean Brink (Treasurer in 1952-53)
Wayne Krueger (Clerk in 1955-56)
Mrs. Harlow Burtness (Director in 1952-53 and 1955-56)
Stanley Burtness (Treasurer in 1955-56)
Melvin Thostenson (Clerk in 1952-53)

Photographs

Rock Hill School. No date. Courtesy of Rock County Historical Society.

Cover of 1905-06 souvenir booklet for Rock Hill School. Courtesy of Rock County Historical Society.

Rock Hill School students and teacher in 1910-11. Row 1: Oscar Engelbretson, Orrion Ness, Elmer Paulson, Otis Saevre, Helmer Foslin, Clara Haugen, Blanche Burtness, Sophia Synstegard, Helma Thostenson, Margaret Braaten, Lillian Burtness. Row 2: Melvin Simonson, Herman Burtness, Carl Foslin, Ted Thostenson, Mabel Bement, Maude Larmer, Anna Paulson, Agnes Saevre, Agna Runaas, Sigde Engelbretson, Geneva Haugen. Row 3: Oliver Haugen, Sigurd Johnson, Gullick Olson, Julius Johnson, Isaac Saevre, Clara Simonson, Clara Himle, Josie Simonson, Fern Olson. Row 4: Albert Paulson, Oscar Haugen, Melvin Runaas, Sam Simonson, Minnick Runaas, Olaus Olson, Jessie Worthington, Mabel Burtness, Mabel Synstegard, Jennie Haugen. Mrs. Alvin Runaas (teacher).
Courtesy of Luther Valley Historical Society

Rock Hill School during the 1947-48 school year. Courtesy of Rock County Historical Society.

Rock Hill School in November, 1960. (Source: The Janesville Daily Gazette, Nov. 30, 1960; p. 13)

Rock Hill School in 1975. Courtesy of Wisconsin Historical Society, Reference Number 83275.

Rock Hill School in June 2015. Courtesy of the author.

Rock Hill School in June 2015. Courtesy of the author.

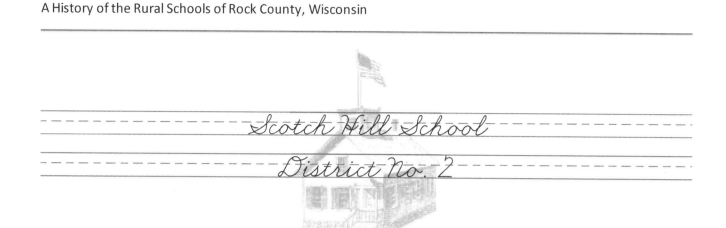

Scotch Hill School
District No. 2

Years of Operation

1840s-1850s – Log structure. Burned down.

Before 1858-1882 (Section 8) on the west side of Scotch Hill Road - just north of Footville-Brodhead Road (aka Rossman Road), across from the cemetery.

1882-1952 (Section 7) on the west side of Scotch Hill Road - just north of Footville-Brodhead Road (aka Rossman Road) south of the cemetery. Later moved to 207 4th Street in Brodhead, WI.

History

SCOTCH HILL COMMUNITY SETTLED BY SCOTCH EMIGRANTS IN 1842
(From an undated newspaper article at Luther Valley Historical Society)

"Every community has a history of its pioneers and the settlement in Spring Valley Township in Rock County, northeast of Brodhead, is no different from the rest. Strictly Scotch in its origin with many of the families related, Scotch Hill offers many historic tales of early life.

The first school was a log house on the corner of the Robert Taylor farm. It had benches along the sides and was also used as a church and for civic meetings. During the winter more than 60 pupils attended classes.

When the log building burned a frame structure was erected and is still in use today. Because the children trampled the wheat fields of the Taylors, he donated a tract of land across the road and the school was moved. Noted for being good spellers, the school's representatives in spelling bees were seldom spelled down.

For many years Sunday school and church services were held in the school with ministers from the Presbyterian church at Brodhead delivering the sermons."

OLD SCOTCH HILL SCHOOL GETS TREATMENT FROM VETERAN MASON
(From an unidentified newspaper clipping dated Aug. 23, 1962 at Luther Valley Historical Society)

"In the fall of 1960 the Henry Williams family purchased the Scotch Hill school house and the lot on which it stood at 207 E. 4th St., for the sum of $1,000. One of the pictures shows what it looked like at that time.

Since then they have made many changes as they wanted it converted into a home. They practically stripped the building – put on a new roof, aluminum siding, press brick window-height all around and a large white outside chimney. This 7-foot wide chimney accommodates the lannon stone fireplace.

Mr. Williams did much of the work himself, insulation, wiring, plumbing, heating, brick and stone work and plastering.

Mrs. Williams enjoys her modern kitchen which includes an electric built-in oven and range, and the brick planters in front of the house.

Aluminum awnings and gutters also add to the value of the home.

From this 20'x44' building, a modern, 4-room comfortable home with bath and utility room was built in Mr. Williams' spare time in less than two years. He is an employee of the Rock County Highway Department with the bridge detail.

The lumber is still good and durable in the 80-year-old building now converted into a modern family home.

The Williams family came to Brodhead in June, 1959. His first job was to lay the stone on the new Brodhead high school. Since then he has worked for contractors and has been self-employed."

Scotch Hill School was sold by sealed bid to Loudon Blackbourn in 1952 for $110.00 and moved to Brodhead for use as a dwelling. It was later purchased by the Henry Williams family (in 1960).

List of Teachers

Circa 1910-11 – Florence Lewis
Beulah Day
1926-27 – Thelma Nyman
1938-39 – Marian Zimmerman
1940-43 – Beulah Paulson (Hadley)
1943-44 – Mrs. Hazel Mau
1944-48 – Mrs. Marian Nyman
1948-49 – Rose Brown
1949-51 – Beulah Paulson
1951-52 – Ada Rhyner

List of Students

Buetow, Fred
Buetow, Walter
Enser, John
Ramey, Bessie
Ramey, Walter
Smith, Belle
Smith, Marguerite
St. John, Ed
St. John, Frank
St. John, Maude
St. John, Myron
Stephens, Roy
Swanton, Katherine
Tulles, Mabel
Van Skike, Robert

Wolf, Amelia
Wolf, Annie
Wolf, Frances

Class of 1926-27

Hawkins, Alerd
Hawkins, Alton
Hawkins, Bobby
Hawkins, Lillian
Hawkins, Russell
Olin, Norman
Olsen, Alice
Olson, Luella
Riese, Pearl
Schwartzlow, Alvin
Schwartzlow, George
Schwartzlow, John
Schwartzlow, Marvin

Graduates in 1944

Caldwell, Marybelle
Rosman, Joan

Some students taught by Marian Nyman in 1946

Caldwell, James?
Culles, Mary J.
Kaderli, Germaine
Meythaler, Bobbie
Meythaler, Daryl
Meythaler, Elaine
Nyman, Rona
Olin, Ramona

Graduates in 1948

Kaderli, Germaine
Swenson, June

Board Members

Lillian Roseman
Frank Rosman (Clerk in 1952-53)
Mrs. Lena St. John (Director in 1952-53)
Clair Meythaler
Claire Wilke
Marian Lang
B. W. Bell
C. D. Wilke
Mrs. Fredrick Duchow (Treasurer in 1952-53)

Photographs

Scotch Hill School. No date, but circa 1910. <u>Back row:</u> Fred Buetow, Walter Buetow, Robert Van Skike, Maude St John, John Enser, Frances Wolf, Amelia Wolf (?), Mabel Tulles, Marguerite Smith, Walter Ramey, Amelia Wolf (?), Frank St John, Myron St John. <u>Front row:</u> Belle Smith, Katherine Swanton, _____ , _____ , _____ , _____ , Annie Wolf, Bessie Ramey, Roy Stephens, and Ed (?) St John. Courtesy of Luther Valley Historical Society.

Scotch Hill School gathering with another school "straight out on Center Street in Brodhead." No date. Teachers known are Buelah Day (Scotch Hill school) and May Day Ross (Hartz school).
Courtesy of Luther Valley Historical Society.

Scotch Hill School. No date, but circa 1911. In front: Roy Stephens. First Row: Belle Smith, Katherine Swanton, _____ , Bessie Ramey. Middle Row: Robert Van Skike, Anna Wolfe, Myron St John. Back row: _____ , Maude St John, Walter Ramey, Frank St John, Marguerite Smith, and Florence Lewis (teacher).
Courtesy of Luther Valley Historical Society.

Scotch Hill School circa 1926-27. <u>Standing in front:</u> Bobby Hawkins. <u>First row, left to right:</u> Russell Hawkins, George Schwartzlow, John Scwartzlow, Pearl Riese, Alice Olson, and Norman Olin. <u>Second row:</u> Alvin Schwartzlow, Alton Hawkins, Marvin Schwartzlow, Alerd Hawkins, Lillian Hawkins, and Luella Olson. Standing in back is Thelma Nyman (teacher). Courtesy of Luther Valley Historical Society.

Scotch Hill School circa 1930's. Courtesy of Luther Valley Historical Society.

Scotch Hill School in 1946. From left: James Caldwell?, Daryl Meythaler, Ramona Olin, Marian Nyman (teacher), Elaine Meythaler, Mary J Culles, Bobbie Meythaler, Rona Nyman, Germaine Kaderli.
Courtesy of Luther Valley Historical Society.

Scotch Hill School during the 1947-48 school year. Courtesy of Rock County Historical Society.

Scotch Hill School in 1949. Teacher is Marian Nyman. Courtesy of Luther Valley Historical Society.

Scotch Hill School in November 1955. Courtesy of Luther Valley Historical Society

Scotch Hill School in June 2015. Courtesy of the author.

Scotch Hill School in June 2015. Courtesy of the author.

Spring Valley Center School
District No. 3

Years of Operation

After 1858-1934 (Section 15)

1934-1957 (Section 15) on Highway 11 (old Highway 20), between Nelson and Bernstein Roads, west of Orfordville, Wisconsin. Located at 15422 W Spiech Road. The location was also given as "west of Pann Road, North side of west Speick Road – dead ends, which is just south of the railroad track that runs from Janesville to Monroe."

Memories

"The Spring Valley Center School was only a building, but the parents of that community and the boys and girls had a sincere love for all people, regardless of their race, color, creed, or social standing. If the people of the Selma, Alabamas all over the world could only open their hearts and minds toward 'Brotherhood' as the people of Spring Valley Center did, what a 'wonderful world' we could have.

The Negro family and the other ethnic groups of this community were as one; they thought, they worked, and they loved as one people – why can't the world emulate their behavior?" – Stanley S. Angell (taught in 1951)

History

HISTORY OF SPRING VALLEY CENTER SCHOOL
By Betty Earleywine

(Courtesy of Rock County Historical Society)

"The Spring Valley Center School was located in Section 15, just off Highway 11, east of Brodhead, on old Highway 20. It had its beginnings in the middle of the 19th century. Tennis Patriquen, who was born in 1847, attended school there and many years later, his granddaughter, Crystal Patriquen Rosheisen, taught school there. Crystal has many memories of Spring Valley Center School as she spent eight years there as a student and later taught there for seven years.

Early records reflect the different times. Wood was used to heat the school. In 1887, Richard Lang was to furnish the wood for $1.65 per cord, 'To be good merchantable wood and no stock less than 2 inches through.' He was also to build a fence around the school for $4. The school board clerk, J. F. Ennis, received $5 per year for his services and the teacher, Mary Nolan, was paid $25 per month. One hundred fifty dollars was raised for school purposes.

The school year was 8 months long. The annual school meeting in 1895 mandated: 'There shall be 8 months of school, starting the middle of April and continuing 2 months. The 1st of Sept. it should commence again for 2 months. The winter term should begin the middle of Nov. and continue 4 months.'

A teacher's contract in the early 1900's would include a report of the teacher's grade in such things as constitution, orthoepy, orthography, physiology and natural philosophy. The 1898 school census lists 63 children between the ages of 4 and 20 in the district. Only 36 were actually enrolled in school, however. In 1905, 26 students were enrolled, among them Tallie and Ruth Everson, Lucetta Dickey and Harry and Lloyd Leng. The average daily attendance in 1905 was 7 and the largest attendance in any one day was 12. In later years, attendance was better. Crystal Patriquen Rosheisen remembers having 15 to 20 students when she taught in the 1920's.

A teacher in a one-room school had to keep a tight class schedule. Winifred Broderick, in 1906-07 had a schedule that included opening exercises at 9 a.m. and then 22 different classes at ten or fiteeen minute intervals until 3:30 p.m. The classes were divided into A and B sections of upper, middle or primary form. The first part of the day was taken with 5 different arithmetic classes. Next came history, language, constitution, reading, geography, and spelling. There was a half hour break at noon. However, students were to be supervised at all times.

Discipline must have been a problem at times. In the early 1900's, clerk minutes record 'moved and carried that the two ___ boys be put in Orford jail for 24 hours with the father's consent.'

By 1910, the price of wood had gone up to $7 a cord and the clerk was paid $10. In 1925, a new floor was needed in the school. The board contracted Mr. Haugen to paint the ceiling and walls, put in the new floor and oil it for $238.50. In 1928, the school year was changed from 8 months to 9 months.

The 1931-32 records list 30 students form the following families: Davidson, Hogue, Vigdal, Burtness, Everson, Christensen, Keesey, Hintz, Ennes, Nording, Knudson, Wendlandt, McGuire and Severson.

A new brick school was built in 1934 by the W.P.A. Students attended school in the Dickey Cheese Factory during the building period. Mrs. Ellen Mahlum (Jean Pinnow's mother), taught at Spring Valley Center during that time.

At every school meeting thru 1938, the voters decided against free text books. Then in 1939, the motion finally carried to furnish them. The 1950 records show $3,500 raise for school purposes, a hot lunch program, and use of a film and traveling library. The clerk's salary was $50 in 1952. The treasurer and director each received $30.

Some of the many teachers (other than those already mentioned) were: Ina Stevens, Richard Egan, Clara Goul, Ida Ten Eyck, Laura H. Risum, Lillian Dybevik Tripke, Cora Thorson Bryant, Winifred Gempeler, Velma Mueller, Philomena Finnane, Mary Finnane, Ester Olsen, Robert Grulke, Standgell and Julia Dietwiler.

In February, 1957, a meeting was called to discuss consolidation. Present were the president of the Orfordville School Board, Merwin Abrahamson; Principal, Mr. McGinnis and Mr. R. Rockwell of Brodhead. It was decided by a vote of 25 to 3 that the district be divided between Brodhead and Orfordville and everyone could go where they wanted.

The school was sold Sept. 14, 1957, at public auction. Mr. Raymond Pann bought it for his wife's parents, the Noble Hamiltons."

Spring Valley Center School was consolidated with Orfordville Village School.

List of Teachers

Ina Stevens
Richard Egan
Clara Goul
Ida Ten Eyck

Laura H. Risum
Lillian (Dybevik) Tripke
Cora (Thorson) Bryant
Winifred Gempeler
_____ Standgell
1887 – Mary Nolan (paid $25.00 per month)
1920's – Crystal (Patriquen) Rosheisen
Circa 1934 – Ellen Mahlum
1938-39 – Velma (Thompson) Mueller
1940-42 – Philomena Malowney
1942-46 – Mary Finnane
1946-49 – Mrs. Esther Olson (Brodhead)
1949-51 – Robert Lee Grulke
1951-52 – Stanley Angell
1952-53 – Mrs. Julia Detwiler of Brodhead, WI
1955-56 – Nola Slaughter of Orfordville, WI

List of Students

Patriquen, Tennis (born in 1847)

Some of the twenty-six students attending in 1905

Dickey, Lucetta
Everson, Ruth
Everson, Tallie
Leng, Harry
Leng, Lloyd

Some students taught by Lillian Dybevik in the 1930's

Anderson, Palmer
Campbell, Lucille (Burtness)
Christensen, Roger
Davidson, Signi
Davidson, Thelma
Hintz, Gilbert
Hoff, Marjorie (Christensen)
Houg, Lena
Houg, Melvin
Houg, Viola
Keesey, Kenneth
Keesey, Lester
Knudson, Howard
McGuire, _____
Nordeng, Pearl
Nordeng, Stanley
Roenneburg, Louise Hintz
Vigdahl, Clifford
Wendlandt, Marvin

Students taught by Mrs. Ellen Mahlum in 1934

Burtness, Lucille
Christenson, Roger

Davidson, Carl
Davidson, Gladys
Davidson, Signe
Davidson, Thelma
Everson, Jean
Hintz, Louise
Keesey, Lester
Nipple, Walter
Nipple, Wayne
Nordeng, _____
Nordeng, George
Rhinehart, Pearl
Sprecker, Evelyn
Sveom, _____
Sveom, Oscar
Vigdahl, Clifford
Wagner, Betty Jane

Graduate in 1942

Vigdal, Charles

Graduates in 1944

Alexander, Robert
Nordeng, Charles

Graduates in 1948

Hofmaster, Ivan
Keller, Eugene
Morgan, Ted

Graduates in 1952

Day, Janet
Hanson, Delbert
Keller, Virgil
Morgan, David

Board Members

J. F. Ennis (Clerk in 1887)
Ray Pann (Director in 1952-53 and 1955-56)
Einar Nelson (Treasurer in 1955-56)
Nathan Potter (Clerk in 1952-53)
Orian Eidahl (Treasurer in 1952-53)
John Bernstein
C.O. Dickey
Kenneth Keesey (Clerk in 1955-56)
Anton Johnson

Photographs

Two photos above: These are believed to be Spring Valley Center School circa 1934 – just prior to being replaced with a new brick school that year. Courtesy of Brodhead Historical Society.

This is believed to be Spring Valley Center School circa 1934 – just prior to being replaced with a new brick school that year. Courtesy of Brodhead Historical Society.

Spring Valley Center School circa 1934. From a newspaper clipping that reads: "Sixty-one years ago, this group of students posed for a group school picture outside the Spring Valley Center School, located on then Old Highway 20, now Speich Road. Seated, left to right: _____ Sveom, Wayne Nipple, Carl Davidson, _____ Nordeng, and Walter Nipple. Center row: George Nordeng, Evelyn Sprecker, Jean Everson, _____ Sprecker, Gladys Davidson, Lucille Burtness, and Betty Jane Wagner. Back row: Oscar Sveom, Clifford Vigdahl, Signe Davidson, Thelma Davidson, Mrs. Ellen Mahlum (teacher), Pearl Rhinehart, Louise Hintz, Roger Christenson, and Lester Keesey. Courtesy of Mrs. Dale (Louise Hintz) Roenneburg via the Luther Valley Historical Society.

Spring Valley Center School circa 1930's. Back row, left to right: Lillian Dybevik (teacher), Howard Knudson, Marvin Wendlandt, Stanley Nordeng, Lena Houg, Palmer Anderson, Marjorie Christensen Hoff, Kenneth Keesey, Signi Davidson, _____ McGuire, and Pearl Nordeng. Second row, left to right: Viola Houg, Lucille Burtness Campbell, _ _____ , Melvin Houg, Lester Keesey, Roger Christensen, Clifford Vigdahl, Gilbert Hintz, Louise Hintz Roenneburg, ___ _____ , _____ McGuire, and Thelma Davidson. Courtesy of Brodhead Historical Society.

Spring Valley Center School during the 1947-48 school year. Courtesy of Rock County Historical Society.

Spring Valley Center School in September 1957. Courtesy of Luther Valley Historical Society.

Spring Valley Center School in 1975. Courtesy of Wisconsin Historical Society, Reference Number 87684.

Spring Valley Center School circa 2012. Courtesy of Luther Valley Historical Society.

Spring Valley Center School in June 2015. Courtesy of the author.

Spring Valley Center School in June 2015. Courtesy of the author.

Spring Valley Center School in June 2015. Courtesy of the author.

Spring Valley Corners School
District No. 1

Years of Operation

1846-Circa 1857(Section 9) – a log structure.

1857-1907 (Section 9) on Dickey Road one eighth mile south of Spring Valley Corners Road.

1907-1957 (Section 9) on Spring Valley Corners Road at Dickey Road – southeast corner of intersection of Gempler, Knutson, Spring Valley Corners and Footville-Brodhead Roads. Located at 1480 S Dickey Road.

Memories

"A never-to-be-forgotten day at the Spring Valley Corners School was the day we heard over the radio that our pupils had won a Zenith radio in an educational contest sponsored by WLS Chicago.

Four social studies programs weekly, for a period of twelve weeks, gave us the background for our project. Our purpose was to show how the knowledge we had gained carried over into every branch of school work. This was developed by means of a large scrapbook illustrating each phase.

A day after the radio announcement, a letter from Station WLS confirmed the happy news, and two days later, a table Zenith radio was delivered, and we knew it was really true." – Arice B. Leng (teacher)

History

SPRING VALLEY CORNERS SCHOOL HISTORY
By the Brodhead Historical Society

(Courtesy of Rock County Historical Society)

"Visit the Depot Museum and you are in for a treat. Along with the railroad memorabilia and 'Grandpa's Memories,' you will find a 'one room school.' There are old desks, slates, and pencil boxes. Behind the teacher's desk is the actual teacher's chair that was used in the Spring Valley Corners School. History comes alive!

Spring Valley Corners School sits on top a hill, 5 miles northeast of Brodhead at the junction of county roads Dickey, Gempler and Spring Valley Corners Road. A log school was built in the 1840s when the area was settled. On Feb. 12, 1857, Spring Valley School District No. 1, Sec. 9, received a grant of land from the University of Wisconsin on which they were to build a school house. The grounds were enlarged in 1886 and 1915.

There were 50 students in the district in 1861, ages 4-26. The families were: Heath, Dahl, Daniels, Boynton, Lawton, Shafer, Harper, Noyes, Smith, Clark, Bowles, Workman, Fuller, Chase, Harris, Harington, Palmer, Krause, Halsey, Fitch and Balis.

Clerk records of 1871 state: 'Resolved to put up hitching posts on each side of the partition fence.' In 1878 they voted 'to sell the moving and setting of the privy to the lowest bidder. James Shafer gets the job for $1.70.' In 1879 it was decided that 'The school children that break out glass and do other damage about the school premises, their parents or guardians, must fix them.' It was moved and carried in 1902 'that we raise $25 to plaster or paper the school house and make it look like a parlor.'

There were 39 students in 1904 including: Leona, Evalina and Dora Hageman, Ethel and Marion Leng, Charlie and Glenn Gibson, Earl Caple and children from the Heath, Liston, Gempler, Palmer, Disch, Fuller, Warn, Wood, Rossiter, Grangaard, F. Hageman and Thompson families.

The school district meeting of 1904 produced a proposal for building a new school and furnishing free text books. After a heated discussion, they were voted down, prompting Ole Grangaard to make the threat, 'we'll bring the 'vimmens' next time and smash this click, by 'uimminy'!' The battle was won in 1907 and a new school house was built, 28 ft. wide, 36 ft. long and 12 ft. high. John Ganzell was the contractor for $1,650 and it was to be built of first class material and by first class workmen. The old school house was sold to Fred Hageman for $30.

The school was used as a church on Sundays until 1915. A Brodhead minister preached there on Sunday afternoons.

Residents voted to raise $100 to build a wood shed in 1918 and any of that money left was to be used to buy War Stamps for District #1. A well was drilled in 1928 and a garage built in 1929. In 1933 it was decided to put a basement under the school and remodel it under the C.W.A. government program. The girl's entry would be eliminated (which had lately been used as a kitchen) and the entry would be at the S.E. corner. An auditing committee was appointed for the first time in 1934. They were to find out why the school received so much money that was not voted. Text books were furnished after 1935. Kerosene lamps were discarded in 1937 when the school was wired for electricity.

On April 18, 1957 the electors voted to dissolve Dist. #1, of Spring Valley and attach it to Brodhead and Orfordville as petitioned by each elector.

The school has been purchased by Ruth Dybevik Barreto and although it has been remodeled it retains much of the character of its former role. The original flooring has been sanded and varnished and the old library cupboards serve as kitchen cupboards today. And you can still ring the bell in the bellfry!"

HISTORY OF SPRING VALLEY SCHOOL DISTRICT NO. 1
By Mrs. Ruth Martin, Secretary of Rock Co. Historian Society, 1957.

(Courtesy of Rock County Historical Society)

"At a meeting of the school commissioners of Common Schools, Town of Spring Valley, April, 1846, the east half of section 4 – 9 – 10 – 15 – 16 be and the same are hereby set off and organized into a school District No. 2.

The District was later change somewhat and reduced in size and changed to District No. 1.

The District Treasurer – Lewis Bowles now living in the district tells this story as he remembers his father telling him that school was first taught in a small log house type of building for a short time at about the same location where the present school stands. This was later torn down and moved and built up again as a residence east of Spring Valley Corners and west of the former Amon Tollefson stone farm home but on the north side of the road. It stood there for many years but has now disappeared.

As far as we know the school was always located on one of the parcels of land about where it is today. In the early days of the stage coach, Spring Valley Corners was on the old stage route from Janesville via Footville cross country to the Corners. A post office established there about that time was in a part of the house now (1957) occupied by Mr. and Mrs. Roy Schenk across the road from the present school. Stone Liston and wife lived there for many years.

The country around the school was quite heavily timbered with lots of oak trees and other timber over the rolling land. The old stage road can be seen to this day where the old stages went up and down the hills and through the timber lands. These lands are now owned by Mrs. Marjorie Staffeld (formerly N. N. Palmer farm), Emma Applegate farm (occupied by Maurice Maveus) and the Lewis Bowles' land across the road from their farm buildings. Lots of hazel brush grew between the openings of the oak trees.

The records show the September meeting in 1866, the District was in debt $15.49 and the next year had but 18 cents in the treasury. They voted to raise $100.00 to pay teacher and $100.00 to paint the school house outside and inside. Mr. A. Shafter furnished 8 cords of wood at $4.65 a cord cut once in two for the stove and $3.00 was the clerk's fee and the only one of the board paid a fee. It was customary to hire a male teacher in winter and a female teacher in summer. Fifty scholars were enrolled this year from 5 to 36 years of age.

Some of the rules for the school in 1866 in regards to attendance were these:

If the child was absent six and one-half days or tardy marks in any four consecutive weeks (sickness excepted) shall render scholar liable for suspension except those under eight years of age.

Scholars who deface or injure any school property or furniture shall pay all damages and be subject to further discipline by the teacher.

There were several pupils at ages 17, 18, 19, 20, 21, and one at 25 and 36 years of age who attended school in the early days.

September, 1867 – voted to raise $125.00 to pay teacher for year. F. B. Smith furnished the 8 cord dry wood at $5.00 a cord.

1868 – The District was again in debt $29.50. This year they voted to build a fence between school and Mr. Shafer, change the hitching posts connected with poles to be set along this fence and a four board fence on the south.

1869 – They voted to pay the clerk $5.00 a year and as church was held in the school house Sundays, F. B. Smith was to receive $5.00 for opening it on Sunday and lock it in the evening. Lightning rods were put on this year – cost, $9.00. February 12th, the board met, Frank Shafer was suspended by Mrs. Harrington, teacher, for disobeying rules. Board unanimously voted to sustain teacher and decided Shafer could not return to school for the rest of the term. He was 15 years old at the time. The yearly cleaning of the school cost $3.50.

1870 – C. F. Dickey furnished 6 cords of wood this year for $36.00 and they voted to have 3 ½ month school in winter and same in summer.

1871 – September 25 – voted to buy a new stove then adjourned for a week for another meeting to discuss about buying a stove and repairs on the school. October 2, 1871 voted to raise $2.50 to repair the old stove and $2.50 for zinc to put under the stove. Raise ceiling overhead 2 feet higher and raise ceiling at walls to 5 feet and resolved to fill between the ceiling and weatherboards to the top of the ceiling with mortar made of lime and gravel and take the two west windows out and close them up and put one of them in the east end and have the black board extend the whole width of the west end. Take up the platform in the east end of school and lay a floor to correspond with the rest of the floor. Remodel seats and move them towards the east end and facing west and to have two coats of plastering put over the whole house. There be raised by tax $100.00 to repair the school and that $50.00 raised for the teachers' wages could be used if necessary to repair school. The work should be began immediately.

1870-71 – Cost $367.50 to operate school

1871 – November 20, Special Meeting. Resolved to give the walls of the school a priming coat of paint. Also to buy a new stove 'without a drum.' Its cost, $20.00, $50.00 more was voted to raise by tax to finish repairing school house and buy the stove and to buy what furniture is needed for the school. Azro M. Bowles was the clerk and resigned after it was built. Wm. Alcott was then elected clerk for two years to fill vacancy. He resigned the next year (1873).

1873 – 15 cord green oak wood was bought for $1.85 a cord delivered from C. F. Dickey sawed in two foot lengths. (Mr. Dickey furnished the wood most of the years until 1880. It was always bought from the lowest bidder). Dipper and wash dish – cost 50 cents. Lime and hair to plaster house – cost $7.10. Plastering the school house – cost $10.75.

1874 – The walls and ceiling were whitewashed for $5.00.

1878 – Voted to build a new woodhouse 12 x 16 with an 8 foot post, cost $35.00. Broom cost 25 cents compared to 1946 cost $1.59. Cost of cleaning school $1.50, and 1950's $25.00.

1879 – Voted the school children that break out glass and do other damage about the school, their parents or guardian must fix them.

1881 – New seats for school – cost $125.00. Cord wood also had increased to $2.00 a cord.

1882 – Voted to keep outsiders out of the school. Bought new seats – cost $90.00

1885 – September 21 special meeting. Voted to buy Lot No. 2 from State of Wisconsin – cost $26.94.

1886 – June 2 paid C. L. Valentine, Register of Deeds 75 cents. On June 18 paid E. C. McFetridge, State Treasurer for Lot No. 2. G. W. Bowles grubbed out the hazel brush and trimmed the trees – cost $7.36. The next year he set the hitching post – cost $2.64.

1887 – March 11. Board met and motion made and seconded that Rhoda Moore and Eva Moore make an apology to the teacher Miss Alcott and the school for their misconduct and disobedience of rules of school on the 10th of March 1887 or they shall be expelled from school for the balance of the term. They both made an apology and were allowed to remain. Rhoda was 17 and Eva 13 years old at the time. Free text books were voted this year also that J. W. Fuller could send his children to this school if he pays his share of expense. According to the number of children. Accepted $5.00 for his two children.

1888 – Bought a Whites Physiological Manikin (sic) for $25.00. The school house was valued at $500.00 and the site $200.00; the apparatus $10.00.

1891 – Bought a flag for the school house – cost $7.75.

1892 – Voted to have nine month school. James Sykes will have charge of the flag.

1893 – A new dictionary was bought – cost $1.20; express $.30.

1895 – July 15 paid Myron Bliss $1.50 to put flagpole on school house – cost $4.25 for first flag pole (for top of school house).

1896 – Paid Will Ackeson $16.00 for painting school and woodshed.

1898 – A new stove was bought from R E. Murdock for $20.00. A new floor was laid – cost $25.00. A bookcase cost $7.50.

1901 – Wash basin – cost $.08.

1904 – November 7 a special meeting to vote on whether to buy free text books and the building of a new school house. The text books were voted against after a lot of discussion. Mr. Ole Grandgaard finally winding up the discussion by saying that we would bring the 'vimmens' along the next time, and smash this 'click,' 'By Yimminy.' Voted against having a new school house. Later at that meeting voted that they have new text books, but wait until the next fall.

1905 – A school bell and order book was bought for $1.75.

1906 – First year the district clerk got paid $10.00.

1907 – March 26, a special meeting voted to build a new school house. April 1, at another special meeting the specifications for the new school house 28 ft. wide – 36 ft. long and 12 ft. high. It is to be built of first class material and by a first class workman. John Cansell was the only bidder. His bid $1,650.00. The district would haul the lumber. June 11, the old seats were sold to the following: James Oliver, Albert Palmer, Mrs. John Gough, N. N. Palmer Stone Liston, Fred Hageman, August Schultz, and Henry Heath all took two at ninety cents each. Ole Vigdahl (1 at .45), Otto Hageman (1 at .25), and Peter Moore (1 at .30).

The old school house was sold to F. Hageman for $30.00. Mrs. John Gough bought the book case for $2.10. P. T. Moore, auctioneer, was paid $2.00. September 19 the first big bell was bought for $30.00. A collection was taken at the church services of $11.81 toward the purchase of the bell. It was customary to hold church services every Sunday in the school.

H. F. Silverthorne furnished the new seats for the new building, cost $103.88. Blackboards cost $23.41. Plaster cost $10.00. Wm. Steuman did the mason work – cost $34.85 and James Moe tended the mason – cost $4.00. The name was painted on the school by F. D. Crosby. Heating plant cost $65.00. George Bahr soldered the deck on the belfry.

1908 – Voted not to have a new flag pole.

1909 – Bought four oil burning lamps.

1910 – Graduated from the dipper to a water fountain – cost $10.75.

1911 – The yard was fenced for $27.11.

1912 – The indebtedness for the new school was all paid off.

1914 – First time all the school board received pay: Clerk - $10.00; Treasurer - $10.00; Director - $5.00.

1915 – Paid J. B. Oliver July 20, $15.00 for land east of school, Lot No. 1. Deed recorded June 29. The first coal was bought. They also burned wood and then used coal in 1923 and eight years later burned wood again to heat the school.

1917 – Had old stove covered with heating and vent jacket – cost $65.00.

1918 – A woodshed was built for $153.00 connected to the school, north side. The next year the woodshed was painted for $15.00.

1919 – A new flag pole was erected. Bought from A. Thompson, cost $37.00.

1920 – Discarded the drinking fountain.

1925 – New lamps were bought for $26.00.

1926 – Voted to look into a line fence between Mr. Pagel's and school property. Maps were bought this year for $20.45.

1928 – Clyde Rossiter [of Orfordville] was paid $233.95 for drilling the well.

1929 – Steinar Haugen built a garage on the school grounds for $130.00.

1930 – Liquid soap made its appearance in use in school room.

1931 – A new stove was bought from Gaarder Bros. Hardware for $100.00 and a new flag cost $6.67 the next year. Five cord of wood was bought from Eugene Clark for $50.00.

1933-1934 – C. W. A. work dug basement under school and other improvements. The basement was all dug by hand and taken out in wheelbarrows.

1935 – New furnace and shovel bought from Brodhead Hardware, cost $301.78.

1937 – Voted to give enough land on corner to make a safe curve in return the grader can be stored on school grounds. If county does not fix curve the grader must be moved. A roof built over front door was put on this year – cost $35.00.

District board salaries were again increased – Clerk $12.50; Treasurer $10.00; Director $10.00.

W. A. Gavey, Orfordville, wired the school for electric lights – cost $82.00. The first light bill of $2.66 was paid November 15, 1937 to the Rock County Electric Cooperative Association. The last bill paid in 1957 was $3.50.

1939 – Teeter totters were added to playground – cost $50.00. A hectograph was also bought for $12.29.

1942 – Lamps were sold to Gardner school for $2.00. This year ten new desks and one chair were bought for $130.75.

1944 – Satrang Hardware was paid $65.00 for pump jack and Nordeng Electric service received $14.88 for installing pump.

1945 – Folding chairs were bought – cost $40.80. Cleaning of the school now cost $14.00, and a broom $1.59 compared to 75 cents in 1875.

It cost around $100.00 for coal to heat the school. The board's salary was raised again this year. Clerk gets $20.00; Treasurer gets $15.00; Director gets $12.50. More chairs were bought – cost $17.40. Voted to scrap the old desks and organ and sell the iron on them. This brought $1.00.

1947 – The blackboards were sanded by Gamble Store for $13.00.

1948 – The board's salary were raised to maximum. Clerk - $20.00; Treasurer - $20.00; Director - $20.00. School house was painted by Melvin Nelson – cost $206.28.

1950 – Crushed rock was hauled into the drive – cost $22.40. Storm windows were put on this year bought from Roderick – cost $78.15. The installing cost was $14.90.

1952 – A mail box was bought from Mrs. Clara Day for $5.00. The boards' salary was raised to Clerk $75.00; Director $50.00; and Treasurer $50.00. The electric lights had increased to $4.50 per month. The expense of operating the school this year was $3,161.91. Ten years before the cost was $1,491.57. Voted the auditors receive $3.00 each.

1956 to 1957 – Cost of operating school was $3,975.40.

1957 – February Board met with Superintendent Upson, Mr. Keithley and Mr. Zanton, Mr. Hannewal, and Mr. Stennerson at Janesville for the purpose of drawing up petition to circulate in dissolvement of district.

March 1 – Ralph Mau and Lewis Bowles circulated petitions. Those that wished to be attached to Orfordville petitioned to that effect and those who wished to be attached to Brodhead petitioned to that effect.

April 18 – A public meeting was held at school to vote on dissolution of District No. 1, Spring Valley and attachment of same to Brodhead District No. 1, Brodhead City Decatur Green County and Spring Valley Rock Co. and to District No. 4 Orfordville Village, Spring Valley, Plymouth, and Avon Township. Mr. Hannewal moved that the petition of the electors of District No. 1 Spring Valley be granted, no one for or against. Seconded by Charles Sarow. Motion carried. Mr. Keithley moved that petition of Spring Valley Center be heard on May 9, 1957, 8 P. M. at Spring Valley Center School.

Students to be transferred to Brodhead: Ralph Mau, Hazel Mau, Oscar Vigdahl, Helen Vigdahl, Raymond L. Staffeld, Marjorie Stafford, Fred G. Kaderli, Wilma Kaderli, Germaine Kaderli, Dwight Hageman, Charlene Hageman, Maurice S. Whitehead, Anna Clark Whitehead, Emil Rabe, Cecile Rabe, and Mary Hageman.

Students to be transferred to Orfordville: W. L. Bowles, Earl Demrow, Roy Schenk, Stanley Dybevik, George Altman, John Powers, Mrs. John Ruef, and Maurice Mavens.

Much credit is due the members of the school board in this district down thru the years. They must of taken their job and responsibilities of protecting the public records of the school seriously (and that is the way it should be) as the treasurer's records are complete from 1866 down thru the year 1957. It shows the orders drawn in the clerk's book or money paid out in treasurer's book and most always both. Neither book is available before 1866, however.

The History is finished, the public is invited to attend the centennial celebration and program June 30, 1957 in the school yard. Each family bringing their own table service, sandwiches and food to pass, also their own beverage. Picnic dinner at noon; program at 2:00 P.M.; Spring Valley School District No. 1.

In closing may we pay tribute to all who had a part in shaping of the Spring Valley Corners School District No. 1 during the 111 years since the establishment of the school district. To the old pioneers who came with courage, faith, and vision to settle here in this new strange country and to carve their homes from out of the wilderness."

The lists of teachers, students, and Officers for this school are gleaned from the aforementioned history by Ruth Martin.

Spring Valley Corners School consolidated with Orfordville Village School. Stanley Dybevik bought it in 1957 and used it as a dwelling.

List of Teachers

1866-67 – C. S. Harrington (salary was $35.00)
1867-68 – Hiram Tourtlott
1868 – Julia Pierce
1868-69 – Clarinda S. Harrington
1869-70 – Lewis Beebe
1870-71 – C. S. Harrington
1871-72 – Albert F. Nott
1872-73 – Julia Pierce
1874 – Helen Smart (part of year)
1874 – Julia Pierce (balance of year)

1875 – Marcelle Clifford (part of year)
1875-76 – Orrie Harris
1876 – Ella Williams (part of year)
1876 – Jane Richards (balance of year)
1877 – Julia Pierce (part of year)
1877 – Jane Richards (balance of year)
1878-79 – Lizzie Grove
1879-80 – Charles Niles (part of year)
1880 – Jennie Sheldon (part of year)
1880 – Charles Niles (balance of year)
1881 – Belle Moore (2 months for $30.00)
1881-82 – Ida Milks (part of year)
1882 – Gertrude Bowen (part of year)
1882-83 – Nellie Day (part of year)
1883 – Gertrude Bowen (part of year)
1883 – Jennie Taft
1883 – Helen Harrington
1884-85 – Nellie Taft (until October)
1885 – Chester Bennett (wages were $40.00)
1886 – Ida Milks (part of year for $40.00)
1886 – Carrie Moore (part of year for $40.00)
1886 – Josephine Alcott
1887 – Minnie Alcott (wages were $20.00)
1887-88 – Emma Wood
1889 – Flora Helmbolt
1890 – Chessie Smiley (wages were $25.00)
1891 – Lettie Hall
1892 – Edna Evans
1893 – Bee Harper (Fall Term)
1894 – Susan Harper
1895 – Malcolm J. Harper
1896 – Lola May Taylor
1897 – Jessie Sprague
1898-00 – Susan Harper
1900 – May Van Skike
1901 – Helen Beebe
1901-02 – Neva Helmbolt
1903-04 – Jessie E. Harper
1904-05 – Gordon Beebe
Sept. 1905 – Feb. 1910 – Mayme Keeley (wages were $40.00 in 1906)
1910 – Ray Fitzgerald (2 months)
1910-11 – Edna Lewis (Miss Hull ½ month; also Mrs. Turn substituted)
1912 – Alice Wilder
1913 – Alice Murray
1913-16 – Talma Straud (wages were $50.00)
1917-18 – Margaret Donahue
1918-19 – Hannah Stuvengen
1919-21 – Pearl Fossum
1921-23 – Cora Thompson
1923-24 – Pauline Kelley

1924-25 – Margaret Drew
1925-26 – Bernice Clark
1926-31 - Cora Thompson
1931-33 – Eleanor Spike
1933-36 – Viola Vigdahl
1936-37 – Florence Palmer
1937-38 – Hazel Mau (Salary $80.00)
1938-40 – Hazel Steele
1940-42 – Vivian (Johnson) Bowles
1942-44 – Bernadine Popanz
1944 – Margaret (Tierney) Drew
1944-45 – Esther Lyons
1945-57 – Mrs. Arice Leng of Box 504, Brodhead, WI (wages went from $197.00 per month in 1948 to $325.00 in 1956-57)
1947 – Mrs. Thelma Olin (substituted for Arice Leng in September, October, and November)

List of Students that attended from 1866 to 1957

Abrahamson, Arthur
Abrahamson, Burnett
Abrahamson, Hilda
Abrahamson, Merwin
Acheson, Tona
Alcott, Anna
Alcott, Minnie
Altman, Kay
Altman, Roy
Anderson, Marvin
Babcock, Arthur
Babcock, Cora
Babcock, Elmer
Babcock, Ester
Babcock, Florence
Babcock, Myrtle
Babcock, Ross
Badertscher, Dick
Badertscher, Jack
Baker, Bertha
Balis, Henrietta
Balis, Thomas
Bartlett, Spencer
Bates, Frank
Bates, Harry (1902-03)
Bates, John
Bates, May
Beach, Alexander
Beebe, Melvin
Beebe, William
Beilby, Anna
Beilby, Eva
Benjamin, Cora
Benjamin, Mary
Benscoter, Hanna
Benscoter, Libbie
Benson, Elizabeth
Bernstein, John
Bliss, Elsie
Bliss, Myron
Bliss, Orbie
Blogette, Mabel
Blogette, Ray
Bonaunet, Maurice
Bonaunet, Ollie
Booth, Harry

Bouthon, Seger
Bowles, Charles
Bowles, Cora
Bowles, Eva (1895)
Bowles, Flora
Bowles, George (1866)
Bowles, Harry
Bowles, Janice
Bowles, June
Bowles, Laura
Bowles, Lewis
Bowles, Louis
Bowles, Lucille
Bowles, Mary
Bowles, May
Bowles, Nellie (1866)
Bowles, Warren
Bowles, Willie
Boynton, Calvin
Boynton, Ellie (1867)
Boynton, Forest (1879)
Boynton, James
Boynton, Jay (1869)
Burnstine, Bennie
Burnstine, Billy
Burnstine, Charlie
Burnstine, Davie
Burnstine, Eddie
Burnstine, Henry
Butaw, August
Butaw, Emil
Butaw, Lena
Caple, Earl (1904)
Caple, Harry
Caple, Helen
Caple, John
Caple, Mae
Caple, Myrtle
Caple, William
Cary, Harold
Cary, Leah
Cary, Marian
Cary, Mary
Cary, Paul
Castle, Millie
Chase, Charles (1866)
Chase, Helen (1866)
Clark, Bernice
Clark, Daniel (1866)
Clark, Eugene

Clark, Farrel
Clark, Florence
Clough, Alfred
Clough, Mary (1866)
Coon, Carrie
Coon, Ida
Coon, Jennie
Coplien, Roger
Cox, Orville
Cramer, Russell
Crawford, Helen
Crawford, Howard
Crawford, Iva
Culles, Mary Jane
Cuygart, Rosa (1896)
Dahl, Frederic
Dahl, Hans (1867)
Dahl, Ole (1866)
Daniels, Fenton (1866)
Daniels, Florence
Daniels, Georgiana (1866)
Daniels, Nettie (1866)
Davidson, Signe
Davis, Theodore
DeLong, Ernie
Demrow, Karen
Dickey, Addie (1874)
Dickey, Frank (1879)
Dickey, Lucy
Disch, Bertha
Disch, Emma (1902-03)
Disch, Odin
Disch, Rena
Disch, Sarah (1902-03)
Douse, David
Dutcher, Clarence
Dybevik, Eunice (Graduated in 1934)
Dybevik, Lillian
Dybevik, Nina
Dybevik, Ruth
Dybevik, Stanley
Dybevik, Wilma
Ewing, James
Fisher, Alberta
Fisher, Beulah
Fisk, Jessie
Fitch, Mary
Fitch, Roxa
Focht, Lily
Frazer, Evaline

Fromholz, Artie
Fromholz, Avah
Fromholz, Emil
Fromholz, Hatred
Fromholz, Otto
Fuller, Albert
Fuller, Charley
Fuller, Edna
Fuller, Franklin
Fuller, Horace
Fuller, Mae (1902-03)
Fuller, Mollie
Garvey, Maria
Geist, Anna
Geist, Frankie
Geist, Lizzie
Geist, Melia
Geist, Rekie (1892)
Geist, Rudolph
Gempeler, Charlene
Gempeler, Hazel
Gempeler, Maybelle
Gempeler, Mildred
Gempeler, Myrtle
Gempeler, Walter
Gibson, Charles (1902-03, 1904)
Gibson, Fordy
Gibson, George
Gibson, Glen (1902-03, 1904)
Gibson, Nellie
Gibson, Willie
Giffort, Bertie
Gosda, Gerald
Gouff, Moore
Gould, Crithors
Gould, Guthram
Graham, Nora
Grangaard, Betsy (1902-03)
Grangaard, Clara (1902-03)
Grangaard, Eleanore
Grangaard, Gilman (1902-03)
Grangaard, Glen
Grangaard, Kenneth
Grangaard, Lena
Grangaard, Oscar
Grangaard, Paul
Grangaard, Signe
Griffin, Alice
Griffin, Josey
Guiel, Andrew

Gulsen, George (1866)
Gulsen, Guthran
Hageman, Beth (Graduated in 1952)
Hageman, Dora (1904)
Hageman, Dwight
Hageman, Elsie (1902-03)
Hageman, Evalena (1902-03, 1904)
Hageman, Faith
Hageman, Leona (1902-03, 1904)
Hageman, Maxine
Hageman, Nathan
Hageman, Pearl
Hageman, Virginia
Hall, Belle
Halsey, Eliza (1867)
Hamblett, Abbie
Hanson, Stanley
Harper, Ella
Harper, Helen
Harper, James (1873)
Harper, Marion
Harper, Susie (1866)
Harper, Tena
Harper, Thomas
Harrington, Helen
Harrington, Minnie
Harris, Emma (1866)
Harris, Orrie (1874)
Hart, Albert
Hart, George
Hart, Mary
Hartin, Charley
Haskins, Edna May (1895)
Hastings, Maggie
Hastings, Mary
Hastings, Nettie
Heath, Emmet (1866)
Heath, Erastus
Heath, Henry (1866)
Heath, Laura
Heath, Matilda
Heath, Robbie
Heath, Roscoe
Hector, Laura
Hegge, Merlin
Heron, Mary
Heyerdahl, Gerald
Heyerdahl, Lorene
Hiatt, Chester
Hill, Mary

Hill, Susan
Hoffman, Annie
Hoffman, Bertha
Hoffman, Betsy
Hoffman, Minnie
Hoops, Clyde
Hoops, Kenneth
Hoops, Philip
Hungerford, Alva
Hungerford, Jerome
Hungerford, Ronnie
Hungerford, Rosella
Hungerford, Willie
Johnson, Bernice
Johnson, John
Johnson, Maggie
Johnson, Merrille
Johnson, Orville
Jones, Bruce
Joranlein, Herman
Joranlein, Mable
Kamps, Jerry
Kamps, Judy
Kamps, Nancy
Kamps, Richard
Kamps, Ronald
Kamps, Ruth Marie (Graduated in 1942)
Keiper, Rosa
Kilday, Kitty
Krause, Lena
Krause, Lizzie
Krause, Sarah
Krueger, Viola
Lawton, Bertie
Lawton, Charles
Lawton, Emma (1866)
Lawton, Herbert
Lee, Bennett
Lee, Helen
Lee, Marvin
Leeport, Georgia
Leng, Elsie
Leng, Ethel (1904)
Leng, Marion (1904)
Leng, Oscar
Liston, Bertha
Liston, Conrad
Liston, Cora (1902-03)
Liston, Mabel
Liston, Oscar (1902-03)

Liston, Sofia
Losey, Georgia
Losey, Jacob
Losey, Josephine
Losey, Lena
Lowe, Lawrence
Lyons, Henry
Matatall, John
Matatall, Willie
Mau, Beverly (Graduated in 1952)
Mau, Ralph
Mau, Raymond
Mau, Stephen
Mau, William
Maveus, Merlin
Maveus, Steven
McCaslin, Bert
McCaslin, Earl
McCaslin, Ethel
McCaslin, Lola
McCaslin, Maggie
McDonald, Irene
McGowan, Mary
McMullen, Barbara
McMullen, William
Miller, Belle
Miller, Bert
Moodie, Darht
Moore, Eva
Moore, Rhoda
Moore, Robert
Morris, Wilbur
Muser, Herman
Muser, Iso
Muser, Jay
Muser, Mayo
Nenneman, August
Nenneman, Gusta
Nenneman, Harry
Nenneman, Herman
Nenneman, Julius
Nenneman, William
Newcomer, Donald
Newcomer, Helen (Graduated in 1942)
Newcomer, Laurabelle
Nipple, Lewis
Nipple, Margaret
Nipple, Walter
Nipple, Wayne
Nodland, Charles

Nodland, Jesse
Noonan, John
Noyes, Grant
Noyes, John (1866)
Noyes, Ruth
Noyes, Wesley (1866)
Nyman, Orville
Nyman, Shirley
Nyman, Thelma
Olin, Donald
Oliver, Tena
Palmer, Albert
Palmer, Bernie
Palmer, Beth
Palmer, Glen
Palmer, Margaret
Palmer, Marjory
Palmer, Maude
Parker, Henry
Patriquin, Edgar
Patriquin, James
Payne, Minnie
Philbrick, Byron
Philbrick, Edward
Philbrick, Frank
Philbrick, James
Pickett, Forest
Pickett, Gaylard
Pierce, Mamie
Potter, Clayton
Potter, Della
Potter, Sophronia
Powers, Barbara
Powers, James (Graduated in 1952)
Powers, Roger (Graduated in 1952)
Powers, Sharon
Rabe, Harland
Rabe, Merlin
Ramey, Ellin
Ramey, William
Raymond, Christabelle
Reuhlow, Albert
Reuhlow, Elsie
Reuhlow, Emma
Reuhlow, Minnie
Rossiter, Georgia
Rossiter, Wesley
Royce, Alice
Royce, Fred
Royce, Harry

Royce, Hattie
Ryan, Frank
Samson, Roy
Schafer, Almeda (1868)
Schafer, Frank (1866)
Schafer, Leona
Scherwin, Irene
Scherwin, Ivan
Schfield, Watson
Schlein, Emma
Schlein, Hampton
Scoville, Freddie
Sellnow, Alvina
Sellnow, Carolyn
Sellnow, Irene
Sellnow, Lester
Severson, Ella (1902-03)
Severson, Eva
Severson, Matilda
Sherman, Lydia
Smart, Edith
Smart, Henry
Smart, Lillie
Smith, Archie
Smith, Charles
Smith, Harley (1866)
Smith, John (1866)
Smith, Laurence (1866)
Smith, Mary (1866)
Smith, Maude
Smith, Orson
Smith, Thomas (1866)
Smith, Viola
Spencer, Frank
St. John, Willie
Staffeld, Nancy
Staffeld, Peggy
Staffeld, Rae
Stewart, George
Stewart, Georgia
Sykes, Harvey (1893)
Sykes, Hattie
Teehan, Francis
Thompkins, Lovilla
Thompson, Carl (1902-03)
Thompson, Dennis
Thompson, Helen (1902-03)
Thompson, Joyce
Thompson, Judy
Thompson, June

Thompson, Theodore
Tourtlelott, Lizzie
Twafman, Willie
Van Skike, Margaret
Van Skike, Robert
Van Skike, Roger
Vigdahl, Amanda
Vigdahl, Anna
Vigdahl, Bertina
Vigdahl, Charles
Vigdahl, Clifford
Vigdahl, Ella
Vigdahl, Geneva
Vigdahl, Isabelle
Vigdahl, Leona
Vigdahl, Lorraine
Vigdahl, Otto
Vigdahl, William (Graduated in 1952)
Vollhartd, Fred
Wall, Belle
Walling, Gilbert
Walling, John
Walling, Mary
Walling, May
Walters, Walter
Warn, Nina
Watt, Alazanna
Watt, Charlotte
Watt, Fremont
Watt, Quigley
Wee, Oscar
Welch, Ernest
Wesenberg, Robert
Whitmore, George (1874)
Wierson, Delores
Wilchelt, Anna
Wilchelt, August
Wilchelt, Bennie
Wilchelt, Bertha
Wilchelt, Jessa
Wilchelt, Ray
Wilchelt, Robert (1891)
Wilchelt, Willie
Williams, Eddie
Williams, Ella
Williams, George
Wood, Norris
Workman, Edith
Workman, Ella
Workman, Lenella

Workman, Sarah (1866)
Wright, Dolly
Wright, Henry
Wright, Herbert
Wright, Louis (1891)
Yusten, Lee
Yusten, Lynn
Yusten, Rusty
Zulke, Clarence
Zulke, Lucille
Zulke, Wilma
Zwygart, Anna
Zwygart, Ernest
Zwygart, Lizzie
Zwygart, Mary
Zwygart, Otto
Zwygart, Walter

Board Members

Clerks

1865 – F. B. Smith
1868 – N. N. Palmer
1871 – Azro M. Bowles (resigned 1872)
1872 – William Alcott (resigned 1873)
1873 – H. J. Lawton (elected to fill vacancy)
1874 – John Smart
1877 – William Alcott
1877 – P. J. Moore (elected)
1880 – H. J. Lawton
1884 – E. L. Wright
1887 – N. N. Palmer
1887 – E. L. Wright
1892 – A. W. Palmer (appointed)
1893-98 – A. W. Palmer (elected)
1899 – Lewis N. Bowles (resigned in 1901)
1901-11 – Otto Hageman (elected to fill vacancy and served 10 years)
1911-14 – J. B. Dybevick
1914-26 – F. R. Hageman
1926-34 – J. B. Dybevick
1934 – Glen Nyman
1935-38 – Oscar Vigdahl
1938-57 – Ralph Mau

Treasurers

1869 – F. R. Smith
1870 – A. Daniels (elected for two years)
1872-75 – S. J. Babcock
1875-78 – H. J. Lawton
1878-81 – Lewis Bowles

1881-82 – S. J. Babcock
1882-83 – James Boynton
1883-97 – J. B. Oliver
1897-July 1900 – R. J. Harper
1900-22 – A. W. Palmer
1922-23 – W. F. Kreuger
1923-25 – A. M. Abrahamson
1925-28 – Mrs. William Nyman
1928-34 – F. R. Hageman
1934-43 – Emil Rabe
1943-52 – Oscar Vigdahl
1952-57 – W. L. "Lewis" Bowles

Directors

1864 – J. Boynton
1867 – George Chase
1870 – Robert Heath
1872 – F. M. Potter
1876 – James Oliver
1879 – C. F. Dickey
1883 – H. J. Stewart
1884-98 – L. N. Bowles (elected to fill vacancy)
1898 – Ole Grosland
1901-09 – Ole Grangaard
1909-21 – Stone Liston
1921-30 – W. E. Bowles
1930-35 – Alfred Abrahamson (resigned)
1935-42 – Gilman Grangaard
1942-45 – Oscar Vigdahl
1945-57 – Dwight Hageman

Photographs

Spring Valley Corners School in 1902-3. Jessie E. "Bee" Harper (teacher). May Fuller Richards, Clara Grangaard, Leona Hageman Gibson, Elsie Hageman, Evelena Hageman Kiethly, next to last Gilman Grangaard. Helen Thompson, Emma Disch, Betsy Grangaard, Ella Severson, Sara Disch, Cora Liston, and Harry Bates (at end). Oscar Liston, Glen Gibson, Charles Gibson, and Carl Thompson. Courtesy of Luther Valley Historical Society

Spring Valley Corners School circa 1910. Courtesy of Luther Valley Historical Society.

Spring Valley Corners School circa 1910. Courtesy of Luther Valley Historical Society

Spring Valley Corners School in the 1920's. <u>Back row:</u> Lucille Bowles, Alvina Zellnow, _____. <u>Second row:</u> Iva Fromholtz, _____ , Lewis Bowles, Ferrel Clark, _____ , Lillian Dybevik, Irene Zellnow. <u>Front row:</u> _____ , _____ _ , Hattie Fromholtz, _____ , _____ , Lester Zellnow, Nina Dybevik. Courtesy of Luther Valley Historical Society.

Spring Valley Corners School in 1937. Courtesy of Brodhead Historical Society.

Spring Valley Corners School circa 1930's. Stanley Dybevik is the third boy from the left.
Courtesy of Brodhead Historical Society.

Spring Valley Corners School in 1942. Back row: Kenneth Grangaard, Maurice Bonaunet, Richard Kamps, Stanley Dybevik, Gilbert Walling. Middle row: Gerald Kamps, David Walling, Donald Newcomer, Russel Kramer. Front row: Margaret Van Skyke, Maxine Hageman, Mae Walling, Larraine Vigdahl, Geneva Vigdahl, Faith Hageman, Virginia Hageman, Eleanor Graangard, Mary Walling, Lara Belle Newcomer. Courtesy of Luther Valley Historical Society.

Spring Valley Corners School in 1944. <u>Bottom row, left to right:</u> William Vigdahl, Mary Hill, Nancy Stafeldt, Beth Hageman, Rae Stafeldt, and Susan Hill. <u>Middle row, left to right:</u> Nancy Kamps, Lorraine Vigdahl Bartelt, Margaret Van Skike Gadow, Maxine Hageman Turner, Jerry Kamps, and Faith Hageman. <u>Back row, left to right:</u> Geneva Vigdahl Johnson, Dick Kamps, Maurice Bonaunet, Kenneth Grangaard, Eleanor Grangaard, and Margaret Drew (teacher). Courtesy of Brodhead Historical Society.

Spring Valley Corners School during the 1947-48 school year. Courtesy of Rock County Historical Society.

May, 1957 – the last day school would ever be held at Spring Valley Corners School. <u>Left to right:</u> Karen Damrow, Kay Altman, Janice Bowles, Stephen Mau, and Nathan Hageman. Courtesy of Brodhead Historical Society.

May, 1957 – the last day school would ever be held at Spring Valley Corners School. Left to right: Kay Altman, Janice Bowles, Stephen Mau, Nathan Hageman, Merlin Maveus and William Vigdahl (in uniform), Ross Heath, and Will Gibson. Names of others is not known. Courtesy of Brodhead Historical Society.

Spring Valley Corners School in June 1957. Courtesy of Luther Valley Historical Society.

Spring Valley Corners School as a home in 1967. Courtesy of Brodhead Historical Society.

Spring Valley Corners School circa 2013. Courtesty of Luther Valley Historical Society.

Spring Valley Corners School in June 2015. Courtesy of the author.

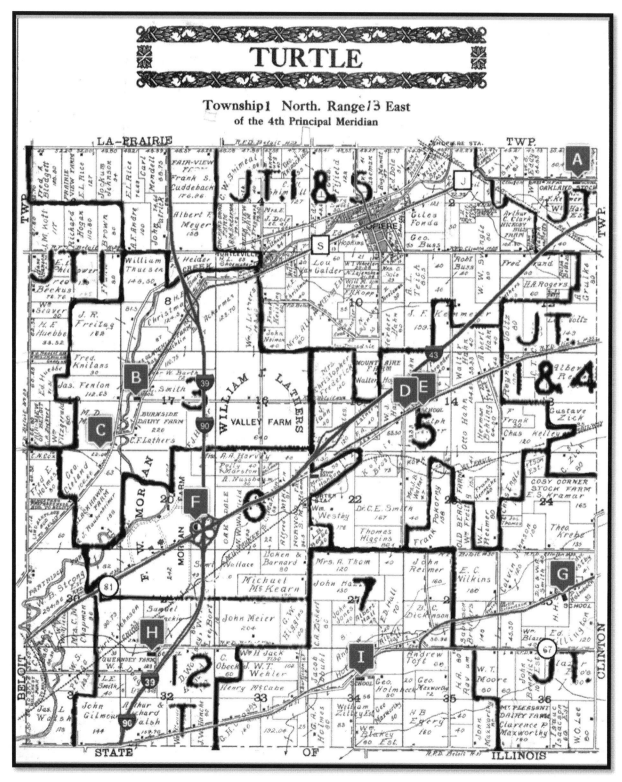

Turtle Township in 1917

Map legend for facing page

A. Chamberlain School - *see page 200*
B. Hart School - *see page 211* (1st location)
C. Hart School (2nd location)
D. Maple Lawn (aka Joel Miner) School - *see page 217* (1st location)
E. Maple Lawn School (2nd location)
F. Morgan Farm School - *see page 219*
G. Murray School - *see page 228*
H. Dougan (aka Daisy Chapin) School - *see page 201*
I. Zilley (aka D. D. Egery) School - *see page 258*

Chamberlain School

Joint District No. 1 with

Clinton, Bradford, and LaPraire Townships

Years of Operation

1867-1937 (Section 1) on County J.

Board Members

Gus Battalio (Clerk)
Glenn Hahn (Director)
Walter Kemmerer (Treasurer)
Walter Waite
Henry Hahn
John Milner

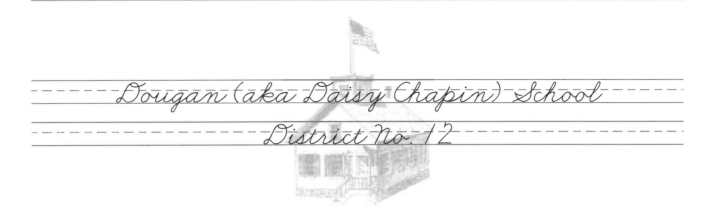

Dougan (aka Daisy Chapin) School
District No. 12

Years of Operation

1866-1920 (Section 32) on Colley Road, between I-90 and Spring Creek.

History

The first entry in the Treasurer's Book was made on March 30, 1866. No extensive records were kept until 1924-25 when pupils were transported and tuition was paid to Beloit School System.

DISTRICT #12 SCHOOL, TURTLE TOWNSHIP
by Eloise ____

(Courtesy of Rock County Historical Society)

"The old country schoolhouse now on the Bartlett Museum grounds originally District #12 School, in Turtle Township. It was located on the northeast corner of the Samuel Colley farm. W. J. Dougan bought this farm from Mr. Colley in 1906. In later years it became the custom to name country schools after prominent farmers in the districts, to wit: Murray, Zilley and Morgan schools. And thus it was that District #12 became known as the Dougan School for the last 10 or 12 years of its existence and is still referred to as the Dougan school district.

My maternal grandparents, Lewis and Eloise Smith and their only daughter, Lura, moved from Shirland, Illinois to the Houston (later Blodgett) farm in 1902. My grandmother became clerk of the school board and with few exceptions we provided room and board for the school teachers for many years.

My mother, Lura, who graduated from high school in 1903, taught the school for two or three years. Some of her pupils were Lydia, Edna (Mrs. George Clark) and Esther Priem, Willie Johnson, Emily Landwehr, Adelaide Greil, Willie Brunhofer, George and Carrie Graves, and Edna Schollmeyer.

Sara Church (Mrs. George Holmes) succeeded mother. I have a stub of one of her paychecks made out by my grandmother, and she was paid $30 per month plus board and room.

Helen Gillette, a relative of the Dougans, came next. She lived with them. Zilla McDowell, a Janesville girl followed. Next came Emma Anderson from Bergen. She had artistic talent and I still have some pictures of Peter Rabbit which she made for me.

Helen Dubois (sic) was the teacher when I started school at the age of 6. Here is the arrangement of the school interior when I started attending. Across the north end of the single room was a raised platform. On it was the teacher's desk, a United States flag on the left and a long recitation bench on the right. Across the north end there was a blackboard with a box of maps at the center. There were four rows of desks of assorted sizes, the smaller ones at the front. A few were double desks. All had inkwells.

Across the rear wall were hooks for our outer clothing. There was also a 5 gallon water crock with a spigot. Each pupil was supposed to have in his desk, his own collapsible drinking cup, a leaky contraption at best. A woodshed extended across the building beyond the back wall and the pot bellied stove, sheathed in a protective jacket, stood conveniently near the wood shed door. Pupils who misbehaved were sometimes sent to the woodshed to think things over.

Midway on the west side of the exterior of the building, was a so-called ventilator – a big sheet metal elbow extending from just above the floor of the classroom to about 18" above the ground. By crawling underneath it was possible to hear what happened when a pupil was kept in at recess. We took turns listening, observing a sort of peck order.

The south and west sides of the schoolyard were fenced with a 5 plank board fence. The north side, fenced only at the west end, sloped down rather abruptly to Spring Brook, which we called the crick. It was not unusual in the spring for some pupils to go wading at recess.

At opposite ends of the west boundary were the two privies. If one needed this facility during school hours, it was necessary to raise either one or two fingers to let the teacher know the action predicted.

At recess we played Anti-I-over the schoolhouse roof, New Orleans, pom, pom, pullaway, many kinds of tag, statuary and tug of war.

Blanche Carpenter (Mrs. Floyd Brewer) was my next teacher. During her term of teaching Leona Diderich, my seatmate, died of a gunshot wound, accidentally self-inflicted, when she dislodged a loaded shotgun from hooks over the outside kitchen door. She and her sister, Mary, always hung their heavy grey sweaters on those hooks and she was attempting to pull hers down when the accident occurred. She lived only a few hours.

Mrs. Ernest Smith was the next teacher. She had to resign when she discovered much to her surprise, after many years of marriage, that she was to become a mother. The school board was shocked when she offered to finish out the year even though her delicate condition might be obvious by that time. It would be a most unwholesome influence on the children, they all agreed. Ronald Dougan finished out that term.

Mrs. Herman Hugle, with her father as a frequent substitute, rounded out the roster of teachers. Mrs. Hugles' father was an expert at mental arithmetic. He drilled some of the upper grade pupils until they could give the correct answer with astonishing speed to a long series of one and two digit numbers added, subtracted, multiplied or divided on command.

The old school house had been condemned in 1910 or thereabouts. At the annual meeting held each June in the schoolhouse, Mr. O. D. Antisdel, Rock County Supt. of Schools, would say that the building was unfit. After considerable haggling and pacing up and down on the sagging floorboards, Mr. Antisdel would be persuaded to grant another year's reprieve. But at last the building was so much in need of major repairs and the enrollment so small, not over 8 or 9, that it was voted to close the school. And transport the pupils to the Beloit School System as tuition pupils. This must have been about 1920 or 1921. The Elson Cab Co was engaged to transport us.

Shortly thereafter the Dougans moved the dilapidated old building to their farm yard to use as a storage shed, the fence was torn down and the school yard returned to cultivation. There now remains no trace of where it stood.

Children enrolled in District #12 at sometime during the years that I attended were: Leona and Mary Diderich, Doris (Mrs. James Bownell) and Norma Higgins, Milton, Albert, Dorcas and Lilas Popanz, Jon Swain, Esther

Dougan, Edna Kraft, John and Grace Hansche, Robert, Margie, George and Merwin Mackie, Margaret and Billie Umland, and a grandson of Smith (Mitt) Graves who built the house and barn on what has long been the Freitag farm."

History of Dougan School
(Author unknown)

(Courtesy of Rock County Historical Society)

"Ronald A. Dougan – a farmer, pupil, and teacher at Dougan School, moved the school to his Hill Farm where it was used as a storage shed. Sentimental attachment prompted him to keep the austere little frame bulding in good repair. Later, he donated the building to the Bartlett Museum where ti was to be restored by the Beloit Chapter of Delta Kappa Gamma – teaching sorority, as the Daisy Chapin Memorial Schoolhouse. She was a former Beloit teacher and principal, for years a curator of the Bartlett Museum and one of Beloit's foremost historians. The school was to be outfitted with early-era desks, chalkboards and other items including the old Strong School (of Beloit) bell."

List of Teachers

1866 – Alice Carpenter
1867-68 – Elizabeth Butlin
1868-69 – Elizabeth Butlin
1869-72 – Elizabeth Perselles
1873-74 – Osbert Jack (3 months); August Perkins (2 months) Mrs. G. A. Love (2 months); Susie M. Hayward (3 months)
1874-75 – Addie Clifford
1876-77 – Addie Clifford
1877-78 – Miss Q. W. Veritatium (?)
1878 – Eunice I. Babbitt
1878-79 – I. W. Hutchinson
1879-80 – Anna Mosher and Anna Simpson
1880-81 – Hattie Munger and Jennie Carpenter (Salary $12.00 per month)
1881-82 – Jennie Carpenter (Salary $12.00 per month, I. W. Hutchinson (Salary $12.00 per month), and Hattie Munger (salary $15.00 per month)
1882-83 – Belle Northrup
1883-84 – No record.
1884-85 – Hattie Colton
1885-86 – Edna Permely
1886-87 – Marie Bailey
1887-88 – Lottie Hayford, Miss Rosenblatt, and Lillian Dean
1888-89 – Lillian Dean
1889-90 – No record.
1891-92 – Ada Jones and Linda Creighton
1892-93 – Linda Creighton
1893-94 – Augusta Zilley (Salary $24.00 per month)
1895-97 – Jesse Jones (Salary $25.00 per month)
1897-98 – Amber Payne and Lizzie Baker
1898-00 – Louise Mills (Starting salary $20.00 per month raised during year to $25.00)

April-June 1900 – Kitty Barrett
1900-01 – Minnie Bird, Myrtle Cranston, and Gertrude Robinson
1901-02 – Sarah Clark
1902-03 – Lillian Hahn (Salary $20.00 per month)
1903-05 – Lura Smith (Salary $25.00 per month. Graduated from high school previous June)
1905-06 – Floy Carter (Salary up to $30.00 per month)
1906-07 – Lillian Latta (Salary $35.00 per month) and Helen Brand (last two months)
1907-10 – Sara Church (Mrs. George Holmes). (Salary $30.00 per month)
1910-11 – Helen Gillette (Salary $40.00 per month)
1911-12 – Ethel Sperry (Salary $35.00 per month)
1912-13 – Anna Wheeler (Salary $37.00 per month)
1913-15 – Zella McDowell (Salary $37.00 per month)
1916-17 – Helen L. DeBois (Salary $50.00 per month)
1917-18 – Blanche Carpenter (Mrs. Floyd Brewer) (Salary $50.00 per month)
1918-19 – Mrs. Ernie Smith (Emma Anderson?). Ronald Dougan finished out the year when Mrs. Smith became pregnant.
1919-20 – Mrs. Herman Hugle with her father as a frequent substitute.
No further records kept until 1924-25 when pupils were transported and tuition was paid to Beloit School System.

List of Students

Brunhofer, Willie
Carpenter, Blanche
Denniff, Joe
Diderich, Leona
Diderich, Mary
Dougan, Esther
Dougan, Trevor
Dougan, Ronald
Graves, Carrie
Graves, George
Greil, Adelaide
Hansche, Grace
Hansche, John
Higgins, Doris (Mrs. James Bownell)
Higgins, Norma
Johnson, Willie
Kraft, Edna
Landwehr, Emily
Mackie, George
Mackie, Margie
Mackie, Merwin
Mackie, Robert
Marston, Eloise
Popanz, Albert
Popanz, Dorcas
Popanz, Lilas
Popanz, Milton
Priem, Edna (Mrs. George Clark)
Priem, Esther
Priem, Lydia

Schollmeyer, Edna
Smith, Lura
Swain, Jon
Umland, Billie
Umland, Margaret

Board Members

Eloise Smith (Clerk)
Fred Umland
Mrs. Alice Mae Umland
Roberta Ullius
R. A. Dougan
Mrs. Fred Wallace
R. C. Walsh
Ray R. Lang (Clerk in 1952-53)
Albert Marston (Director in 1952-53)
Ray William Lang (Treasurer in 1952-53)
Melvin McCabe (Director)
Bernie Gordon (Treasurer)
Annie L. Higgins
S. K. Blodgett
Mrs. George Mackie

Photographs

Dougan School. Front row, left to right: _____ , Carrie Gravey?, Adelaide Gruebl?, Edna Priem, and Esther Priem. Back row, left to right: Willie Johnson, Willie Brunhofer?, George Graves, Lura Smith (teacher), and Lydia Priem. Courtesy of Rock County Historical Society.

Dougan School in 1912. Ron Dougan on roof. Other names written on back are Trevor Dougan, Robert Mackie, and Margaret Mackie. Teacher (2nd from left) is Ethel Sparry who lived on Bluff Street in Beloit, WI.
Courtesy of Beloit Historical Society.

Dougan School teacher Zella McDawell. Courtesy of Rock County Historical Society.

Dougan School. Blanche Carpenter, Joe Denniff, and Eloise Marston. Courtesy of Rock County Historical Society.

Dougan School in 1975. Courtesy of Wisconsin Historical Society, Reference Number 82889.

The Dougan School as it appeared in 2014 on the grounds of the Bartlett Homestead Historical Site operated by the Beloit Historical Society in Beloit, Wisconsin. Photo by Clark Kidder.

Hart School
(Called Schuster School after Consolidation)
District No. 3

Years of Operation

1840-1845 (Section 18) in Bennett home

1845-1866 (Section 17) on Bennett land on County S, south of Hart Road.

1866-1957 (Section 17) ¼ mi. northeast of old school, west side of intersection of County S (Shopiere Road) and Hart Road.

Circa 1957-1963 - on 2401 Murphy Woods Road (on Schuster property). A two-room school now called Schuster School.

History

THE HART SCHOOL
By Leona Skogen
(Written in July 1984)
(Courtesy of Rock County Historical Society)

"The first district school began in the home of Alden Isaac and Mary Bennett. The children of this family made up a large part of the school. The Bennett children were Ruth Ann, Phineas, Alden, Mary, Thomas, Charles (died in infancy), Augusta, and Alfred.

This first school started in 1840. Miss Miner was the teacher. Other families besides the Bennetts were Harvey and Tuttle.

In 1845, a frame schoolhouse was built on the Bennett property south of the Bennett-Hart Bridge, on the east side of the road, just at the edge of the woods.

In 1866 the second Hart School was built on Reigart property about a quarter of a mile northeast on Shopiere Road. It was used until 1957. At that time a two-room school was built on Schuster property on Murphy Woods Road and was called Schuster School. Within a few years the district discontinued and was divided, part going to Beloit and part to Clinton.

The Northwest Ordinance of 1787 declared that free education was to be provided in the new states. As soon as the Town of Turtle was organized schools got immediate attention.

On July 29, 1847 the school commissioners for the common schools of Turtle met at the home of Joel Miner. They numbered the districts, identifying each in the wilderness of woods and creeks. They often were given the name of a well-known settler such as Samuel Hart. The school was given number four and called Hart School. Later the number was changed to three.

Samuel W. Hart and his wife Sarah came from Paris, N.Y. In 1859, they bought 440 acres on Shopiere Road. He was a leather tanner and merchant. They had nine children. He was very prominent in local politics and promoting education.

Those who attended Hart School remember the entrance with caps, coats, boots and dinner pails along the walls. There was a sink, water pail and cooler kept in one corner. Pupils were assigned duties to keep the entrance in order and the cooler filled. The kids enjoyed this because it gave them a chance to be out of the classroom for a spell and they could mix a little pleasure with their work.

The school was remodeled several times. In the early days there was a small platform in front for the teacher's desk. In a rear corner was a jacketed stove. On this food was kept warm in winter by placing glass jars in a roaster half filled with water. The older boys carried in wood from a woodshed outside the school. There was one just outside the front door. Each morning a cooler was filled with fresh water.

At the front of the classroom was a long recitation bench with a high back. Classes in turn were called to the front to recite. Blackboards were placed between windows and also in front of the room. Pull down maps hung over the blackboards. A large globe on a pulley hung down from the ceiling. The library consisted of shelves under the windows. Many of the books were read over and over. In later years a large box of books traveled from school to school. This was a real treat for the pupils.

Softball was the usual game each spring with neighboring schools competing for the best team on Playday. This was a day set aside each spring for a gathering of schools to compete in various activities.

In winter everyone took turns sliding down the hill behind the school. Every kind of 'made up' sled was used, including three-cornered pieces of tin and old dishpans. When the ice was ready everyone hurried to eat lunch so they could play or skate on the creek. Those without skates usually had sleds or just played tag on the ice. In spring there was 'rubber ice' and sometimes a ducking in the cold water.

Arbor Day was a fun day. All the kids helped clean the yard by bringing rakes, spades and hoes to school. In a long line they would rake the schoolyard from one side to the other. A tree, bush or flowers were planted in the yard. Of course this would be followed by a picnic and games.

May Day was another fun day to recall. May Day baskets were made from paper in all sizes and shapes each with a handle. Wild flowers were gathered for the baskets. These baskets were taken home at night. Usually they were hung on doors to surprise another child by leaving the basket and quietly running off.

Halloween was always a time for foolishness. On one occasion a bag rack belonging to Henry Schallmeyer was placed on top of the schoolhouse. The next day he saw to it that the big boys took it down again and returned it.

Another time Jon Stabler found a horse's harness on one of his milk cows. He was very angry as they knew he would be. Corn shocks were often taken from fields and placed in unusual places."

The Hart School is listed as a State Graded School in the 1955-56 directory. It became part of Beloit Union High School District Jt. 1 after closing.

List of Teachers

1840 – Miss Miner
Mary Bennett
Clara Eddy
Miss Goodall

Charles McLenegan
Emmett Scriven
Jennie Carpenter
Winnifred Carpenter
Della Tuttle
Jennie Tuttle
Rena Gilman
Della Southard
Katherine McGlauchlin
Lenore Cadman
Maud Crippen
Norma Higgins
Esther Ellis
Arlene Hagar
Leona Skogen
Nellie Bostwick Van Galder
1938-43 – Mrs. Ora Haas
1943-44 – Mrs. Evelyn Alderson
1944-46 – Arlene Schollmeyer
1946-47 – Mrs. Mildred Lippens
1948-53 – Mrs. Ellen Wildermuth of Rte. 2, Clinton, WI
1955-56 – Mrs. Leona Skogen (Principal) of Beloit, WI
1955-56 – Hazel Bown of Beloit, WI
1961-62 – E. C. Heyerdahl of Orfordville, WI; Principal; Grades 7-8
1961-62 – Mrs. Esther McCutchan of 320 Forest Park Blvd., Janesville, WI; Grades 1-2
1961-62 – Mrs. Betty Webb of Milton Junction, WI; Grades 5-6
1961-62 – Mrs. Ida Mae Proper of S. Bluff Trailer Park, S. Beloit, IL; Grades 3-4
1962-63 – Mrs. Esther McCutchan of 320 Forest Pk. Blvd., Janesville, WI. Taught Grade 1.
1962-63 – Mrs. Lucille Belke of 1426-1/2 Henry, Beloit, WI. Taught Grade 2.
1962-63 – Mrs. Leona Friske of 20 S. Concord, Janesville, WI. Taught Grade 3.
1962-63 – Mrs. Mary Thym of 2577 White Oaks, Beloit, WI. Taught Grade 4.

List of Students

Andre, Archie
Andre, Elsie
Capron, Clarence
Capron, Grace
Capron, Sam
Carpenter, Edward
Carpenter, Jennie
Carpenter, Winnifred
Christman, Alta
Christman, Farmer
Christman, Harrison
Garlick, Murray
Garlick, Ruby
Hard, Fred
Harvey, _____
McGlouchlin, Charles
McGlouchlin, Hanna

McLenegan, Annie
McLenegan, Archie
McLenegan, Charles
McLenegan, Sam
Murphy, _____
Ross, Nellie
Ross, Spencer G.
Scriven, Ernest
Scriven, Jesse
Tuttle, DeWayne
Tuttle, Hattie
Tuttle, Jennie

Graduate in 1942

Schollmeyer, Donna

Graduate in 1944

Fink, Larraine

Graduate in 1948

Knueppel, Julia

Graduates in 1952

Coburn, Carol
MacGowan, Terry

Graduates in 1962

Allen, Cheryl
Belcher, Kathleen
Charland, Stuart
Fitch, John
Marxen, Dale
Roeker, David
Wintlend, William
Witt, Christiane

Families in the District

Pioneer families included: Bennett, Harts, Billing, Smith, McGlaushlin, Raymond, Flory, Tuttle, Hoadorn, Palmer, Britten, Murphy, Holmes, Ross, Carpenter, Scriven, Andre, McLenegan, Patrick, Christman, Page and Hilton.

Board Members

Jean MacGowan (Clerk in 1952-53)
Mrs. Mary Boggs (Director in 1952-53)
Selmer Skogen
Walter Gornet (Treasurer in 1952-53)
Mrs. Lois Coburn
Clifford Hazelwood
Henry Schollmeyer
Virginia Coleman
Nellie Henning
Wallace Carlson (Clerk in 1955-56)

James McGuire (Director in 1955-56)
Cyril Finnegan (Treasurer in 1955-56)
Forrest D. Knueppel (Clerk in 1961-62)
Harold E. Roeker (Director in 1961-62)
Arthur Kind (Treasurer in 1961-62)
Robert MacGowan

Photographs

Hart School in 1936. Courtesy of Beloit Historical Society.

Hart School in 1936. Courtesy of Beloit Historical Society.

Hart School during the 1947-48 school year. Courtesy of Rock County Historical Society.

*Maple Lawn (aka Joel Miner) School
District No. 5*

Years of Operation

1852 – _____ (Section 14) north of County X, just east of Walker Road.

Before 1873-1947 (Section 14) south of County X.

History

HISTORY OF MAPLE LAWN SCHOOL
By Leona Van Landingham and Tracy Grulke

(Courtesy of Rock County Historical Society)

"In 1860, Miner was in school. Farmers would try to get wolves on horseback, passed the school. In 1860 George, son of Joel Miner, attended school.

Began by Will Gates who was Superintendent of Turtle Town Schools. In 1852-53 officers met in Sept. 1852. They were Joseph Post, Joel Miner, Edward Bradley, and David Blood.

At another meeting Joel Miner was Moderator and Librarians Hamlin Treat, Herman Barrett, and David Blood attended.

In 1852, Catherine Dockstader was the teacher – salary $50.00 a month. In 1864 C. M. Treat taught a winter term for $30.00 a mo. School value was $150.00. M. T. Treat and Alex Thom."

List of Teachers

1852 – Catherine Dockstader (paid $50.00 a month)
1864 – C. M. Treat (winter term for $30.00)
Frances McCabe (Babcock)
Florence Babcock
Jenette Johnson
Jennie Kilpatrick
Elda Schaffner (Ehrlinger)
Marian Larson (Higgins)
1938-39 – Edna Mohr
1940-41 – Perle Skinner
1941-42 – Zola Dietrich
1942-43 – Evelyn Alderson
1943-44 – Arlene Schollmeyer (Hager)
1944-46 – Frances Conley
1946-47 – Eleanor Von Hayden

List of Students

Grulke, Tracy
Nyberg, Irene
VanLandingham, Mrs. J. C.

Families in the District

Fred Gebroeder, Ralph Miner, Bater, Herman Behling, Kelly, Engebretson, Fred Hahn, Chant, and Walker.

Board Members

Mrs. Herbert Hahn (Treasurer in 1952-53)
Mrs. Carl Hahn (Clerk in 1952-53)
Leonard Beadle (Director in 1952-53)
Volney Schroeder
Albert Hahn
Charles Walker
Arnold Hahn
Mrs. Tom Higgins
Mrs. Otto Hahn

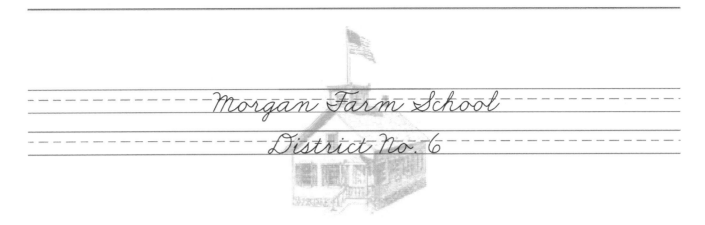

Morgan Farm School
District No. 6

Years of Operation

1848-1920's (Section 20) in the northeast corner of the intersection of Milwaukee Road and Highway 15.

1920's-1938 (Section 20) moved to the opposite corner (exact direction not given).

1955-____ (Section 29-30) on 1611 Lee Lane at Milwaukee Road.

History

MORGAN FARM SCHOOL
DISTRICT #6, TURTLE
By Helen Wildermuch
(Written September 1984)
(Courtesy of Rock County Historical Society)

"The early records of Morgan Farm School, District #6 of Turtle have been found. No record of a land transaction giving land for school use was found in the records of the County Registrar of Deeds. The clerk and treasurer's books which were believed to have been turned over to the Beloit School district could not be located at the time of this writing.

The Town of Turtle Clerk's record book beginning in the year 1846 records the making of a new school district #6. I quote this record keeping the original spelling and putting in parenthesis words which could not be clearly made out either because of penmanship or because of aging.

'We the commfisioners of the common schools in and for the town of Turtle (pursuant) to notice duly met on the 13 day of May 1848 at the house of E. P. (Sasy) and set off the following (described) sections and parts of sections to constitute a new School District No 6 in Section 19, 20, 30, 29, 31, 32 and (W 1/2) of 21, 28 and 33, in Town ( ) N. Also (Sec) 6, 5, and W ½ of 4 with the exception of the E ½ of SW qs in Town 1 North Range 13, East. R. F. Murray and H. Donalson; Comm of Con-Schools. Attested J. A. Harris; Town Clerk.'

The clerk's records show several alterations to districts in the township in these years. No record of money issued to District 6 was found until March 19, 1849 – a year later, when an order for $32.70 was written to school district #6.

The town Clerk's records also show a town superintendent of schools. The records give no indication of the duties of this township superintendent. Even though his relationship to Morgan school is not clear, reference to these records is included in this paper for general interest in early school history. On March 20, 1854, William Gates claimed $20 for superintendant of schools for the Town of Turtle. H. J. Murray drew $11.00 on March 27, 1857, for the school superintendent. The following record is shown for the appointment of Mr. Treat: 'At a meeting of the Board of Supervisors held this fifteenth (15) day of October AD 1861, said board did appoint Mr. C.

M. Treat to fill the vacancy in the office of School Supt, occasioned by the reisgnation of E. D. Farham, this day received, accepted. Attested W. Atwood Bond; Town Clerk – by order of Board Sup.

A later Town of Turtle clerk's record book, starting with the date 1868, records the following officers for District #6: L. E. Smith, Philo Porter, Director. Aug. 18, 1869, S. H. Slaymaker; Treasurer. In 1875, J. R. Dole replaced one of the officers and in 1878, B. F. Hannahs was on the District #6 board.

From the name and location of the school, it can be assumed that the land was obtained from the Morgan family but more research is needed to determine the type of agreement. The school was first located at the NE intersection of Milwaukee Road, Highway 15, and a road leading back to the Morgan home. According to Harry Wallace the road at that time continued to the Chicago, Milwaukee, and St. Paul Railroad. There at Morgan Switch, vegetables, cabbage, and sugar beets were shipped. A section of the road can still be seen. Presently the Shell Gas Station is located very close to the original location of the school.

Because of flooding in the original location the school was later moved to the opposite corner of the field but still on Highway 15. The second location can presently be identified by a few trees which grew in the school yard and are now seen in the NE clover leaf of the Highway 15 – I-90 intersection. The school was located directly across the road from the lane which lead to the Samuel Wallace residence.

Some of the maple trees lining this lane can still be seen and help locate the setting of the school. The exact date of moving the school is not known but it was in the early 1920's.

Mamie Strang Wallace, who taught in the school from 1918 to 1921 recalls the water being so high that they couldn't get into the school. She remembers a team of horses brought them to school and came to get them when school was out when the water was so high.

A class picture, owned by Mildred Rey, and taken in 1923 or '24, can be easily identified as being in the second location. The school was then built with a basement and had several steps and cement porch. This places the moving of the school sometime between 1921 and 1924.

Paul Han remembered helping move the school with horses on rollers according to his wife Revella. Mrs. Han contributed a class picture taken when Paul was in first or second grade – 1907 or '08. The picture makes an interesting comparison with the picture taken in 1923 or '24 shortly after the school was moved. Paul is the little boy in the front row and Revella thinks his brother is just behind him.

Mamie Strang Wallace also recalls that she had a box social to raise money for hot lunches. 'The boys and girls were good to help prepare the lunches,' she writes. 'One lad became a chef in a large restaurant.' This lad is Lewis Marston who was chef, among other places in the Congressional restaurant serving both houses of Congress.

Harry Wallace who probably started in Morgan in 1912 or '13, also remembers the high water which flooded the school. He remembers that his teacher walked from her home on the east side of Beloit built the fire and was ready for pupils by 8:00. She also did her own janitor work. He couldn't remember the teacher's name but possibly it was Hazel Doyle who taught there just before Mamie Strang Wallace.

Fannie Viehman Tuck whose son Fred went to Morgan in the late 20's – early 30's was impressed by the hot lunch program Mrs. Murphy started. The method was simple. A pan of water was put on a hot plate. Pupils brought whatever they wished to be warmed in a pint jar. Fannie Tuck also remembers that Mrs. Murphy had three school programs a year. In a play for one of these programs Fred played the part of one of a family on a train trip. He always considered the pupils who were in this play family as his school family. In March when Fred was in fourth grade the Viehmans moved out of the district. Fred walked down the railroad track to keep attending Morgan School for the rest of the year, probably a walk no farther than he had walked before. And he still had the company of Les and Ralph Wallace as they cut through the property of Sam Wallace on the first part of their way home.

I attended Morgan School for the eight years of my elementary schooling – 1925-1933 – and have the following recollections which are probably typical of any rural school of this period.

The school was one main room with a hall as you entered with hooks for our coats. Boots removed here saved much cleaning in the school room. This hall was also useful in games during a rainy day recess when one person or team had to go away from the main group.

A larger hall in the back of the building lead to the basement stairs and back door. This hall made the main room much easier to heat. Here the water cooler or drinking fountain was kept. Water was carried in from a hand pump in the school yard. There was a stand with wash basins where we were each required to wash before lunch. Shelves provided storage for books not in use and for our dinner pails. Each hall was used for individual study – an excellent place to practice flash cards with a friend or individually, or to memorize a poem, since low voices here did not disturb pupils in the main room.

The basement was large enough for games like pusy-wants-a-corner or hop scotch, on a rainy day. There was a coal bin and the furnace. The hot air pipe for the furnace extended to the back of the schoolroom. The register giving forth heat was high enough so that only the teacher and taller pupils could reach the mittens which were hung by their thumbs to dry.

The teacher's desk was always in the front of the room. Mrs. Murphy, who was my teacher grades 2-8, may have moved her desk to different spots in the front of the room but it was always up front. Next came the recitation bench where each class was called for their instruction. The four or five rows of pupil's desks had three to five desks in a row. The desks in each row where joined together. Smaller desks for first graders were on the left of the room. As we grew in grade level and size we gradually moved right into larger desks.

When I first started school we had no electricity but kerosene lamps in brackets on the walls. On a dark day light was inadequate. I remember the teacher standing by the window reading to us when there wasn't enough light for us to see at our desks.

Class work followed the state course of study, which was set up for odd and even years enabling the combination of grades. Third and fourth grade, fifth and sixth, seventh and eighth, were easily combined for language where they had one set of pictures and stories for even years and another for odd years. Even this made better than twenty classes every day.

First grade classes always came first in the morning and after each play period. Lower grades followed on up to the seventh and eighth grade. This enabled the teacher to explain their assignment to lower grades. The older pupils could remember an assignment given the day before or read it from the blackboards which were in front and between windows on each side of the room.

Seventh and eighth grade reading consisted of classics such as 'Rip Van Winkle,' 'Legend of Sleepy Hollow,' 'Evangeline.' Mrs. Murphy always read the next days' lesson aloud to seventh and eighth grades. I can remember planning my work so that I had time to listen to these stories.

Recesses were fifteen minutes each morning and afternoon for the upper grades. Lower grades were excused first giving them longer play time – shorter school time. Noon hour was usually half an hour in winter and an hour in spring and fall. Since the length of the noon hour determined the time of closing school for the day, this had to be cleared with parents. The big bell called us in at the end of recess. It was considered a privilege to pull the rope which rang the bell. The county superintendent or supervisors came periodically to visit. We looked forward to their visit because teacher and supervisor talked during recess. This always took longer than fifteen minutes giving us a 'long' recess.

When the weather was nice we ate our lunch outside. When it was cooler, sitting in the sun with our feet dangling over the edge of the cement porch was a favorite place to eat lunch. At one time during my school years, our mothers decided to take turns bringing us a hot lunch. This didn't work too well because we didn't always like what someone else's mother brought. Each bringing our own food in a glass jar to be heated in the pan of hot water worked much better.

Games played during recess were hide-and-go seek, pompon pull-away, anti-i-over, soft ball and of course other things we had to practice for Play Day. Play Day, sponsored by the county YMCA was a big all day event which included all schools in the township. Events included soft ball, our favorite, volley ball, horse shoe, relay races, ball throws, broad jump, and bean bags for the little ones. Sometimes Play Day was held in the grove on the Boynton farm very near our school. Sometimes it was at Murray School. Events were tightly scheduled. We had to keep close track of the events we were in to be sure we didn't miss them. Besides we liked to watch the adults of our district as they competed with other schools. A big thing of the day was the stand selling pop cooled in a tub of ice water. Pop was not an everyday thing in those times. Occasionally we would have a practice for Play Day beforehand with Maple Lawn School. It was fun to leave school for a ball game, especially since we always chose a school with which we were evenly matched for these practice games.

Each year we had a social to raise money. For days ahead we practiced our plays and recitations and probably some songs. We often didn't have a music teacher and music wasn't one of Mrs. Murphy's special talents, so music wasn't emphasized. The plays Mrs. Murphy selected were usually funny, at least we felt so and enjoyed them. Our parents seemed to approve. They came to Turtle Hall on the night of our performance, paid their admission, ate the light lunch (which they had provided). We had some extra money for things like play ground equipment, or pictures for the wall.

Good Friday was another special day. We brought our rakes and raked the lawn. Older ones raked and younger ones carried leaves.

Another thing we looked forward to was the arrival of the county book box. This was a small collection of books, not more than twenty or thirty in each box, as I remember, which circulated around the schools. Each school kept it a period of time, possibly a month. I can also remember that I could be disappointed if the book box came with nothing to my particular liking. It did help us find books to fill our reading circle requirements. If we read so many books each year – was it six? – we got a seal to put on our reading circle certificate. These books had to be from different groups, social studies, fairy tales, and biography. I'm sure I would never have read anything but fiction if it hadn't been for these requirements.

We had county exams in seventh and eighth grade. All seventh and eighth graders in the county went to a center where these written exams were taken. Passing the exams certified completion of eighth grade and permitted us to take part in the county eighth grade graduation. I remember spending considerable time in the hall with old county exams, memorizing exact answers to specific questions.

One year we also had a County Music Appreciation Contest. For this we were given a selection of classical records and brief biographies of the composers to study. The test again taken at a center, consisting of recognizing the selections played, correctly spelling the name of the selection and the composer, and then a few questions on the biographies. Looking back it was for me a successful introduction to classical music.

Walking home from school is another integral part of my memories. In the morning my brothers and I were able to ride with my father as he hauled the milk to Beloit. But after school we walked. When we walked 'around the road' it was a little over two miles. Sometimes we went that way to walk with friends. The shortest way cross-lots was only about a mile. Time-wise this was probably the longest way because it went past Grandma's and meant a stop to raid her pantry with its good pound cake. We stopped to read her funnies in the Rockford Morning Star. To get home we had to cross the creek and railroad. Cross-lots meant stepping stones in the creek and all sort of things to explore as we came through the fields.

I have tried to orient these memories of my school days in Morgan Farm School toward my feeling as a child. While they have the peculiarities of my personality and the aching of Mrs. Murphy, they are probably basically very similar with other memories of this period of life in a rural school. For this reason they were included in this paper to try to give a picture of life in a rural school.

Because of small enrollment the school was closed in 1938 and the pupils were transported to Beloit. Isabel Halderson has confirmed that the contents of the school were auctioned probably in 1943. More research will be needed to learn what actually happened to the building.

During the '40s a subdivision developed in the western section of the district increasing the number of students. With the influx of these urban members, a new three room school was built within the Turtle Ridge subdivision. School board members at this time were Dr. Eisel Le Masters, Director; Mrs. Everette Beguin, Clerk; and Hugo Budzien, Treasurer.

In 1962 with the Common School District Consolidation Act the school was again faced with what must have been a traumatic decision. A 2.6 square mile sector of the district which was basically urban was annexed to the Beloit School district. The rest, which was basically a rural area, became a part of the Clinton Consolidated School District.

Morgan School stands today as a part of the Beloit school system. Its history as a one room school and then a three room school are still remembered by this school community."

List of Teachers

Circa 1917 – Hazel Doyle
1918-21 – Mamie (Strang) Wallace
Circa 1926-33 – Mrs. Murphy
Dora (Conlon) Higgins
Kathryn (St. John) Johnson

List of Students

Hahn, Paul (Circa 1907-08)
Marston, Lewis (Circa 1919-21)
Tuck, Fred (Circa late 1920's-early 30's)
Wallace, Harry (Circa 1912-13)
Wallace, Lester
Wallace, Ralph
Wallace, Sam
Wildermuch, Helen (1925-33)

Students in 1900

Bumsted, Floy Marston
Gates, Frank
Gates, George
Gates, Ida
Hannahs, Alex
Hannahs, Ben

Hannahs, Lenora
Hannahs, Mark
Marston, Albert
Marston, Roy
McKenzie, Clara
Montanye, Della
Porter, Frank
Steinberg, Anna

Students in 1924

Bauman, Gladys
Bauman, Les
Decker, Bob
Hammell, Howard
Johnson, Ted
Lippens, Andy
Lippens, Ray
Marsden, Gordon
Ulrich, Agnes
Ulrich, Gertrude
Ulrich, Frank
Ulrich, Mary

Board Members

L. E. Smith (1868)
Philo Porter (Director in 1868)
S. H. Slaymaker (Treasurer in 1869)
J. R. Dole (1875)
B. F. Hannahs (1878)
Kathryn (Mrs. Ted) Johnson (Clerk)
W. R. Halderson (Director)
Hugo Budzien (Treasurer, 1940's)
Mrs. Everette Beguin (Clerk, 1940's)
Dr. Eisel Le Masters (Director, 1940's)
Vern Jeckert
Mrs. Alice Livingston
Mrs. Fred Wallace
Al Jack
Mrs. Artis Halderson
Arthur Hahn

Photographs

Morgan School in 1900. <u>Behind fence, left to right:</u> Floy Marston Bumsted, Anna Steinberg, Miss Libbey (teacher), Roy Marston (twins), and Frank Gates. <u>In front of fence, left to right:</u> Mark Hannahs, Albert Marston, Ida Gates, Clara McKenzie, Lenora Hannahs, and Della Montanye. <u>On steps:</u> George Gates, Alex Hannahs, Ben Hannahs. <u>On lower step</u> is Frank Porter. Courtesy of Rock County Historical Society.

Morgan Farm School in 1907. <u>Front row:</u> _____ , _____ , and Paul Hahn. Boy in back row behind Paul Hahn is one of Paul's brothers. Courtesy of Rock County Historical Society.

Morgan Farm School in 1924. Back row: Agnes Ulrich, Dora (Conlon) Higgins (teacher), Mary Ulrich, Howard Hammell, Andy Lippens, Gordon Marsden, and Ray Lippens. Middle: Gladys Bauman, _____ , _____ Lathers?, Gertrude Ulrich, and Les Bauman. Bottom row: Bob Decker, Ted Johnson, and Frank Ulrich.
Courtesy of Rock County Historical Society.

Murray School
Joint District No. 8 – 2 with Clinton Township

Years of Operation

1847-1872 (Section 25) on Highway 67

1872-1955 (Section 25) on County P about a quarter mile west of S Clinton Corners Road. Located at 7242 E County P.

History

HISTORY OF MURRAY SCHOOL DISTRICT NO. 9 (LATER 8 AND 2)
By Irene Dresser Sommers

(Courtesy of Rock County Historical Society)

"According to the clerk's minutes of Murray School 'it was founded September 22, 1844 by order of the commissioner of common schools of said town (Clinton). By order of said commissioner the first school district meeting was held in the house of Hiram Raymond on October 21, 1844. William S. Murray was chosen moderator and Jesse Leverich was elected clerk pro tem.'

At a meeting on October 23, 1847 it was decided to collect a tax of $50 to finish the school house. Adjourning to Friday the 29 they voted to pay B. D. Murray $8 advance for flooring and an additional tax of $25.

In 1849 'time for giving proper notice having passed by through the misapprehension of the director no annual meeting of the district was held, but a special meeting was called and duly notified to be held October 1.' $21 for teacher for summer school, $40 for teacher for current school year, $15 for fuel, $14 for building school house, $3 for repairs on school house and for furniture for school, are listed as the business conducted.

In May 1852 there were 11 males and 7 females in Clinton Township, and 13 males and 23 females in Turtle Township between the ages of 4 and 20.

Minutes are recorded for annual meetings for the years 1847, 1849, 1850, 1852, 1853, 1855, 1856, 1858, 1867, 1869, 1871, 1872, 1873, and 1879.

It was first referred to as district 8 and 2 in the 1853 meeting. Also that year $6 was allowed for H. H. Smith for fence on site 'upon receiving deed for same.' There was apparently quite a struggle in the district to get a deed for the site but this was never done and upon the dissolution of the district the land reverted to descendents of Henry Smith as was voted in the 1871 annual meeting.

Due to expansion of the district it was voted in 1855 to build a new school house. This was followed in 1856 by voting $120 for repair of the old school building. October 2, 1869 they decided to 'form a committee to ascertain the cost of a new school house.' The meeting was adjourned to October 16 whereupon they rescinded the previous meeting's proceedings.

The meeting on September 25, 1871 was an eventful one. 19 voted to let the school house site remain where it was (12 against). $50 was voted to buy ½ acre of land from H. H. Smith and $500 for building school house. The committee was given one week to find a site for the school house. The next month it was resolved the school board shall not expend any money for school house 'until title is obtained for old site with an additional half acre.' A ballot vote authorized the board to spend no more than $600 for the building. A motion to change the site lost - a motion to reconsider and table motion carried.

By 1872 problems were resolved. A contract was let to Chandler and Hatch for $575 for the new building. A half acre was purchased from H. H. Smith for $50. The old school building was sold to William Murray for $15.35. There are no further records of the district.

The school building stood virtually unchanged from its completion until its purchase by J. A. Christiansen when the move was made to go to Clinton. A front entry was added at some time.

In 1933 a Civil Works Project made possible the excavation for a basement and the installation of a furnace. This necessitated a change in the rear of the building as the wood shed made way for a back entry and steps to the basement.

Running water was never put in. The hand pump in front continued to provide clear, cold water. When my father attended Murray School he helped carry water from a spring on the Smith farm while my sister helped bring it in pails from the two close neighbors (1908-1916).

Electricity came through in 1936 when REA lightened and illuminated the entire countryside.

Murray School received its name from the Murray family. William S. was one of the first six settlers in Clinton Township. He served prominently in town affairs taking an active part in the organization of the township, serving as chairman of the board. He represented the district in the state legislature. Members of the Murray clan were large land owners in the district. The records do not reveal when the name Murray was selected.

At one time Sunday school was held in the school house on Sunday afternoons. This started around 1906 and continued for several years.

The first and last day of school picnics were eagerly awaited by all the residents, as were the school programs. Murray usually had one in the fall (it was quite an incentive for good behavior and grades for if things weren't 'up to snuff' – no program); a Christmas program and one in the spring. Sometimes a box social was held in conjunction. In an earlier day when married teachers were not allowed this gave the local fellows a chance to impress the 'school Mom' with a sizable bid on what they thought was her box. Sometimes teachers married someone in the district and became a permanent resident.

The township Play Days brought the adults together in the spring as they met at the schoolhouse in the evening, after chores, to practice for the competition between schools in the township. Murray always had an excellent men's volleyball team.

During the 1940's a community club enjoyed pot luck suppers once a month and then played '500.' These continued until the school consolidation in 1955. For many years neighbors gathered here for bridal showers for young ladies of the settlement.

Two of our sons, my father, grandfather and this writer attended Murray School – Irene Dresser Sommers, R. 1, Clinton, Wis."

REMEMBER OLD MURRAY SCHOOL?
By Ardis Boynton

(This story ran in the Clinton Topper newspaper, Oct. 16, 1975; p. 12)

"It is September and I am sitting at my desk in the old Murray School, about 1910. It is a warm, sunny day, and thru the open windows I can hear the autumn humming of the crickets and grasshoppers, and an occasional 'katy-did.' The neighbor's chickens are cackling and crowing, the ducks paddle about and quack, in the brook back of the school house, a calf blats and its mother moos her answer. All is quiet in the room, except for the occasional rustle of a page turned or the tapping of a pencil as the pupils work at their lessons. There is such a wonderful feeling of peace and security, confidence in the world. Suddenly a voice says, 'second grade reading class stand,' and I come back to the present with a start. It's just another one of those nostalgic dreams, a 'rerun' of scenes of yesteryear.

So, in retrospect, I look about the sunny school room, with its very high ceiling, and long windows, kerosene lamps with bright reflectors along the walls and blackboards between the windows. A hanging globe, which could be raised or lowered for study, cases of pull down maps, one for each continent, picture of Washington and Lincoln and panels of Audubon bird pictures and a big pendulum clock adorned the walls. There was an old fashioned organ, the teacher's desk, with a slanted top, which she had to raise to reach her supplies, and neat rows of double desks, bolted to the floor. The front ones were for the small pupils and gradually were larger toward the back for the older pupils. Those desks were sometimes used as a method of punishment, because, if a boy misbehaved the teacher might sentence him to sit with a girl the rest of the day, and that made him an object of ridicule with the rest of the boys. The only thing that kept the girl from feeling that she was being punished too was the fact that she was setting an example for good behavior, and the sympathy of the rest of the girls. I can't remember that a girl was ever sentenced to sit with a boy. Sometimes 'pals' were allowed to sit together, as long as they did not break any rules.

At one end of the room an entry jutted into the room, with doors opening, on the right and left, into alcoves where there were hooks to hang wraps and a bench for dinner pails.

At the other end, doors opened into the library and the woodshed. Beside the woodshed door stood the old wood burning stove, with a high metal jacket around it, which was supposed to diffuse the heat; but only seemed to send it all up to the ceiling, until someone conceived the idea of cutting an opening in the jacket, with a sliding closure, which could be opened when it was too cold.

The library contained a big cupboard in which there were some reference books and a few 'story books,' by such authors as Louisa May Alcott.

That room answered more than one need. When a pupil misbehaved he might be banished to that room, forbidden to open the cupboard, to meditate or study until he decided to behave. On the other hand, good behavior might win a reward of going in there to study, or for two or three to work on a project.

Then there was the water supply. That was carried in a pail, by the older boys and girls, from the nearest neighbor. The pail was set on a bench, with a long handled dipper, which served everyone. Later, when ideas of sanitation became more prevalent, there was a cupboard, divided into small compartments, in which a white enameled cup with a number on it, and each pupil had his own cup, but they all still dipped into the same pail. Finally a stoneware bubbler replaced that method and then a well was drilled in the school yard and each pupil brought their own cup.

In the last few years of the rural schools, the county promoted Play Days, when each school in a township entered teams in men's, women's and children's kitten ball, volley ball and many other contests. There would be a play day in each township and the champions there entered the County Play Day. That brought every one out for practice in the spring, on Sundays and 'after chores' in the evening.

When P.W.A. days came along the Murray school house was raised and a basement was built under it. It had plenty of windows, and made a fine place to play on stormy days. A coal-burning furnace was installed. There was a hot plate and saw horse tables, electric lights in the school room and a yard light. The old woodshed became a coat room with wide cement steps to the basement. About the only thing that did not change was those two little buildings in the farthest corners of the back yard [the boys' and girls' outhouses]!

Teachers' wages went up too, gradually, to almost $200 a month, and of course her work was much lighter 'with all those modern conveniences'!

In order to graduate from the rural District School, every pupil had to pass an examination on all the subjects studied, given by the County Superintendent's office. It was a very thorough examination but there were very few who ever 'flunked out' and many students went on to honors in high school and college.

The demise of the Rural District School left a void, which nothing has yet been discovered to fill.

Then there was the teacher, the most important cog in the rural education system, and they were dedicated people in those days. They loved teaching and were truly interested in their pupils' progress. They loved most of them and were loved in return. Oh, I'll have to admit that once in a while there would be one who was an ogre to some of the pupils, as well as an occasional pupil who was an ogre to the teacher.

Teacher was the 'hub' of almost everything that went on in the school was well as a 'cog' in the system.

In nineteen ten her salary was about forty-five dollars a month, out of which she paid two or three dollars a week for room and board. Earlier the salary had been much less, and she 'boarded around' in the homes in the district. She might have anywhere from 10 or 12 to 50 or 60 pupils in all eight grades. Our school was one of the largest and a good teacher could keep three classes going at once: one in their seats doing a written assignment, one in the recitation seats, and one at the blackboard, probably doing arithmetic problems.

She taught the 'three R's' – Geography, Physiology, History, Spelling, Civics, Agriculture – which was really more a study of plants and animals. The first three were taught in every grade, with others started in fifth or sixth. We were fortunate that our school had two large wooded areas nearby with dozens of kinds of flowers and trees, also a swamp, with many more varieties. We had many bird hunts and flower gathering days. I still remember the big beds of violets, purple, yellow and white, blood root, mandrakes, shooting stars, anemones, brakes, wood ferns and maiden hair ferns.

Every morning there would be fifteen minutes for 'opening exercises' which usually was singing or sometimes reading from a book by the teacher. Fifteen minutes of every day was devoted to writing in our 'copy books' following a model at the top of the page. Often we had spell-downs or oral arithmetic – no pencils allowed, 11x12 plus 4-7 plus 10-16 equals?

Oral questions in Geography and history, done like a spell-down, were fun too.

The teacher's duties didn't end with just teaching pupils. She had to build the fires in the morning and keep them going all day. She swept the floors and kept the school room in order. Of course she could enlist the aid of the older scholars, but it was her responsibility. She helped the small ones with their wraps in the winter and comforted the small ones when that was needed. She kept order in the school yard during noons and recesses, and often; played games with her pupils. Games in those days could be Drop-the-handkerchief, Prisoner's Goal, Tag, Run-around-the-bases, Hide and Seek, Anti-over, or London Bridge. In winter the most fun was Fox and Geese when there was snow. Indoors we might play Spin-the-platter, Musical Chairs, Fruit basket Upset, Skip-to-my-Lou, or Winkum. In the spring the instant that teacher said 'Classes dismissed,' everyone leaped to their feet and yelled, 'pitcher,' 'catcher,' 'first base' or some other position on the team as they all raced to the ball diamond, both boys and girls.

There was plenty of social life in those old rural school days too, and a fine fellowship and loyalty among friends. There was always a picnic the first day of school for the whole family and a picnic, with a program by the pupils, on the last day of school. There was a Christmas tree, a program and treats for everyone. The Christmas tree was lighted with candles and I marvel that we never had a fire from them. There was an Arbor Day program and then everyone pitched in to help rake the school yard and plant trees, flowers and shrubs. There would be one or two box socials during the year, when a lot of the young men would vie for the teacher's box and run it up to four or five dollars, which was a lot of money in those days.

Murray School had a Community Club too, which met every month with a pot-luck supper and card games."

In early years Murray School had an orchestra, which was highly regarded, and played at dances over a wide area.

List of Teachers

William Treat
Achsah Lewis
J. Montgomery
Lucy M. Smith
Mary O. Hale
M. Carrie Harris
Ella Hayward
M. E. Winne
M. G. Park
Ella Raymond
C. Bennett
Blanche Carpenter (Brewer)
Lucy Rice
Celesta Dyson
Maude Crippen
Emma Barth
Flora Robinson
Rosetta Blaser
1914 – Rachel (Beals) Weirick
1928 – Alice Murphy
Virginia Snyder
Barbara Ledman
Minnie Egery
1938-41 – Janette Snyder Kohls
1941-42 – Ilah Goldsworthy
1942-45 – Mrs. Ellen Wildermuth
1945-46 – Mrs. Florence Doering
1946-49 – Frances McCabe (Heyerdahl)
1949-53 – Mrs. Hylah Kolman of 1660 Chapman St., Beloit, WI
1955-56 – Mrs. Hilda Burns of Beloit, WI

List of Students

Andell, Dorothy
Anderson, Christine (Gustafson)
Bandlow, Edward
Bandlow, Francis
Bandlow, Leonard
Bandlow, Richard
Bates, Howard
Bates, Lester
Boynton, Ardis (Dresser)
Champney, Winifred
Cole, Connie (Larson)
Dresser, Ardis
Dresser, Carrie (Harris)
Dresser, Marston
Fosmoen, Carrie
Fosmoen, Gertrude
Fosmoen, John
Friday, Paul
Gustafson, David
Hessler, Annie
Higgins, Marion (Larson)
Holman, Amanda
Holman, Selma
Holmes, Jean (Dresser)
Kohls, Alfred
Jacobusse, Wallace
Johnson, Stanley
Kelsey, Edith (Hogan)
Kelsey, Margaret (Hogan)
Klein, Nellie (Wright)
Kramer, Hiram
Kramer, Mable
Kramer, Olen
Kramer, Rollin
Krebs, LeRoy (1930's-40's)
Lee, Alice
Lee, Carrie
Lottig, Walter
Moore, Vernon
Ocher, Gladys (Reimer)
Reimer, Gladys
Rohr, Dorothy (Reimer)
Sommers, Edwin
Sommers, Irene (Dresser)
Sommers, LeRoy
Spence, Anna Mae (Sommers)
Straub, Patty (Johnson)
Twist, Faye (Lovesee)
Westby, Hazel

Wildermuth, Bob

Students taught by Miss Alice Murphy in 1928

Bradford, Elmer
Dresser, Eunice
Dresser, Irene
Dresser, Jeanette
Keifer, Ila
Larson, Marvin
Lowery, Ella
Lowery, Lavina
Moore, Alan
Moore, Elaine
Morse, Donald
Nionz, Irving
Reimer, Billy
Reimer, Dorothy
Sommers, Edwin
Sommers, Esther
Sommers, Lawrence
Sommers, Le Roy
Wright, Elsie
Wright, Isabel
Wright, Laurs
Wright, Nellie

Some students attending in 1940

Barber, Dolly
Barber, Jasper
Gaulke, Floyd
Gustafson, David
Gustafson, John
Johns, Arlene
Langholotz, Betty
Schwengler, Stewart
Shull, Bud
Shull, Helen
Sommerude, Ella
Torkelson, Betty
Torkelson, Jean
Torkelson, Marlin
Trush, Ann

Graduates in 1942

Torkilson, Marlin

Graduates in 1944

Sommerud, Ella Ruth
Zelonski, Clifford

Graduates in 1952

Anderson, Elsie
Byerley, Ken

Gustafson, Wallace
Helwig, Hyacinth
Moore, Howard
Schull, Helen
Wood, Jonathan

Families Living in the District

Early days: Murray, Smith, Benedict, Blaser, Leverich, Hammond, Burdick, Dresser, Halliday, Isham, Livingston, Olds, Owens, Pierce, Beach, Giles, Sherwood, Crockett, Gault, and Roth.

Later families: Moore, Lee, Wilkins, Westby, Stoney, Thorson, Torkilson, Nussbaun, Zick, Millington, Champeny, Klingbeil, Wright, Sommers, Gilbertson, Holman, Bandlow, Fosmoen, Kramer, Bates, Kohls, Freitag, Johnson, Jacobusse, Bradford, Gustafson, and Larson.

Board Members

Stanley Johnson (Clerk in 1952-53 and 1955-56)
Edwin Summers (Director in 1952-53 and 1955-56)
William L. Riemer (Treasurer in 1952-53 and 1955-56)
David Gustafson (Director)
Marvin Torkelson
C. A. Larson
E. C. Dresser

Photographs

Murray School flag raising ceremony on September 21, 1895. Courtesy of Rock County Historical Society.

Murray School. No date, but circa 1906. Edward Bandlow, Paul Friday, Carrie Lee, Amanda Holman, Ardis Dresser, Hazel Westby, Dorothy Andell, Annie Hessler, Leonard Bandlow, Marston Dresser, Alice Lee, Carrie Fosmoen, Selma Holman, Winifred Champney, Gladys Reimer, Lester Bates, Mable Kramer, Gertrude Fosmoen, Francis Bandlow, John Fosmoen, Hiram Kramer, Howard Bates, Rollin Kramer, Oren Kramer, Alfred Kohls, Richard Bandlow, and Vernon Moore. Courtesy of Rock County Historical Society.

Murray School teacher, no name, but circa late 1910's. Courtesy of Rock County Historical Society.

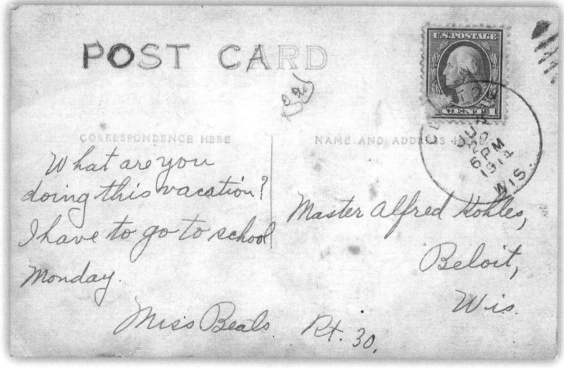

Murray School in 1914. Front and back of a photo post card. Miss Beals was teacher.
Courtesy of Clinton Historical Society.

Murray School. No date, but circa late 1910's. Courtesy of Rock County Historical Society.

Murray School in the late teens or early 1920's. Courtesy of Clinton Historical Society.

Murray School circa 1930's or 1940's. Leona Skogen is teacher on far left. Courtesy of Clinton Historical Society.

Murray School circa 1930's or 1940's. Courtesy of Clinton Historical Society.

Murray School circa 1930's or 40's. Leona Skogen is teacher on right and Leroy Krebs is on back left.
Courtesy of Clinton Historical Society.

Murray School circa 1930's or 40's. Courtesy of Clinton Historical Society.

Murray School in 1928. <u>Front row:</u> Lawrence Sommers, Irving Nionz, Donald Morse, Billy Reimer, Alan Moore, and Elmer Bradford. <u>Center row:</u> Laura Wright, Nellie Wright, Lavina Lowery, Eunice Dresser, Irene Dresser, Elsie Wright, Esther Sommers, and Elaine Moore. <u>Back row:</u> Edwin Sommers, Marvin Larson, Jeanette Dresser, Dorothy Reimer, Miss Alice Murphy (teacher), Ila Keifer, Ella Lowery, Isabel Wright, and LeRoy Sommers. Courtesy of Clinton Historical Society.

Murray School on September 30, 1938. Courtesy of Clinton Historical Society.

Murray School in 1940. Names on back are written in this order: Marlin Torkelson, Ella Sommerude, John Gustafson, Jasper Barber, Ann Trush, Betty Torkelson, Dolly Barber, David Gustafson, Helen Shull, Floyd Gaulke, Jean Torkelsen, Arlene Johns, Betty Langhlotz, Stewart Schwengler, and Bud Shull. Courtesy of Clinton Historical Society.

Circa 1940's Murray School gathering. Courtesy of Clinton Historical Society.

Photos taken the same day as prior photo at a circa 1940's Murray School gathering.
Courtesy of Clinton Historical Society.

Murray School during the 1947-48 school year. Courtesy of Rock County Historical Society.

Murray School in 1975. Courtesy of Wisconsin Historical Society, Reference Number 86583.

Murray School in May 2015. Courtesy of the author.

Murray School in May 2015. Courtesy of the author.

Shopiere School
Joint District No. 1-5 with LaPrairie Township

Years of Operation

1856-1927 (Section 3) on East Buss Road.

1927-1982 at 5417 E Buss Road.

List of Teachers

1934-35 - Irene (Jones) Pratt

List of Students

Students in 1934-35

Benedict, Wesley
Christopherson, Robert
Dressel, Dorothy
Hellar, David
Hellar, Harvey
Jackson, Delores
Jackson, Jean
Jenkins, Norman
Kangar, George
McCabe, Elinore
McCabe, Kathryn
Needham, Dean
Needham, Jean
Nehls, Henry
Porter, Alice Marie
Porter, Howard
Reese, Norman
Roberts, Judd
Rummage, Leslie
Shuckbarth, Lyle
Swingle, Rodney
Telfair, Beverly
Telfair, John
Tompkins, Leroy
Tompkins, Willis
Warner, Eva

Photographs

Shopiere School girls in 1934-35. Names in order written on back: Delores Jackson, Elinore McCabe, Alice Marie Porter, Jean Needham, Dorothy Dressel, Jean Jackson, Beverly Telfair, Kathryn McCabe, and Eva Warner. Courtesy of Rock County Historical Society.

Shopiere School in 1934-35. Names in order written on back: Wesley Benedict, Henry Nehls, _____ Porter, Eva Warner, Beverly Telfair, Elinor McCabe, Jean Jackson, Alice Marie Porter, Howard Porter, Jean Needham, Dorothy Dressel, Kathryn McCabe, Dolores Jackson, Harvey Hellar, George Kangar, Lyle Shuckbarth, David Hellar, John Telfair, Willis Tompkins, Judd Roberts, Robert Christopherson, Norman Reese, Leroy Tompkins, Rodney Swingle, Dean Needham, Howard Porter, Leslie Rummage, Norman Jenkins, and _____. Irene (Jones) Pratt was teacher at the time. Courtesy of Rock County Historical Society.

Shopiere School in 1975. Courtesy of Wisconsin Historical Society, Reference Number 86591.

Shopiere School in May 2015. Courtesy of the author.

Shopiere School in May 2015. Courtesy of the author.

Shopiere School in May 2015. Courtesy of the author.

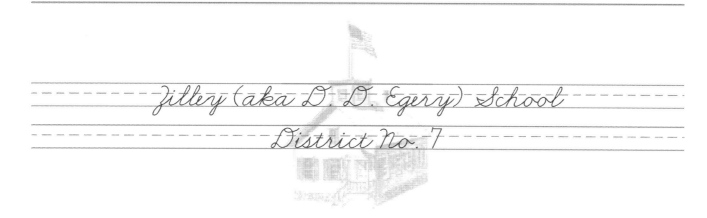

Zilley (aka D. D. Egery) School
District No. 7

Years of Operation

1847-1869 (Section 34) on State Line and County P on the southeast side of the intersection (south of Hwy 67).

1869-1955 (Section 34) at same location. Named changed to Zilley School circa 1912.

Memories

"Christmas was an exciting and busy time at Zilley School, Eighteen eager children and myself preparing a Christmas program that would make them feel important and the neighborhood proud. I was always amazed at the gross amount of talent and poise that could be found among eighteen supposedly ordinary children." – Margaret Splinter (teacher)

"I grew up in Turtle Township and went to the school called Zilley. It was the same school my father, George Toft, attended when he was growing up. His father was a member of the school board and dad told many funny experiences when he was a child.

The school was one room with a shed attached to the back where the wood was kept to heat the school in the cold weather. There was a huge furnace in one corner of the room and in the winter all of our coats, hats and mittens were put around it to dry. The room smelled of wool. We always walked to school no matter the weather. I loved to climb through the snow drifts on the side of the road and by the time we got to school, one mile each way, we would all be soaking wet. We had to get all the wet clothes off and they were put around the furnace to dry.

The room had blackboards on one wall and the front wall. The students sat in rows, the smallest in the front and the oldest in back. When the older ones had to take tests written on the blackboards they had to sit in the front seats to see. This caused a number of incidents, some of which resulted in someone being punished. Punishment either standing in the corner, or, horrors, you had to sit – if you were a boy – with a girl, and if a girl, a boy. If you dropped a pencil it was stand in the corner. We would decide to be real brave and drop a pencil. Into the corner we went, soon another dropped a pencil, another corner filled, etc.

At Christmas time someone would bring in a large tree and we decorated it with popcorn and cranberry strings. Paper wreaths were made for it and real candles were put on the branches. The students learned poems, songs and plays which were presented to the whole neighborhood. The parents and siblings were there and it was scary to have to get up in front of all those people. The candles were lit on the tree, Santa came and each child got a bag of goodies. There was always some candy, popcorn balls, peanuts, and even sometimes an orange. These were real treats in the depression years. Some of the parents would bring a gift for their child but not many. After the program the candles would be blown out, the tree would go to the lucky family who brought it and we would go home for our Christmas vacation.

There was a pump in the school yard and the drinking water was pumped out. The boys would take their shoes off, put them on the cement platform, and play barefoot at recess. The older boys liked to tease the little girls so we decided to get even and when they were playing we filled the shoes with water and waited for them to yell at us. If they did, they got punished, not us. The teacher knew the boys had started it. Some of the eighth grade boys were bigger than the teacher but they knew she meant business and a few times they felt the switch she had for extreme punishment. They didn't run home to mom because they knew they would get worse at home for misbehaving in school.

Our teacher was a widow who married the grandfather of one of the students. We figured he would get preferred treatment, but she was just as stern with him as everyone else. We loved her dearly. She was an excellent teacher and we learned. I started school in 1927 at the age of five. There were four of us, three boys and me. We started first grade, we went into second grade and did all the required work, started doing third grade work and completed that so we went from second grade into fourth. We went through eight grades and graduated from grade school in a ceremony at the Marshal high school in Janesville. That was a thrill. From there went to Beloit High School. I was eleven years old. I graduated high school at age fifteen. Much too young.

I will never forget my school years and the education I got. We had one teacher and eight grades in one room but we got a wonderful education. We studied and we learned. If we didn't pass, we stayed back a year and our parents didn't try to influence the teacher to pass us. We learned good manners, learned to respect our elders and learned to respect authority. We were always welcomed in high school because the teachers knew we had been taught good manners and had a good education. I am just sorry that when my children were growing up they didn't have the kind of education I got in that one room school. – Edith K. (Toft) St. John, July 31, 2005

Edith K. Toft (left) poses with her former teacher Mrs. Egery in 1955.
Courtesy of Edith K. (Toft) St. John.

Zilley School in 1955. Courtesy of Edith K. (Toft) St. John.

History

ZILLEY SCHOOL DISTRICT NO. 7
by Phil Holmes

(Courtesy of Rock County Historical Society)

"All available records at this late date of 1984 indicate that Zilley School originated at the one location which it has always occupied until it was consolidated with Clinton Community School System in 1955. The legal description being 'the northwest corner of the southwest quarter of the northeast quarter of Section 34 Township 1 Range 13 east,' eventually to become a part of Turtle Township. At that time Rock County had been organized, but Wisconsin was still a territory.

The Abstract of that description of land states it's acquisition from the United States Government to one Obed Gillman March 3, 1843. A later entry of 'Gillman to A.G. Murray' March 1, 1856 describes the Southwest Quarter of the afore mentioned Northeast Quarter of said Section 34, and I quote, 'Excepting a Schoolhouse lot seven rods square taken out of the northwest corner thereof.' This pretty well established that Zilley School originated sometime between 1843 and 1856.

Those were eventful years in the history of our community. The Blackhawk wars were over, Wisconsin was not yet a state until 1848 but Rock County was organized in 1839 and in this manner land was offered for sale by the United States Government, Washington, D.C. As soon as an office was opened for this purpose in Milwaukee there was a rush of buyers. Most of the land in what later became Turtle Township in 1846 was taken up in the early 1840s by families with their children. One such family was the Daniel D. Egery family in 1840. Mr. Egery became active in community affairs and community development such as roads, etc. By 1847 there was D. D. Egery road and D. D. Egery School. But Egery School was not on Egery road nor was it on Egery farm.

Whatever building had been provided in 1847 was purchased by D. D. Egery in 1869 for $10. The original site apparently considered appropriate, a new building was built that year on what was later to become the Zilley farm, and for the time being was called Turtle School District No. 7.

In 1877 William C. Zilley became owner of the property from which the Schoolhouse lot had been selected. The Zilley family then became prominent in the community for two generations. Also, since their home was convenient to the schoolhouse, several of the school teachers lived in the Zilley home.

School records show that during most of those years 'Turtle School District No.7' was used as the name of the school. However, between the years of 1912 and 1916 the School became known as ZILLEY SCHOOL DISTRICT No. 7, and so it has been ever since.

School District boundaries were appropriate to what would be considered convenient walking distances, of that time. Up to approximately 2 miles as the crow flies. Much too much for 1984 standards. The District was bounded on the south by the Illinois State Line and on the west by the City of Beloit, and a bit of the old Dougan District. To the east was Murray District and to the north was Maple Lawn and Morgan.

All of these rural schools in addition to the Hart School and Shopiere School for many years held an annual 'Play Day' about the last day of the school year. That was a fun day for inter-school competition in sporting events. There was something for everyone to participate in such as volleyball, kitten ball (soft ball), bean bag throwing for first graders, foot races, etc. Games for everyone in all eight grades. There was soft ball competition for men's teams and women's teams too. In those days it was unlady-like for women to wear shorts or jeans so the mothers were game and played ball wearing bloomers which were knee length and very baggy. The air virtually rang with cheering and laughing. Even corn cultivating seldom kept the men away from 'Play Day.'

For this Day competition was always keen, enthusiasm at a high pitch throughout the day and to the delight of the youngsters there was a refreshment stand, known as a 'pop stand' with ice cream and candy bars and lots of pop, a real treat during those years of rural one room schools.

Zilley had its share of teachers too. Some of whom married locally to become a permanent part of the community.

At least a partial list of teachers pretty much in the order of their service are as follows: Jennie Carpenter Cleland, Albert Henry, Miss Lillian Barrett, Mattie Schain 1911, Hazel Setzer 1912, Ina Truesdell 1913, Janet McAdam 1914, Hazel Evans 1918, Josephine Fanning 1919, Rosetta Blazer 1920, Ruth Canary 1923, Alcie Knutson 1935, Carrie Lee 1924, Minnie Highland 1925, Leona Skogen 1948, Margaret Schollmeyer 1951. Consolidation 1955.

Mattie Schain became Mattie Schain Elgeston of Shopiere neighborhood. Hazel Setzer married Charlie Maxworthy who had attended Zilley and lived within the district. Rosetta Blazer never married but lived out her life on the local Blazer farm and remained a warm friend of Zilley School children all the days of her life. Alice Knutson married Andy File living close by. Minnie Highland had been widowed by the death of her first husband and she became the third wife of Harry Egery, grandson of Daniel D. Egery from the first part of our story, and lived out her life on the Egery farm. The many years she taught suggests that she must have been a super good teacher. What with eight years of her teaching the writer of this can attest to that.

It should be interesting to recall that the school building did receive extensive improvements during the late 1930s via a government program designed to create work to help alleviate effects of the great depression. A full basement with a heating system was added and electric lights too. So it was no longer quite the same one room schoolhouse it had been for so long with its potbellied stove and kerosene lamps. It even had an attached shed for the teacher's car. However, it never did get flush toilets nor running water.

Upon consolidation the property reverted back to the R. B. Meech Family who were the owners at that time. Since then the revered Northwest corner of the Southwest Quarter of the Northeast Quarter of Section 34 Township 1 Range 13 east has been permanently detached and sold as a private dwelling.

Thus ended an era which was testament to the quality of character of those who carved this great Nation. The only blight is the plight of the Indian, for those who knew Blackhawk well knew well how he dearly loved this land too."

❦

The following article ran in an undated and unidentified newspaper:

ZILLEY DISTRICT SETS GATHERING ON SUNDAY

"The present term in Zilley School is the last as the district decided at the fall school meeting to consolidate with the Clinton School District.

Most everyone regrets to see the little country district school passing from the scene but it is in keeping with our American way of Progress.

Millions of our children in the past received the fundamentals of education in the one room district school.

The history of Zilley district is close to that of many thousands of others throughout this free America that we are so proud to be a part of.

Daniel D. Egery and family came to Wisconsin with the New England Emigrating Co. in 1837 and in 1839 Rock County was organized. Wild land was offered for sale and Mr. Egery purchased a large tract near and along the Wisconsin-Illinois State Line.

Of course Mr. Egery was only one of many early settlers that arrived from the East to carve out homes in this New West.

Other pioneer families who came to settle in this district were the Crosbys, Jacks, Ross, Blakey, Favour, Deming, Zilley, Everett, Smith, Ingersoll, Hall, Hill, and Maxworthy.

As they settled down and sent for their families and friends back East, their first thoughts were of churches and schools.

A school district was soon formed and a building erected.

In the year 1869 the present school building was erected and it has been in continuous use to the present time.

It has been called Zilley School many years, but before that was known by family names of residents of the district.

Records show that when the new building was erected the old building was purchased by D. D. Egery for $10.

It is interesting to know that a 4th generation of the Egery family and a fifth generation of the Crosby family attended this school the past year.

A few descendants of the early settlers still reside in the district, Emma Crosby Thomas, Florence Egery Gunderson and Charles G. Maxworthy, the last two having spent their entire lives in the district.

The two earliest pupils of the school now living are Clara Blakey Daniels and Celia Blakey Evans, who now reside on Merrill Avenue, Beloit.

The oldest living teachers of the district are Jennie Carpenter Cleland and Mr. Albert Henry, who both reside in Beloit, and Miss Lillian Barrett of California.

Last fall when it was decided to close the school, it was suggested that the annual school picnic be made the occasion for inviting as many of the old pupils, teachers and residents and their descendants as could be found by personal cards and messages inserted in the local papers.

The committee which was appointed to arrange for the homecoming has been busy gathering names and addresses of former pupils, teachers and residents of the district and hope that no one has been left out.

If YOU are a former pupil, teacher or resident of the district, you are cordially invited to attend the picnic. Dinner will be at 12:30 . . ."

Zilley School became part of Clinton Community Schools after consolidation. It was later purchased and used as a dwelling.

List of Teachers

Alice File
Albert Henry
Lillian Barrett
Jennie (Carpenter) Cleland
Circa 1910 – Grace Wheeler
1911 – Mattie Schain
1912 – Hazel Setzer
1913 – Ina Truesdell
1914 – Janet McAdam
1918 – Hazel Evans
1919 – Josephine Fanning
1920 – Rosetta Blazer
1923 – Ruth Canary
1924 – Carrie Lee
1925 – Minnie (Highland) Egery
1935 – Alice Knutson
1938-50 – Mrs. Leona (Schollmeyer) Skogen
1951-53 – Margaret (Schollmeyer) Splinter of Rte. 3, Beloit, WI

List of Students

Daniels, Clara (Blakey)
Evans, Celia (Blakey)
Gunderson, Florence (Egery)
Maxworthy, Charles G.
St. John, Edith K. (Toft) – (started in 1927 at age five)
Thomas, Emma (Crosby)

Students attending in 1910

Bennett, Jenny
Draves, Clara
Friar, Faye

Gunderson, Clarence
Hazley, Edna
Hazley, Helen
Hilton, Harold
Holeman, Amanda
Holeman, Minnie
Holeman, Selma
McCabe, Marguerite
McCabe, Martin
Ravnum, Harry
Ravnum, Rosie
Reimer, Nellie
Toft, George

Graduate in 1942

Meech, Esther

Graduates in 1944

Gunderson, Berwyn
McCabe, Edward
Reimer, Harry Eugene

Graduates in 1948

Kirkpatrick, Betty
Kirkpatrick, Donna
Rufer, Dorothy

Graduates in 1952

Beilke, Thomas
Rufer, Donald

Board Members

Lester Wallace (Clerk in 1952-53)
Mrs. Wyona Meech (Director in 1952-53)
Mrs. Florence Gunderson (Treasurer in 1952-53)
R. B. Meech
Mrs. Martha Riemer
A. J. Toft

Photographs

Zilley School during the 1947-48 school year. Courtesy of Rock County Historical Society.

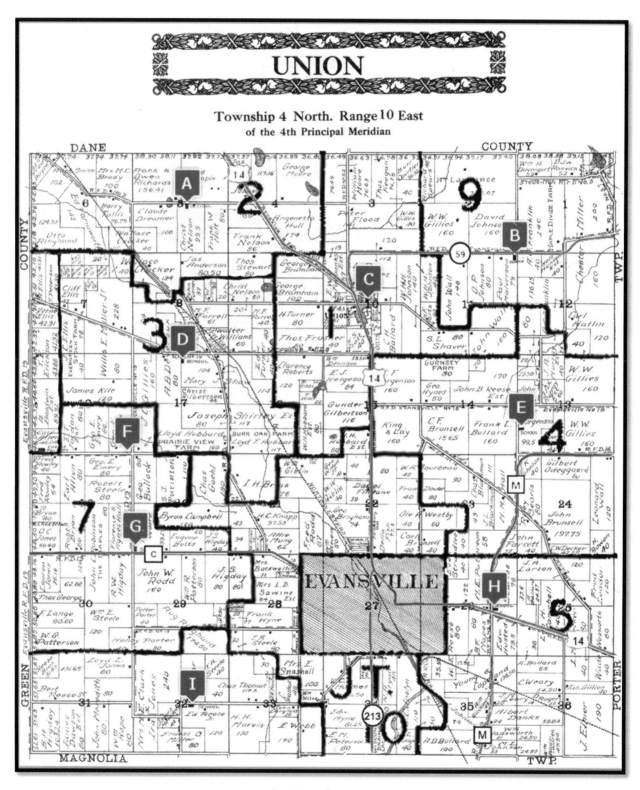

Union Township in 1917

<u>Map legend for facing page</u>

A. Holt School - *see page 286*
B. Franklin School - *see page 282*
C. Union School - *see page 323*
D. Butts Corners School - *see page 277*
E. Tupper School - *see page 310*
F. Emery School - *see page 281*
G. Pleasant Prairie School - *see page 288*
H. Brown School - *see page 268*
I. Tullar School - *see page 300*

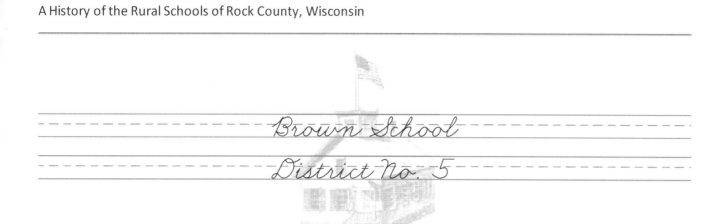

Brown School
District No. 5

Years of Operation

1869-1962 (Section 26) on County M at Highway 14 – northeast corner of intersection.

Memories

"I'll never forget the year 1959 when I was teaching at the Brown School and we saw a barn, east of our school, burn. About eleven o'clock that day I happened to look out the window and notice smoke coming from under the eves of the barn. We knew the family was aware of the fire as we saw them run to the house. The children and I stood at the windows watching and in seconds the whole barn was in flames. As the wind was in the east the flames were blown toward the school house. Parts of the burning barn were blown into the fields and were starting grass fires. It was getting very hot by the windows in the school building so I decided the children and I had better leave. I loaded all ten of them in my car and drove far enough away where I know we would be safe. The children brought their lunches with them, but none of them felt like eating.

The barn burned to the ground, but our school did not catch fire. We returned to school, but did not accomplish much as the excitement of the fire was still with us." – Claramae Moldenhauer (teacher)

"You went down to Janesville and got all of the books that were new. It was such a thrill. We used to go down to C & M books and get the workbooks that you needed and you ordered all these books. You went into the room where they had all of these. You usually worked a week without." – Virginia Fenn Mauerman (attended in 1946-1949)

History

HISTORY OF BROWN SCHOOL
by an unknown author

(Courtesy of Rock County Historical Society)

"Brown School was built before 1873 on land donated by a man named Brown. The schoolhouse is in Section #26 at the intersection of County Trunk M and Highway 14.

The district, #5, is composed of Sections #25, #26, #35 and #36. The schoolhouse is on land once owned by Adam Luchsinger whose granddaughter, Ruby Templeton taught there for fourteen years, from 1922-1936.

Some families from 1873 were: Mitchell, Blackman, Sartell, Jones, Spencer, Ahara, Wolcott, Campbell, Allen, Palmer, Johnson, Montgomery, Spencer, Ferris, Smith, Wadsworth, Ballard, Carpenter, Stiles, Fitch, Beale,

Woodworth, Weary, Dennison, Decker, Richards, Searles, Patterson, Barnard, Larson, Croak, Reese, Trickel, and Koepp. Descendants of the Woodworth family live in the district.

The teacher's bell was given by Elva Story Weary in 1937 and is now in possession of her granddaughter, Lois Weary Patterson. Three generations were students here, Elva Story Weary, Russell Weary, and Lois Weary Patterson.

Morris Woodworth tells of school being dismissed so the students could watch the soldiers marching past in 1917. At that time his teacher was Miss Ruth Berryman.

In 1928 the Goodwill Club was formed. It started as a Mothers' Club and still functions as a community club, meeting regularly.

The school closed in 1962, the last teacher being Claramae Moldenhauer. The building is still standing but is in bad repair.

Some teachers are: Marion Purinton, 1910, Wilva Vaughan, 1911 and '12, Nellie Maloy, Mrs. Keegan, Mrs. Trambly, Ruth Berryman, Lola Webb, Lil Haney, Ruby Templeton, 1922-1936, Inis Miller Haakenson, Virginia Fenn, Marg Wilder Cary, Frances Lang, Ruth Templeton, Mildred Franklin, Bonnie Vandervort, Claramae Moldenhauer, 1956-'62."

THE BROWN SCHOOL HISTORY
By an unknown author

"The Brown School was built about seventy-nine years ago. The building was painted brown until 1933 when it was painted white.

The school seemed to be overshadowed by the city of Evansville and so it was never a social center of the community.

It seemed interesting as I went through the record book to read of the expenses. Every year it seemed that a broom had to be bought. The expenses also inclued [sic] a water pail and a dipper but one year instead of buying a new pail they just had a new bottom put in it for ten cents.

I thought that the school lunch program carried out by Mrs. Grant Haney during the years 1920-1923 was rather interesting. Every morning she had to be out to the school at seven to start on the hot dish. The lunch was prepared on an old kerosene stove. Money for the lunch was made through programs and the farmers helped furnish milk, fruit and vegetables.

Each child was served in a big white cup but first each child washed his hands and wiped them on his own towel which the child took home each Friday night to be washed.

Mrs. Haney said it was hard to make hot lunches without water on the school ground. She decided she would have a well. She raised the money through a box social. Some of the men helped with the work and the school had its new well."

(Source: Area Research Center, Andersen Library, University of Wisconsin-Whitewater, Whitewater, WI; Rock 39, Box 3, Folder 16.)

Brown School was attached to Evansville School District after closing.

List of Teachers

1910 – Marion Purinton
1911-12 – Wilva Vaughan
Nellie Maley
Mrs. Keegan
Mrs. Trambly
1917 – Ruth Berryman
Lola Webb
Marge (Wilder) Cary
1920-23 – Lil (Mrs. Grant) Haney
1922-36 – Ruby or Ruth Templeton
1938-41 – Inis (Miller) Haakenson
1941-46 – Mrs. Beverly (Hart) Jenny
1941-50 – Virginia (Fenn) Mauerman
1950-53 – Mrs. Frances Lange of Rte. 2, Evansville, WI
1955-56 – Mildred Franklin of Evansville, WI
1956-62 – Mrs. Claramae Moldenhauer of 325 W. Main, Evansville, WI

List of Students

Weary, Elva (Story)
Weary, Russell
Woodworth, Morris (attending in 1917)

Students attending in 1933

Arneson, Philip
Arneson, Ruth
Barnard, Elsie
Barnard, Ethel
Barnard, Lee
Barnard, Paul
Cowell, Lucille
Decker, Katherine
Haeft, Marjorie
Janes, Donald
Klusmeyer, Lois
Meichtry, Thomas
Reese, Ruth
Richards, Beatrice
Richards, Emily
Weary, Lois

Graduates in 1942

Melvin Janes
Jeanette Reese

Graduates in 1944

Bourbeau, Donald
Kopp, Walter C.
Warner, Hazel M.

Graduates in 1948

Reese, William
Taylor, John
Trickel, Jeanette
Valentine, Diane

Graduate in 1952

Spersrud, Jane

Graduates in 1962

Nipple, Judith Ann
Trickel, Patricia L.

Board Members

Herbert Christensen (Clerk in 1952-53)
Glen Trickel (Director in 1952-53, 1955-56 and 1961-62)
Mrs. Ivan Reese (Treasurer in 1952-53 and 1955-56)
Mrs. Bert Richards
Harold Klusmeyer
Laurence Jones
Wade Woodworth
Ernest Kopp (Clerk in 1955-56)
Russell Weary
Arnold Rupnow (Clerk in 1961-62)
Norman Krumwiede (Treasurer in 1961-62)

Photographs

Brown School in 1927. Courtesy of Rock County Historical Society.

Brown School in 1933. Ruby Templeton (teacher, on back left), Emily Richards, Katherine Decker, Elsie Barnard, Marjorie Haeft, Lois Weary, Beatrice Richards, Ruth Riese, Ethel Barnard, Lucille Cowell, Lee Barnard, Lois Klusmeyer, Paul Barnard, Thomas Meichtry, Philip Arneson, Donald Janes, Ruth Arneson, and _____?
Courtesy of Rock County Historical Society.

Brown School music festival in 1944. Courtesy of Walter C. Kopp.

Eighth grade graduation diploma for Walter C. Kopp from Brown School, dated June 1, 1944.
Courtesy of Walter C. Kopp.

Brown School during the 1947-48 school year. Courtesy of Rock County Historical Society.

Brown School in 1975. Courtesy of Wisconsin Historical Society, Reference Number 29548.

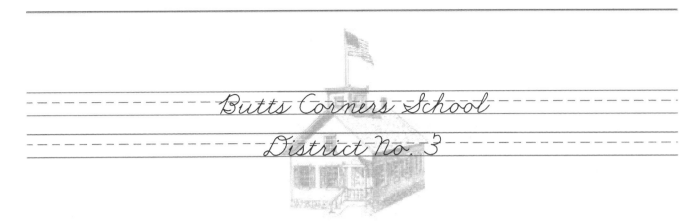

Butts Corners School
District No. 3

Years of Operation

Before 1858-1915 (Section 17) on Evansville-Brooklyn Road. (Butts Corners Road), Butts Corners - about 1/2 mile east of Pleasant Prairie Road.

1915-1962 (Section 17) at same location. Located at 17029 E Evansville-Brooklyn Road.

History

THE HISTORY OF BUTTS CORNERS SCHOOL
By an unknown author

(Courtesy of Rock County Historical Society)

"The original Butts Corners School was built prior to 1873, one and one half miles west of Highway 14 in Section #17 on Butts Corners Road.

In 1915 the old building was moved east to the Morris Williams farm and used as a granary. The new school was built on the original site. Distirct #3 is composed of Sections #7, #8 and #17, North ½ of Section #18, west ½ of Section #16 and west ½ of Section #9. The school was named for the Butts family who lived on the four corners east of the school. A great granddaughter of the Butts family still lives in Evansville. She is Mrs. Ray Knapp.

In 1962 when the rural schools were all closed the grounds were sold and the building is now a residence.

Some of the early families are: Miller, Ellis, Delaney, Richardson, Deveraux, Ingalls, Burgess, Frnacis, Butts, Erancie, Montgomery, Shivley, Hubbard, Kile, and Peach. Some later families: Goehl, Devlin, Templeton, Woodstock, Farrell, George, Turner, Williams, Maas, Jones, Thomas and Allison Butts, not related to the original Butts families. Descendants of the Templeton, Maas and Ellis families still live in the district.

There was a Mother's Club and a Community Club which still meets. Clifford Ellis who started school at the age of 4 in 1895 and who is now 94 years young tells of one day when farmers were riding by on horses with the harness on. The teacher said, 'There has to be a fire. You are all excused to go to the fire.' The house burned on what is now the Krajeck farm. He also tells of being with his brother Arthur catching gophers at noon. They put one in the teacher's desk and about scared her to death."

The school was supported by the Butts Corners Community Club with an annual flower and seed sale in the spring of each year.

Butts Corners School was attached to Evansville School District after closing. It is now being used as a dwelling.

List of Teachers

Cecil Popanz Schultz
Ruth Milligan
Annie McGuire
Olga Neilson
Beth Miller Woodworth
Miss Porter
Bernice Keehn
Mrs. Harry Loomis
Etta Hubbard Smith
Lil Haney
Joyce Spencer
Delores Luchsinger Carson
Claramae Moldenhauer
Ruth Templeton
Janice Abey Horstmeyer
1938-39 – Beth Uehling
1940-41 – Ella Bullis
1941-42 – Closed
1942-43 – Erma Smith
1943-44 – Joyce Montgomery
1944-46 – Clara Reese
1946-50 – Helen Ginner
1950-51 – Jeanene Werle
1951-56 – Mrs. Dolores Parsons of Evansville, WI
1962 – Hazel Murphy of 329 N. Madison, Evansville, WI (last teacher)

List of Students

Ellis, Arthur
Ellis, Clifford (started at age four in 1895)

Graduates in 1952

Ringhand, Roger
Templeton, Kenneth

Board Members

Ralph Maas (Director in 1952-53)
Kenneth Ellis (Clerk in 1952-53)
George Krajcek (Treasurer in 1952-53, 1955-56 and 1961-62)
Claude Willoughby
Mrs. Ed Ellis
Mrs. Beulah Thomas
Allison Butts (Director in 1955-56 and 1961-62)
Melvin Sanner (Clerk in 1955-56)
Willis Miller

Photographs

Butts Corners School during the 1947-48 school year. Courtesy of Rock County Historical Society.

Butts Corners School in 1975. Courtesy of Wisconsin Historical Society, Reference Number 84079.

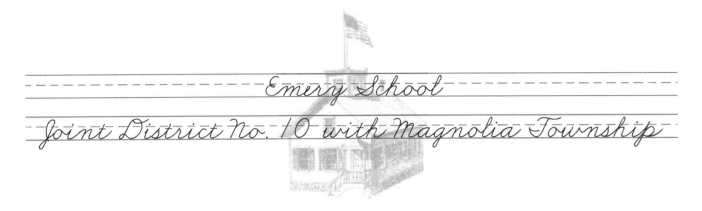

Years of Operation

1873-1900 (Section 18) on Emery Road at Pleasant Prairie Road – northwest corner of intersection. Joined Magnolia in 1900.

History

HISTORY OF EMERY SCHOOL
By an unknown author

(Courtesy of Rock County Historical Society)

"There was great dissatisfaction over the location of the Pleasant Prairie School. The north part of the district still thought it should have been an equal distance from them so in 1873 a schoolhouse was built on land donated by Fred Emery at the four corners of what were later called Emery and Pleasant Prairie Roads.

This was a clapboard building practically the same dimensions as District #7 and was known as District #10. The district was composed of Section #18, north ½ of Section #19, south ½ of Section #17 and north ½ of Section #20. The building was one mile east of the Rock-Green County line in Section #18.

School was held here until 1900 with the exception of a few years when it was closed for lack of scholars.

In 1929 the building was sold to Pete Libby and he moved it one half mile east and made it into a dwelling. It is now the home of the Alan Butts family.

Some of the early family names are: Emery, Alan, Rowley, Stevens, Baldwin, Eggleston, Farmin, Swin, Bullock, Deveraux, and Antes. Descendants of the Emery, Alan and Dunbar families still live in the neighborhood. Elmer Alan still lives on the Alan Homestead.

Mrs. Lil George Haney was the last teacher from September 10 to December of 1900. There is no record of clubs or other teachers.

The above information was taken from the notebook of Mrs. H. H. Robinson."

Emery School is now being used as a dwelling.

List of Teachers

1900 – Mrs. Lil George Haney

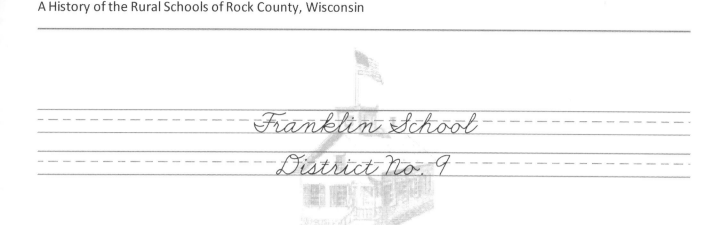

Franklin School
District No. 9

Years of Operation

1858-1916 (Section 11)

1917-1962 (Section 11) on Highway 59 at Franklin Road – southeast corner of intersection, west of Cooksville, Wisconsin.

Memories

"Hobbies, pets and learning – school is a place for all. One of the pets of the children of the Franklin School was a little turtle. Nameless, this little fellow lived in his glass bowl day after day. The highlight of his day would come during the noon hour after lunch. The children would take the turtle out on the gravel drive, put him down and head him away from the schoolhouse. But no, he would turn around and head straight back for school. Why? Could it have been the new encyclopedias just purchased, brimming with knowledge, or the new pressure system recently installed?" – Clara Reese (teacher)

History

THE HISTORY OF FRANKLIN SCHOOL
By an unknown author

(Courtesy of Rock County Historical Society)

"Franklin School or District #9 as it was called until 1920 is located in the northeast corner of Section 11, on Highway 59 about 1 ½ miles west of the village of Cooksville.

[On] December 18, 1858 Lydia Clark deeded one acre of land for the school. The cost was $30.00. Oliver Franklin has the original deed.

A red brick school was built just a few feet east of the present building. It was simply called District #9 until 1920 when it was named for the Franklin family.

In September of 1916 the district borrowed $2500.00 for ten years at 10% interest to build a new school. [On] May 16, 1917 a special meeting was called for the purpose of raising an additional fund of $500.00 for building the new school. The board had added $45.00 to the load fund. The money was to be used for the building. The outhouses were left to the board to provide.

The Franklin District was composed of Sections 1 and 2, and the north half of Sections 11 and 12.

Construction was begun immediately and pupils moved into the new building in the fall of 1917. The building is identical to the Butts Corners School but 6 feet longer. Martha Norum Norby was the first teacher in the new school which was of clapboard instead of brick. A fence was added in 1918. The old building remained for many years before being razed.

Water was hauled to the school until 1924 [and] then a well was drilled. A pressure system was installed in 1941 and a telephone in 1938.

In 1962 when all the rural schools were closed Oliver and Crystal Franklin bought the building and grounds. They remodeled the building into a very comfortable home and moved in in 1969.

Some of the older family names are: Loomis, Merrill, Buxxell, Davenport, Leedle, Gillies, Doherty, Davis, Chapin, Hayward, Clark, Johnson, Elwood, Rowley, Lamb, Nesbit, Lawrence, Mason, Cushman, Wall, Foss, Champney. Some later families: Ehredt, Dahl, Davenport, Renvick, Hanson, Hatlen, Green, Winn, Heinzarth, Ellis and Miller.

Now there are Franklins in the district and Phelps and Dahls in the area. A Mother's Club was formed in the '30s and still meets monthly.

Clara Meulemans who taught in 1923, '24, '25, and '26 was a lady who had a wooden arm and was a very strict disciplinarian. She also had a rather short temper and was known to use her wooden hand as a means of administering discipline."

Author's Note: A list of teachers from 1906 to 1962 followed and is incorporated into the list below.

List of Teachers

Jenny Murray
May Johnson
Pearl Heffel
Lucile Moore
Clara Oberg
Myrtle Fletcher
Buelah Cole Kloften
Lucile Johnson
Gladys Anderson
1917 – Martha Norum Norby
Alva Benway
Mary Ludden
Marie Jenson
Alice Bowen
1923-26 – Clara Muelemans
Amber Kleinsmith
Isabelle Crocker
Bertha Odegaard
Ruth Franklin
Marie Jenson
1938-39 – Gladys Peterson
1942-45 – Dorothy Thompson
1945-46 – Mrs. Bert Jones
1946-48 – Mrs. Amy Wall
1948-53 – Mrs. Clara Reese of 322 W. Main St., Evansville, WI
1955-56 – Yvonne Vorpagel of Edgerton, WI
Merlin Anderson
John Prein
1961-62 – Mrs. Erma Smith of 106 Division, Brooklyn, WI

List of Students

Graduates in 1942

Clark, Walter
Ellis, Marvin
Shantz, Dorothy

Graduate in 1944

Ellis, Frances

Graduates in 1948

Ehredt, Patricia
Ehredt, William
Franklin, Mildred
Severson, Carol

Graduates in 1952

Foss, Beverly
Franklin, Oliver George

Graduates in 1962

Dahle, Linda K.
Young, Phyllis Jean

Board Members

Mrs. Oliver Franklin (Clerk in 1952-53, 1955-56 and 1961-62)
Dean George (Director in 1952-53, 1955-56 and 1961-62)
John Heritage (Treasurer in 1952-53 and 1955-56)
Donald Elmer (Treasurer in 1961-62)
Wilbur Ehredt
Austin Tronnes
Lloyd E. George
Mrs. Carl Klitzman
Ernest Miller

Photographs

Franklin School during the 1947-48 school year. Courtesy of Rock County Historical Society.

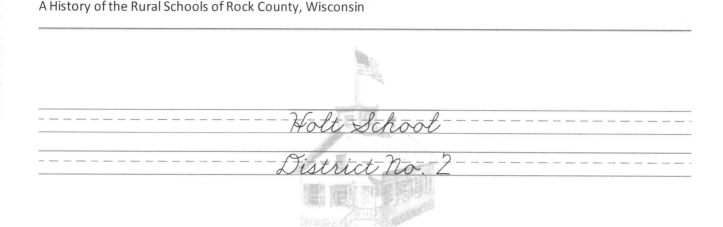

Holt School

District No. 2

Years of Operation

Before 1858-1920 (Section 5) on Holt Road one half mile west of Highway 14 and about a half mile east of Crock Road. Consolidated with Brooklyn.

History

HISTORY OF HOLT SCHOOL
By an unknown author

(Courtesy of Rock County Historical Society)

"Holt School was built before 1873, probably about 1858, on land owned by Henry Holt. It is located on Holt Road about ½ mile west of Highway #14. The district, #2, was composed of all of Sections #4, #5, and #6. The building is in Section #5.

In 1912 or when the district was combined with Brooklyn, the children were transported in a horse drawn bus at first, later a motor bus. It was supposedly the first school bus system in Wisconsin. Holt paid tuition to Brooklyn.

Phil Smith who went to Holt but now lives just out of the district tells of Lyle Tullis and him hitching a ride on the bus which went into the ditch and turned over. He and Lyle got out and hurried home but there was a lot of excitement before that fact was discovered, as the driver thought they were still in the wreckage. Needles to say they were punished.

Some of the early families were: Wheelock, Snyder, Devine, Lovejoy, Slawson, Johnson, Richardson, Chapin, Nelson, Winston, Whitcomb, Schell, Alberti, Crocker, Stewart, Holt and Yarwood. Later families: DeRemer, Nielson, Smith, Boynton, Winters, and Armstrong.

The school was closed before 1920 and I could find no records of teachers, clubs, etc. and there was no community club. The building has been a residence for many years."

Holt School was sold after it closed and was used as a dwelling.

List of Students

Smith, Phil
Tullis, Lyle

Board Members

Philip Johnson
Ben Stewart
Herbert Armstrong
Perlie Calhoun
Hans Nielson

Pleasant Prairie School
(Likely first called Robinson School)
District No. 7

Years of Operation

1840-1866 (Section 29) – possibly known as Robinson School.

1866-1872 (Section 20) on Pleasant Prairie Road, south of County C.

1872-1962 (Section 20) on Pleasant Prairie Road at County C – northeast corner of intersection. Located at 17532 W County C. Emery joined in 1900.

Memories

"The present building was completed in 1872 at a cost of $1,494.00, with the bricks being hauled by wagon from Rockford, Illinois. The first teacher's salary was $18.00 per month in summer and $30.00 per month in winter. The enrollment in 1872 was 38. The school operated continuously until 1962 and ended with an enrollment of 26." – Doris Roberts (teacher)

"Pleasant Prairie School, currently a private home, is built of brick. There was no well, so water was brought in cans from neighboring farms. If the water ran out during the school day, a couple of the older boys went to get more. Two outhouses behind the school served the boys and girls separately. The building was heated by, first, a wood burning furnace in the basement and later converted into a coal burning furnace with a stoker, thus making the work easier. The boys had the job of removing the clinkers as needed. The school sat on about an acre of land at the corner of County C and Pleasant Prairie Road. About the only play equipment was a dangerous set of swinging chains from the top of a pole and a couple of teeter-totters. The chains of the swing swung around when the kids let go – an accident waiting to happen – with a bump on the head. The children sledded in a neighborhood pit in winter, a great place to enjoy the snow.

I, Jack, attended Pleasant Prairie School for all eight grades, beginning in the fall of 1939 until graduation which was a county-wide eighth grade graduation ceremony held in Janesville, possibly at the Court House, I just don't remember where, for sure.

Mine was a class of four students, the same four, for most of those eight years. Two girls, Jeanie Golz and Lilas Dunbar, and two boys, Don Allen and myself, Jack Leeder. Interestingly, we four celebrated our 50th class reunion together!

The school enrollment ranged from 15-21 students over the years, which included siblings of several families. Our family had five in school at one time, Rodney, Dale, Janice, Dean and Jack. My younger brother, Lee, started school about the time Rodney and Dale graduated.

We had four different teachers over the years. Miss Gransee taught two years, Mrs. Moldenhower stayed for four, while Mrs. Ruby Templeton and Mrs. Clara Reese each taught for one year.

The teacher's job was to teach all eight grade classes, to keep order in the school and to build the fire when needed. Am sure they did more than that on a daily basis.

We students swept the floor, carried water, heated the many jars of soup and hot chocolate on the hot plate in a pan of hot water during the cold winter months and did other tasks. In the fall, after school started, one day was spent cleaning up the yard so the school board member could bring his hay mower to mow the long grass grown up over the summer. After the work was done, we enjoyed hot dogs and fresh buns brought by the teacher to eat along with our lunches. Then, I think, we had time to play! No classes that day.

We lived about a mile from school on County C and usually walked or rode our bikes. There was a rare ride now and then with our dad when he hauled milk to the creamery in Brooklyn or in bad weather. Classmates lived anywhere from one-half mile to a mile and three-quarters away from us. If bad weather in winter made the roads impassable, of course, school was closed.

The daily school routine was pretty normal for country schools and city schools. We had classes in reading, arithmetic, spelling, science and social studies. My favorites were the radio programs on WHA from Madison, LET'S DRAW and music class. The children in the lower grades had a daily recess of playing kittenball or in winter, Fox and Goose in the snow. Sometimes, we rode our bikes around the yard. If a child misbehaved, he or she had to remain in his or her desk and miss out on recess. And, I'm sure, the parents were swiftly informed of the deed!

The Christmas program was always a special event to look forward to every year. All the parents came and just filled the school to see the school play and listen to the singing of all the favorite songs of the season.

In Spring, all the rural schools township wide gathered at Leota Park in Evansville for a PLAY DAY of Kittenball, sack races and relay races. Lots of fun!

MEMORIES! Lots of them. Sometimes we boys, and maybe some girls, would hide behind the snow banks and wait for a car to go by and then fire some snowballs at the car. Well, one time, the driver turned around, and stopped and talked to the teacher about the event. He turned out to be a sheriff's deputy! That was the last time we threw snowballs at cars!!

Then, many times we pretended we didn't hear the school bell ring while playing and would be late for class.

During WWII we all helped out by picking milkweed pods used for the war effort. I'm still not sure what they were used for. I used to think the silk part was for making parachutes or was it 'down' for pillows? We also, if we had a dime, brought it to school and bought a war stamp each week and when we had enough stamps saved, traded them for a war bond. My younger brother, Lee, and I had enough for a $25.00 bond between us. We still have the bond.

In the late 1940's after WWII, the boys and girls of Rock County schools were invited to go by a special train form Janesville to Chicago for a day of sightseeing. We went to a museum and the Armour Packing Co. – hundreds of children, the teachers and some parents went, including my mother and Jean's mother, Rosie Golz, I remember. We took sack lunches with us. I think Mr. Donald Upson was Superintendent of the Rock County Schools at that time." – Jack Leeder

Five of the William and Gladys Leeder family attended Pleasant Prairie School at the same time – Rodney, Dale, Janice, Dean and Jack. They are standing at the entrance to the school. Courtesy of Jack Leeder.

Pleasant Prairie School students Jack Leeder, Don Allen, Jean Golz, and Lilas Dunbar posed for this photo in the schoolyard. Courtesy of Jack Leeder.

History

HISTORY OF PLEASANT PRAIRIE SCHOOL
by and unknown author

(Courtesy of Rock County Historical Society)

"The first records show that school was held in 1866 in the schoolhouse directly across the road, County Trunk C, from the present building. Anna Blakely received $52.82 for teaching the first term. The district was composed of Sections #19, #29, #30 and the south ½ of Section #18. After Emery School closed in 1900 the districts were combined. The present school is in Section #20.

After many special meetings and much discussion in the early 1870s it was decided to build a new school and ¾ acres of land were bought from Vinson Cooley for $60.00. J. A. Hoxie drew up plans and specifications for which he was paid $5.00. They were very detailed as to lumber, nails, etc. J. A. Ellis and his brothers were the builders and in 1872 it was completed at a cost of $1494.80. The treasurer's book shows brick hauled from Rockford, building of privies $5.00 each, seats $210.00, wood .50 per cord, fencing the yard $20.00. At the time in 1872 there were 38 pupils.

W. B. Patterson bought the old building for $20.00 and moved it with his other buildings. It was used as a shop and granary and was still in use in 1965.

Early in the 1920s a new porch was needed and it was decided to put in one of cement. All the neighbors helped, supervised by Robert Steele who was an enthusiastic promoter of cement. This was such a success that Mr. Wolfe wanted to cement the basement so the little children would have a place to play in rainy weather. This later was a community project cheered all the way by Mr. Wolfe.

A discussion came up as to naming the school and several were suggested. Mr. J. C. Robinson suggested Pleasant Prairie and that seemed to please everyone thus Pleasant Prairie was born and the school had a name instead of being just called #7.

It was customary to have 8 months of school, a 3 ½ or 4 months winter term which was to be taught by a man and a spring term.

In 1924 a cistern and pump were installed but water for drinking still had to be carried from a neighboring farm. Charlotte Brunsell Collins tells of herself and Mildred Allen Howard carrying water from her home in 1934 and '35. She said by the time they reached the school there wasn't much left in the pail. She and Millie started giggling and as the supervising teacher, Hattie Fredrichs was there they were banished to the hall, since they couldn't stop giggling.

In 1920 the Pleasant Prairie Community Club was organized and still meets monthly. There was also a neighborhood Kitten ball team.

Some of the older families were: Gibbs, Zenas Dooley, Morris, Winston, Hyne, Haley, Patterson, Collier, Freehauf, Palmer, Higday, Cooley, Hall, Waldo, Gibson, Siver, Alan, Robinson in 1880, Hatfield, Jones, Porter, Emery, Steele, Wolfe, Bryan, and Brunsell. Some later families were Cushman, Golz, Libby, Francis Hagen and Maas.

Many fine teachers were employed, but one unusual group of sisters taught here: Belle Lloyd Bryan 1898, May Lloyd Miles '92-'95, Bernice Lloyd Patterson '95-'96 and Edna Lloyd Bryan 1901.

Lil George Haney went to school here and later taught here. She was here from 1912 through 1919.

One family had three teachers who completed 8 grades here. They are: Ruth Alan Templeton, Kenneth Alan and Arlene Alan Rice. Ruth Templeton also substituted here and had a career total of teaching of 45 years.

Several families of three or four generations attended Pleasant Prairie. They are: Annie Hyne Jones, Orville Jones, Mildred and Donald Jones, May Emery Robinson, Hugh H. Robinson, Madge and Olive Robinson, Phil and Harold Robinson, Ruth Ann, Kathryn and Barbara Robinson.

[A list of teachers from 1866-1962 followed and is given below]

The school closed in 1962 with an enrollment of 26. The building was sold to Floyd Frances and has had several owners. It is now an attractive home.

Most of the information above was obtained from the notebook of Mrs. H. H. Robinson and from the clerk's book from 1866-1939."

Pleasant Prairie School was attached to Evansville School District after closing.

Newspaper Articles

An article on the students being on WCLO radio station in Janesville: Evansville Review, January 15, 1942

List of Teachers

Anna M. Blakely (first teacher – wages were $52.82 for teaching the first term)
Hattie Dibble
S. F. Main
Anna M. Firth
Philip H. George
Lizzie J. Clark
E. B. Hasey
M. E. Babcock
J. A. Sarvin
E. J. Rowley
J. Alles
J. Allen
Jenny Allis
Mary A. Shesson
Mary Butz
Eleanor Allen
Lizzie Baker
Eleanora Allen
N. E. Libby
Sarah Cadwallader
Sarah E. Bennett
Eleanora Patterson
Eva Janes
Lizzie Baker
George Blakely
Emma Glenan
Lizzie Baker
Eva Howard
S. Bryan
M. L. Hoskins

Emma Stearns
Carrie Janes
May Bemis
Jennie Steele
Lizzie Van Patton
L. M. Van Patton
Lila Luddington
Flora Janes
Inis Maxon
Lottie Roberts
H. B. Waite
Alice Steele
Kittie West
Mary Hughes
Mattie Waters
Martha Carson
Ella Clifford
Myrta Sadler
Mabel Starkweather
1892-95 – May (Lloyd) Miles
1895-96 – Bernice (Lloyd) Patterson
1898 - Belle (Lloyd) Bryan
E. J. Holt
Eunice Budd
Pearl Campbell
Nellie Purington
Margaret Walker
Lulu Weaver
1901 – Edna (Lloyd) Bryan
Cora Fairbanks
Belle Dennison
May Moore
Bessie McMurray
Minerva Jones
Harriett Blake
Maud Shreve
Lizzie Miles
Mina Shreve
Esther Nordrum
1912-18 – Lil George Haney
Irene Loomis
Grace O'Leary
Mrs. Meister
1923-25 – Frances Bell
1926-29 – Mary Montgomery
Mrs. Potter Porter
1931-33 – June Ramsey
1935-36 – Ruth Maas
1936-38 – Orpha McLaughlin
Mrs. Ray Manion

Clara Reese
1938-39 – Frances Francis
1940-43 – Helen Gransee
1944 – Mrs. Clara Reese
1943-44 – Helen Klug
1944-46 – Ruby Templeton
1946-48 – Mrs. Claramae Moldenhauer
1948-62 – Mrs. Doris Roberts of 124 N. First, Evansville, WI (the last teacher at this school)

List of Students

Alan, Kenneth
Atkinson, Judith (Dennison)
Babler, Linda (Dennison) (beginning in 1950)
Boettcher, Sue (Dennison)
Burns, Alice (Dennison)
Collins, Charlotte (Brunsell)
Crans, Beverly (Dennison)
Cronin, Dawn (Dennison)
Dennison, Arthur
Glock, Brenda (Dennison)
Haney, Lil (George)
Howard, Mildred (Allen)
Leeder, Dale
Leeder, Rodney
Reddy, Dorothy (Thompson)
Rice, Arlene (Alan)
Templeton, Ruth (Alan)
Traxler, Rebecca (Dennison)

Graduates in 1942

Crawford, Rodney
Denison, Fred
Dunbar, Raymond
Hunt, Emma
Lange, Marvin

Graduates in 1944

Dunbar, Alma A.
Leeder, Janice I.

Students taught by Ruby Templeton in 1944-45

Abey, Janis
Allen, Donald
Allen, Janet
Dunbar, Betty
Dunbar, Lilas
Dunbar, Wayne
Elmer, Joan
Farrel, Charles
Golz, Jean
Harnack, Carol

Hunt, Howard
Leeder, Dean
Leeder, Lee
Templeton, Ardis

Graduates in 1948

Allen, Donald
Dunbar, Lilas E.
Golz, Jean
Leeder, Jack

Graduates in 1962

Harding, Dolores
Harding, Robert
Harnack, Dolores
Porter, James

Board Members

Mrs. Grace Brunsell
Mark Brunsell (Clerk in 1952-53 and 1955-56)
Harold Robinson (Director in 1952-53)
Mrs. Wilma Maas (Treasurer in 1952-53, 1955-56 and 1961-62)
Willis Harnack (Director in 1955-56)
Elmer Allen
Walter George
Mrs. Elsie Hunt
Austin Hunt
Mrs. Sarah M. Dunbar (Clerk in 1961-62)
Howard J. Hunt (Director in 1961-62)

Photographs

Pleasant Prairie School in 1944-45. <u>First row, left to right:</u> Carol Harnack, Charles Farrel, Lee Leeder, Jack Leeder, Betty Dunbar, Ardis Templeton, and Janis Abey. <u>Second row, left to right:</u> Janet Allen (or Joan Elmer?), Lilas Dunbar, Dean Leeder, Wayne Dunbar, Donald Allen, Jean Golz, and Howard Hunt. <u>Back left:</u> Ruby Templeton (teacher). Courtesy of Jack Leeder.

Pleasant Prairie School during the 1947-48 school year. Courtesy of Rock County Historical Society.

Pleasant Prairie School in June 2015. Courtesy of the author.

Pleasant Prairie School in June 2015. Courtesy of the author.

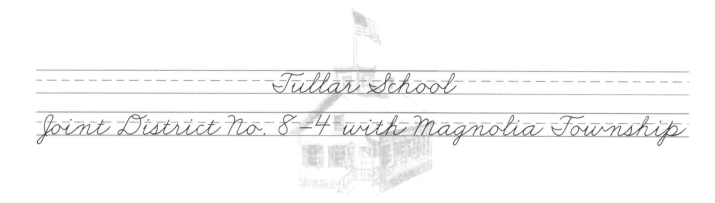

Tullar School
Joint District No. 8-4 with Magnolia Township

Years of Operation

1860-1962 (Section 32) on Croft Road – just east of Finn Road.

Memories

"One day at Tullar School, as we were getting ready for dismissal, the flag chairman went out to get the flag. The wind was blowing very hard and took the rope and flag out of his hand. We were quite disturbed as to what to do, when one of the parents came after his child and was able to get the flag with a long stick, for which we were very much relieved and thankful." – Hazel Murphy (teacher)

History

HISTORY OF TULLAR SCHOOL
by an unknown author

(Courtesy of Rock County Historical Society)

"Tullar School was built about 1860 on land owned by M. M. Tullar. The district, #8, was composed of Sections #1 and #32 and the southwest half of Section #33. The building was in Section #32 on Croft Road and the district was named for the Tullar family. It was a very well built brick building, supposedly the sturdiest in Union Township.

There was an active Mother's Club and an Extension Club called the Neighborly Club which continued to function for a few years after the school closed in 1962. In 1984 the building was demolished to make room for a new home built by Franklin Leeder.

Some of the early families were: Carter, Tullar, Francis, Higday, Jackman, Powell, Taggart, Robinson, Jones, Keyes, Bryan, Gibbs, Zenas, Hatfield and Snashall. Later: Finn, German, Webb, Lewis, Lamb, Disch, Parsons, Haynes, Waelti, Klitzman, Francis, Abey, Milbrant, Croft, and Ringhand.

Some teachers are: Mrs. Newman, the first teacher, Marica Van Wort, Loa Webb, Hazel Behling Green, Alma Janes, Arlie Ramsey, Corinne Murwin Apfel, Ina Bly, 9 years, Marion Holm, Madelyn Rowald, Cornelia Tilley, Claramae Moldenhouer, Frances Francis, Elizabeth Baker, Miss Elanor Villella, Harold Miller, Jean O'Brien, Hazel Murphy, Irma Smith and Helen Ginner in 1961 and '62, the last teacher."

Tullar School was supported by the Neighborly Club. John and Dennis Bullard of the Tupper School played in the rural band at the teachers' convention in Madison in February 1956. Tullar School was attached to the Evansville School District after closing.

List of Teachers

1860 – Mrs. Newman (first teacher)
Marcia Van Wort
Loa Webb
Hazel Behling Green
Alma Janes
Arlie Ramsey
Ina Bly (taught 9 years)
Marion Holm
Madelyn Rowald
Eleanor Villella
Harold Miller
Jean O'Brien
Hazel Murphy
Irma Smith
1925-26 – Corinne Murwin Apfel
1938-41 – Cordelia Tilley
1941-42 – Julia Williams
1942-44 – Mrs. Cordelia Tilley
1944-46 – Claramae Moldenhauer
1946-47 – Frances Francis
1947-51 – Elizabeth Baker
1952-53 – Mrs. Helen Ginner of Brooklyn, WI
1955-56 – Harold L. Miller of Evansville, WI
1961-62 – Helen Ginner

List of Students

Kopp, Walter (attended in 1937-39)

Class of 1925-26

Anderson, Anna
Anderson, Estella
Anderson, Nellie
Croft, Hazel
Croft, Louis
Croft, Mabel
Croft, Mildred
Croft, Thomas
Disch, Ardys
Jones, Clifford
Jones, Dorothy
Jones, Ralph
Klitzman, Virgil
Lamb, Donald
Lamb, Ruth
Morrison, Bernice
Morrison, Doris
Scherer, John
Scherer, Willie

Thornton, Avis
Thornton, Rex

Graduate in 1942

Parsons, Theodore

Graduates in 1944

Dewey, Mary Jane
Douglass, Rodney
Seils, Harold
Steindl, Eldora

Graduate in 1948

Steindl, Charlotte

Graduate in 1952

Croft, Sue Ann

Board Members

Mrs. Eleanor Swartzlow
Mrs. Dorothy Schrader
Ora J. Green
Mrs. Lawrence Miller
D. F. Finnane
Mrs. Ernest Miller
Mrs. O. F. Popanz
E. L. Dewey (Clerk in 1952-53)
Geraldine Topp (Clerk in 1955-56)
Eldon Klitzman (Director in 1955-56)
Spencer Porter (Treasurer in 1952-53 and 1955-56)
Orville Popanz
Merrill Hyne

Birdell Douglas served as clerk of the Tullar school board and was re-elected several times.

Ben Disch served as a member of the board in the 1940's to at least 1952-53.

Photographs

Tullar School in Fall of 1925. Photo by teacher Corrine Apfel. Courtesy of Rock County Historical Society.

Tullar School in Spring 1926. Courtesy of Rock County Historical Society.

Tullar School during the 1925-26 school year. Teacher Corinne Apfel's 1923 Ford is shown in the photo.

Tullar School in Fall 1925. Teacher Corrine Apfel is on far left.

Tullar School in Spring 1926.

Tullar School Reader's Circle Certificate dated June 3, 1938 for Walter Kopp. Courtesy of Walter Kopp.

Tullar School Reading Circle diploma for Walter Kopp dated May 1939, and signed by teacher Mrs. Cordelia Tilley.
Courtesy of Walter Kopp.

Tullar School during the 1947-48 school year. Courtesy of Rock County Historical Society.

Tullar School in 1975. Courtesy of Wisconsin Historical Society, Reference Number 84100.

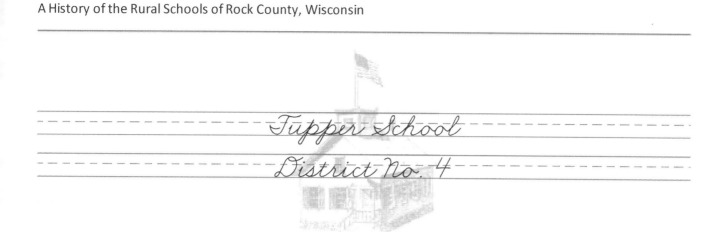

Years of Operation

1846-1868 (Section 13) on the south side of Bullard Road and Murray Road, which extended straight across to County Trunk M.

1868-1959 (Section 13) a quarter mile north of County Trunk M on Tupper Road.

History

HISTORY OF TUPPER SCHOOL IS REVIEWED
By Ellen Bullard

(Courtesy of Rock County Historical Society)

"Exactly 15 years ago, in the July 18, 1959 issue of The Evansville Review, School District No. 4, known as Tupper District, a 113 year old school was officially annexed July 10, 1959 to the Evansville School District No. 6.

At this time District No. 6 assumed the liabilities and assets of District No. 4. No opposition to the closing of the school was presented by the Evansville or Tupper School boards when they met June 8, 1959 at the old school house. Twenty two children from the Tupper School entered Evansville Elementary School as a result of this decision. Two other pupils, Sharon Bullard and Gordon Odegaard entered high school as freshmen and those already in high school were John and Dennis Bulard and Ruth Johnson.

It wasn't easy for some of the older generation to vote for the closing of the old landmark for its history was intertwined with that of the families of the community. But members of the district had to face between a big building program to meet state education requirements or annexation.

Tupper District was started in 1846 when a transfer of one half acre of land from John Tupper, for whom the school was named was made to the district. The first school house was built at the south end of Murray Rd., which continued at that time straight across County Trunk M. In 1868 another transfer from John Tupper to the school district was made and the school house was moved to this new half-acre lot which remained the site of the school until the present time.

In looking back it was found that one member of the Bullard family had been on the school board every year since 1866, Frank Bullard, father of Laurence, was elected to the school board for 56 consecutive years. Other Bullards who served are Hiram, Elmer, Lawrence, Robert and Ellen. This covers a period of 98 years.

First entry in the treasurer's books was Nov. 10, 1867, from Hiram Bullard with William Morrow serving as treasurer. Jane Cleveland was hired as teacher with wages of $120. In 1867 the school started with a small income: Tax for teacher's wages, $10; tax for wood, $30; state and county tax, $78.22.

The late Sylvia (Tupper) Colony, aunt of Laurence Bullard, was one of the early teachers, beginning in 1890 at a salary of $20 per month for a period of three months.

Myrtle Green, who retired from the Evansivlle School System, began teaching at Tupper in 1900 at $25 per month.

Alma Brunsell Sumner, mother of Will Sumner of Evansville, began her teaching career at Tupper in 1907 at $30 a month. This was the first time that a nine month term had been held.

Soon after this period a steady rise in teacher's wages took place with Clara Furseth receiving a wage of $100 a month in 1920.

Hazel Murphy, who still resides in Evansville, began her 26-year career of teaching in the same school in 1925.

In 1924 a new slate blackboard was installed at a cost of $21.97; a 50-foot well was dug in July of 1925, by John Hockett at a cost of $14; the first electricity was installed in September, 1939.

The school was run in 1884 at a cost of $41.85 per year but in 1958 the cost had reached $4,500.

Some of the teachers who will be remembered at Tupper School are Olive Warren, Nath Libby, F. Janes, R. Ahara, Cora Cadwallader, Sylvia Tupper, Edith Graves, Martha Carson, Nina Jones, Myrtle Green, Emma Holt, Marie Green, Maude Gibbs, Marie Eberlein, Alma Brunsell, Alice Murray, Charity Winsor, Robert Hall, Clara Lamb, Hazel Bourbeau, Alice Milbrant, Clara Furseth, Mary Baird, Hazel Murphy, and Berdette Weissphennig.

In 1959, when the school was closed, Mrs. Fred Heller served as clerk on the school board; Mrs. Robert Bullard was treasurer, and John Brunsell, director."

HISTORY OF TUPPER SCHOOL
by unknown author

(Courtesy of the Rock County Historical Society)

"Tupper School was founded in 1846 when a transfer of one half acre of land was made from John Tupper to the district, which is composed of Sections 13, 14, 24, east ½ of Section 15 and east ½ of Section 23. It is District #4. The first school was located on the south side of Bullard Road on Murray Road, which at that time extended straight across to County Trunk M. The building was in the Southwest quarter of Section 13.

In 1868 another transfer was made by John Tupper to the district of one half acre of land which remained the site of the school to the present time. It was one quarter mile north of County Trunk M on Tupper Road.

The school was named for the Tupper family.

The first entry in the treasurer's book was November 10, 1867 by Hiram Bullard. There was a Bullard on the School Board all of the 113 years existence of the school.

Jane Cleveland was the first teacher being paid $120. for the school year.

Sylvia Tupper Colony, aunt of Laurence Bullard, began teaching in 1890 at a salary of $20 per month for three months.

Myrtle Green began teaching in 1900 at $25. per month.

Alma Brunsell Sumner mother of Will Sumner, Jr. began her teaching career at Tupper in 1907 at $30. per month. This was the first time a nine months term was held.

Wages rose steadily after that. In 1925 Hazel Murphy received $125. per month. She taught Tupper for twenty six years, form 1925 to 1951. She had a life total of 45 years teaching.

In 1924 a slate blackboard was installed at a cost of $21.97. A fifty foot well was dug in 1925 by Jon Hockett at a cost of $104. Before that water was carried from a neighboring farm. Gillies Spooner remembers carrying water with another student and by the time they reached the school sometimes little was left. Elecricity was installed in September of 1939 and a telephone in 1950.

In comparison, the school was run at a cost of $41.85 per month in 1884 but by 1959 expenditures had increased to $4,500 for the year.

The whole school went to the nearby George Severson farm to hear President Coolidge's inauguration speech on the radio in 1924.

Some of the family names from the 1860s and later are: Whellock, Dudley, Carvell, Tupper, Bullard, Bishop, Cunningham, Boyd, Tuttle, McMillan, Clark, Blackman, Abbott, Lockwood, Van Patten, Demster, Ballard, Gillett, Jones, Searles, Norton, Jorgenson, Murray, Phelps, Odegaard, Gillies, Spooner, Wall, Cole, Brunsell, Holm, Barnard, Elmer, Pearson, Graves, Hall, Glidden, Moe, Siles, Ehredt, Leeder, Hermanson, and Reese. Louis Reese was born on the farm in the district and lived there all his life which ended December 28, 1983. A grandnephew now lives on the farm.

Five generations of the Bullard family attended Tupper. Robert Bullard still lives in the district as do Odegaard, Phelps, Jorgensen and Spooner families.

Tupper had a Mothers' Club, and the community club, We Are Neighbors, was formed in connection with the school and functioned until 1960. It was truly a community center.

The district had to decide between a big building program to meet state standards and annexation so on July 10, 1959 District #4, and the 113 year old school was officially annexed to Evansville, District #6 at which time District #6 assumed the assets and liabilities of District #4. In 1959 when the school closed Mrs. Fred Heller was clerk, Mrs. Robert bullard, treasurer, and John Brunsell, Jr. director.

The school house was razed in 1974 and a home built on the grounds. It is the home of Mr. and Mrs. Ray Weigand." [A list of teachers followed and are incorporated into the list below.]

The following article appeared in the July 18, 1974 edition of the Evansville Post, Inc.:

MEMORIES OF OLD TUPPER SCHOOL BURN IN FLAMES OF ROTTED WOOD

'Forty years ago, I'd been happy to set fire to it myself,' said one alumnus laughingly when told the old Tupper school, on Bullard Rd., would be torn down to make way for a new home.

He didn't really mean it he said, and there are others who attended the old frame school house on the hill who feel a little bit sentimental about it. One of these is Louis Reese who still lives down the road a bit, the farm he was born on almost 68 years ago. He remembers lugging water to the school from the farm on which the school ground had been carved out of. It is now occupied by Robert Wustmann who purchased it recently. He also remembers going out to the nearby woodshed to get wood for the big round wood-burning stove.

Mrs. Alice Denison, who taught at the school for five years, from 1915 to 1919, said it was a good district to teach in. 'Everyone was nice to me. The children were well behaved.' Louis Reese is one of her former students.

Hazel Murphy said the years she taught at Tupper school were 'wonderful years. The children were good.'

Miss Murphy who taught at the school for 26 years, helped train any number of student-teachers from the Rock County Normal School, Janesville, while teaching at Tupper.

Several of the students came out from the Normal School for one week in spring and two weeks in fall.

Miss Murphy taught for 45 years, including six years as substitute teacher in the Evansville school system. The Evansville school children also happened to be well-behaved, attentive children remembers Alice Murphy. She added that she is really glad the old school house is being dismantled. 'It has looked so bad lately that I'm glad that is being torn down.'

Mrs. Henry Julseth, who attended school as Isabel Bullard, remembers the Christmas programs, the little plays and recitations that the school put on for the entertainment of the parents, and the beautifully decorated baskets at the box socials, held once a year.

She remembers one occasion when a boy was to be punished for a transgression by remaining after school, his chum opened a window from the outside from which the culprit escaped.

Mrs. Robert Bullard, who was school district treasurer when the old school was closed in 1959, has a small bronze bell momento [sic] which was used to announce that the school was in session in the mornings, at recess, and at noon hour. There was a Bullard on the School Board every year of the 113 years of the school district's existence.

Mrs. Grace Brunsell, who graduated from the school in 1908, remembers such teachers as Emma Holt, Maud Gibbs and Alma Brunsell Sumner, and also remembers the fun that took place at the school such as the box socials and the other special school entertainments.

The school was closed in 1959 when School District No. 4 (Tupper School) was annexed to the Evansville School District (No. 6). It had been decided that the many improvements and additions that were necessary to meet state education requirements meant a big building program. The choice was between annexation and an extensive building program.

Tupper School began in 1846 when a one-half acre of land on Murray Road was transferred from the land of John Tupper for whom the school was named. Later, the school house was moved to another Tupper one-acre plot on Tupper Road. Berdette Weissphennig who taught the school for five years, was the last teacher. She had 22 pupils that year. Members of the last School Board were John Brunsell; director; Mrs. Fred Heller, school clerk; and Mrs. Robert Bullard, treasurer.

The school included two entrances, boys on the left and the girls on the right. The entrances were partitioned off from each other and each had a small cloakroom. There were outhouses, popularly known as Chick Sales at one time, for the two sexes - - and the woodhouse.

Mr. and Mrs. Raymond Weigand will put up a new one-story home on the old school house landsite after the old building is down. Ray Weigand is agricultural teacher at the Evansville High School."

HISTORY OF TUPPER SCHOOL DISTRICT
By an unknown author (circa 1946-47)

"Some of the early pioneer settlers of Tupper School district were Stilman Bullard, John Tupper, Gillman Searles, Hiram Bullard, Jonathan Blackman, Hiram Bishop and James Bullard.

The Hiram Bullard farm now occupied and owned by Laurence Bullard has been in the same family for more than one hundred and one years. The house on this farm is a brick structure and was erected in 1868 by Hiram Bullard. An Indian trail may also be seen in the woods on this farm.

The second highest hill in Rock County may be seen on what is now the farm owned by John Brunsell. The early stage coach road between Janesville and Madison passed by this farm.

The original school building is still being used and is located on land which was purchased from the John Tupper farm. It is a frame structure and has gradually been modernized from time to time.

Some of the first teachers were Jane Cleveland, Olive Warren, Flora Janes, Sylvia Tupper, Cora Cadwallader, Edith Graves, Maude Ludington and Myrtle Green. The most any one received per month was $25. And the least $16. per month.

While Miss Olive Warren was teaching, a messenger, who came on horseback, came to the school door and told her Lincoln had been shot. He was going from place to place delivering the news of the assassination, which was soon after April 14, 1865.

In 1883 the entire expenses for maintaining the school were $79.95. They used cord wood for fuel, and the other supplies were a broom and a box of chalk.

Frank Bullard was elected treasurer in 1891, and held the same office until his death Sept. 10, 1942. This office is now being held by his son Laurence Bullard.

Lester Bullard, another son of Frank Bullard, helped build the Panama Canal, serving as an engineer. He died in 1947.

The present teacher Miss Hazel Murphy has taught in the district for twenty-two years continuously and is now receiving $200 per month for the school year 1946-1947."

(Source: Area Research Center, Andersen Library, University of Wisconsin-Whitewater, Whitewater, WI; Rock 39, Box 3, Folder 17.)

List of Teachers

1865 – Olive Warren
1867 – Jane Cleveland (first teacher)
1890 – Sylvia (Tupper) Colony
1900 – Myrtle Green (received $25.00 per month)
1907 – Alma Brunsell Sumner (began her teaching career at Tupper – received $30.00 per month)
Maude Ludington
Nath Libby
Flora Janes
R. Ahara
Cora Cadwalladar
Edith Graves
Martha Carson
Nina Jones
Emma Holt
Marie Green
Maude Gibbs
Marie Eberlein
Alice Murray
Charity Winsor
Robert Hall

1912 – Clara Lamb
Hazel Bourbeau
1915-17 – Alice Milbrant (aka Alice Denison?)
1920 – Clara Furseth
Mary Baird
Verna Schmeling
1925-51 – Hazel Murphy (received $125.00 per month in 1925 and $200.00 per month in 1946-47)
Helen Naysmith
1952-53 – Robert Hedman of Rte. 3, Evansville, WI
Bonnie Vandervort
Circa 1955-59 - Berdette Weissphennig of Evansville, WI (the last teacher)

List of Students

Brunsell, Grace (graduated in 1908)

Students attending in 1912
Bullard, Isabel (Mrs. Henry Julseth)
Reese, Esther
Reese, Florence
Reese, Louis

Class of 1926-27
Anderson, Elizabeth
Ballard, Evalyn
Ballard, Homer
Ballard, Wayne
Bone, Alvin
Bone, Norman
Brunsell, Edith
Brunsell, Rollo
Bullard, Larry
Graves, Edith
Graves, Jim
Jorgensen, May
Jorgensen, Phil
Julseth, Vera
Moe, Agnes
Moe, Leonard
Moe, Ruby
Odegaard, Alice
Odegaard, Gerda
Phelps, Beth
Phelps, Dana
Phelps, Esther
Phelps, Roy
Spooner, Elizabeth
Spooner, Gillies
Starks, Albert
Starks, Bessie
Starks, Frank
Sturdevant, Alta

Sturdevant, Dorothy
Sturdevant, LeRoy
Sturdevant, Thelma

Graduates in 1942

Brunsell, Ruth
Jorgensen, Robert
McPherson, Marlan

Graduate in 1944

Brunsell, Richard

Class of 1954-55

Brunsell, Connie
Brunsell, Steve
Bullard, Dennis
Bullard, John
Bullard, Sharon
Bullard, Vicki
Erickson, Jean
Erickson, Joyce
Heller, Kenney
Odegaard, Gordon
Odegaard, Suzy
Phelps, Joyce Ann
Rawley, Clifford
Spanton, Donny
Spanton, Judy
Spooner, Gail
Spooner, Mary
Spooner, Tom
Wilson, Claria
Wilson, Jerome

Class of 1958-59

Brunsell, Connie
Brunsell, Dale
Brunsell, Steven
Bullard, Sharon
Chapin, Kanny
Fiese, Candy
Fiese, David
Fiese, Russell
Fiese, Vicky
Heller, David
Heller, Kenny
Heller, Richard
Johnson, Jimmy
Jorgensen, Steven
Odegaard, David
Odegaard, Gordon
Odegaard, Suzie

Spanton, Donald
Spanton, Joyce
Spanton, Judy
Wilson, Clariece

Board Members

Hiram Bullard (1867)
William Morrow (Treasurer in 1867)
Norman Odegaard (Clerk in 1952-53 and 1955-56)
Albert Starks (Director in 1952-53)
Robert Bullard (Treasurer in 1952-53)
Gilles Spooner
Joe Tait
Lawrence Bullard (Treasurer in 1940's)
Harley Brunsell
Katherine Hatlen
John Brunsell (Director in 1955-59)
Frank Bullard (Treasurer circa 1891-1942)
Elmer Bullard
Ellen Bullard
Ed Jorgenson
Mrs. Fred Heller (Clerk in 1959)
Mrs. Robert Bullard (Treasurer in 1955-59)

Photographs

Tupper School during the 1947-48 school year. Courtesy of Rock County Historical Society.

Tupper School in 1954-55. First row: Vicki Bullard, Judy Spanton, Steve Brunsell, Clarice Wilson, Joyce Erickson, and Mary Spooner. Second row: Suzy Odegaard, Joyce An Phelps, Connie Brunsell, Donny Spanton, and Kenney Heller. Third row: Gordon Odegaard, Jerome Wilson, Tom Spooner, Clifford Rowley, Sharon Bullard. Fourth row: Jean Erickson, Gail Spooner, John Bullard, and Dennis Bullard. Berdette Weisphennig was the teacher at the time. Courtesy of Rock County Historical Society.

Tupper School. "Building a Wigwam." Courtesy of Rock County Historical Society.

3-14
—Gazette photo
SPACE TOURISTS—Some of the sights seen on a trip through space were described by pupils of the Tupper School, Rte. 1, Evansville, on WCLO Schooltime. They were, front row from left, Steve Brunsell, David Heller, Dale Brunsell, Don Spanton, Jim Johnson; second row, David Fiese, Richard Heller, Steve Johnson, Kenny Chapin; third row, Joyce Spanton, Vicki Bullard, Vicki Fiese; fourth row, Clarice Wilson, Candy Fiese, Judith Spanton, Connie Brunsell, Kenneth Heller; back row, Miss Berdette Weissphennig, teacher, Russell Fiese, Gordon Odegaard, Sharon Bullard, Susie Odegaard.

Newspaper clipping from The Janesville Gazette, Janesville, Wisconsin, March 14, 1959. Pictured are Steve Brunsell, David Heller, Dale Brunsell, Don Spanton, Jim Johnson, David Fiese, Richard Heller, Steve Johnson, Kenny Chapin, Joyce Spanton, Vicki Bullard, Vicki Fiese, Clarice Wilson, Candy Fiese, Judith Spanton, Connie Brunsell, Kenneth Heller, Russell Fiese, Gordon Odegaard, Sharon Bullard, and Susie Odegaard.

Tupper School Is Demolished

The 128 year old Tupper School which is located on Tupper Road, north east of the city of Evansville, is now in the process of being torn down. See story on Page 8 of this issue.

Newspaper clipping from the Evansville Review, July 18, 1974, p. 1, col. 1-3, Evansville, Wisconsin.

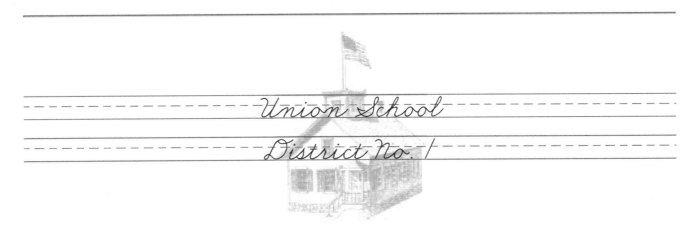

Years of Operation

1841-1877 (Section 10) – A log building.

1877-After 1955 – on East Union Road a quarter mile east of Highway 14. Located at 15100 W East Union Road.

History

Union School was attached to Evansville School District after closing.

List of Teachers

1892 – O. G. Green
1942 – Marion Holm
1944 – Geneva Bacon
1948-56 – Mrs. Ruth Templeton of 315 Lincoln St., Evansville, WI
1961-62 – Rosella Borgen of 213 N. 6th, Madison, WI

List of Students

Students attending in 1892

Brunsell, Fred
Davis, Leslie
Elwood, Ray
Fairbanks, Cora
Fairbanks, Frank
Fairbanks, Maud
Fairbanks, Milton
Frost, Dora
Gillies, Maud
Johnson, Johnny
Johnson, Olga
Jorgensen, Ed
Jorgensen, Henry
Lee, Minnie
Sweeney, Jim
Sweeney, Mary
Wall, Daisy
Wall, Harley

Students attending in 1898

Benway, Edith
Fairbanks, Flora
Benway, Sid
Dennison, Belle
Stewart, Hattie
Barry, Edna
Frost, Adele
Benway, Julia
Wall, Harley
Knutson, Jens
Knutson, John
Frost, Frank
Stewart, Bill
Brunsell, Fred
Scotsberg, _____
Jepson, Ann
Brunsell, Dora
Fairbanks, Edith
Lincoln, Minnie
Davis, Blaine
Gibbs, Earl
Fairbanks, Frank
Benway, Mabel
Wall, Daisy
Jepson, Clarence
Jepson, Agnes
Rosa, Lora
Wall, Lennie
Ham, Charlie
Brunsell, Alma
Ham, Kate
Brunsell, Clara
Wall, Floyd

Graduate in 1942

Wall, Carol

Graduates in 1944

Larson, Louise
Rosa, Cathryn

Graduate in 1948

Matson, Darlene

Graduates in 1952

Hopper, Gordon
Rosa, Harris
Seversen, Patricia
Wilson, Janice

Board Members

Mrs. Charles Kaste (Clerk in 1952-53, 1955-56 and 1961-62)
Mrs. Lawrence Rosa (Director in 1952-53 and 1955-56)
Kenneth Gilbertson (Treasurer in 1952-53 and 1955-56)
Delores Quam (Director in 1961-62)
Donald R. Cornwell (Treasurer in 1961-62)

Photographs

Union School during the 1947-48 school year. Courtesy of Rock County Historical Society.

Union School in 1975. Courtesy of Wisconsin Historical Society, Reference Number 83459.

Union School in June 2015. Courtesy of the author.

Union School in June 2015. Courtesy of the author.

Index of Names

Bowles, Louis 176

Bowles, Lucille 176, 185

Bowles, Mary 176

Bowles, May 176

Bowles, Nellie 176

Bowles, Vivian 175

Bowles, W. E. 181

Bowles, Warren 176

Bowles, Willie 176

Bown, Hazel 213

Boyle, Grace 27

Boynton, Ardis 230, 233

Boynton, Calvin 176

Boynton, Ellie 176

Boynton, Flora Belle 29

Boynton, Forest 176

Boynton, J. 181

Boynton, James 176, 181

Boynton, Jay 176

Braaten, Margaret 131

Bradey, Janet 54

Bradford, Elmer 234

Bradford, Florence 26

Bradie, Jackie 54

Brady, Janet 55

Brandt, John 120

Brannon, Patricia 31

Brigham, Bernice 28

Brink, Jean 132

Brinkman, William 55

Brooks, Harold 92

Brooks, Melvin 92

Brooks, Violette 92

Broughton, Doris 31

Brown, Anna 31

Brown, Bernice 28

Brown, Rose 141

Brunhofer, Willie 204

Brunsell, Alma 324

Brunsell, Clara 324

Brunsell, Connie 316

Brunsell, Dale 316

Brunsell, Dora 324

Brunsell, Edith 315

Brunsell, Fred 323

Brunsell, Grace 295, 313, 315

Brunsell, Harley 317

Brunsell, John 312, 317

Brunsell, Mark 295

Brunsell, Richard 316

Brunsell, Rollo 315

Brunsell, Ruth 316

Brunsell, Steve 316, 321

Brunsell, Steven 316

Bryan, Belle 293

Bryan, Edna 293

Bryan, Madelene 306

Bryan, S. 292

Bryant, Cora 155

Bryant, Fannie 29

Bryant, Mamie 28

Bryant, Oran 132

Bublitz, Laura 28

Bublitz, Wilma 28

C

Drafahl, Peter 52, 55

Draves, Clara 263

Dressel, Dorothy 252

Dresser, Ardis 233

Dresser, Carrie 233

Dresser, E. C. 235

Dresser, Eunice 234

Dresser, Irene 228, 234

Dresser, Jeanette 234

Dresser, Marston 233

Drevdahl, Gladys 31, 106

Drew, Margaret 29, 130, 175

Drew, Mary 29

Duchow, Mrs. Fredrick 142

Duggan, Betty 94

Duggan, Robert 66

Dunbar, Alma A. 294

Dunbar, Betty 294

Dunbar, Lilas 288, 294

Dunbar, Lilas E. 295

Dunbar, Marian 51, 53

Dunbar, Raymond 294

Dunbar, Sarah M. 295

Dunbar, Wayne 294

Dunn, Gladys 27

Duoss, Clara 29

Duoss, Esther 29

Duoss, Isabel 31

Dutcher, Clarence 177

Dwyer, Virginia 28

Dybevick, J. B. 181

Dybevik, Eunice 177

Dybevik, Lillian 30, 155, 160, 177

Dybevik, Nina 177, 185

Dybevik, Ruth 168, 177

Dybevik, Stanley 173, 177, 187

Dybevik, Wilma 177

Dyson, Celesta 232

E

Eberlein, Marie 314

Eddy, Clara 212

Eddy, Florence 30

Egan, Richard 154

Egery, Minnie 232, 263

Ehlenfeldt, Myrtle 27

Ehlert, Rodney 112

Ehlert, Roy 113

Ehredt, Patricia 284

Ehredt, Wilbur 284

Ehredt, William 284

Ehret, Harriet 92

Ehrlinger, Rachel 26

Eidahl, Orian 156

Ellis, Arthur 278

Ellis, Clifford 277-278

Ellis, Esther 213

Ellis, Frances 284

Ellis, Kenneth 278

Ellis, Marvin 284

Ellis, Mrs. Ed 278

Elmer, Donald 284

Elmer, Joan 294

Elwood, Ray 323

Empereur, Marilyn 54

Hale, Mary O. 232

Hall, Belle 178

Hall, Elida 22, 28

Hall, Lettie 174

Hall, Robert 314

Halsey, Eliza 178

Ham, Charlie 324

Ham, Kate 324

Hamblett, Abbie 178

Hamblett, Eliza D. 122

Hamblett, Eva 28

Hamilton, Lulu D. 28

Hammell, Howard 224

Han, Paul 220

Haney, Lil 270, 278, 294

Haney, Lil George 281, 291, 293

Hannahs, Alex 223

Hannahs, B. F. 224

Hannahs, Ben 223

Hannahs, Lenora 224

Hannahs, Mark 224

Hannewell, Alice 30

Hannewell, Lorraine 30

Hanry, A. G. 52, 54

Hansche, Grace 204

Hansche, John 204

Hansen, Verdelma 94

Hanson, Delbert 156

Hanson, Marie 27

Hanson, Nina 29

Hanson, Rosalyn 31

Hanson, Stanley 178

Hard, Fred 213

Harding, Dolores 295

Harding, Robert 295

Harnack, Carol 294, 296

Harnack, Dolores 295

Harnack, Willis 295

Harper, Bee 174

Harper, Ella 178

Harper, Helen 178

Harper, James 178

Harper, Jessie E. 174

Harper, Malcolm J. 174

Harper, Marion 178

Harper, R. J. 181

Harper, Susan 174

Harper, Susie 178

Harper, Tena 178

Harper, Thomas 178

Harriet, Bill 38

Harrington, C. S. 173

Harrington, Clarinda S. 173

Harrington, Helen 174, 178

Harrington, Minnie 178

Harris, Emma 178

Harris, J. W. 124

Harris, J.M. 36

Harris, M. Carrie 232

Harris, Mr. 124

Harris, Orrie 174, 178

Hart, Albert 178

Hart, George 178

Hart, Mary 178

J

Jack, Al 224

Jack, Osbert 203

Jackson, Delores 252-253

Jackson, Jean 252

Jacobs, Ella 27

Jacobs, Genevieve 27

Jacobson, Ella 20

Jacobson, Hyla 30

Jacobson, Louise 38

Jacobusse, Wallace 233

James, Ruth 29

Janes, Alma 301

Janes, Carrie 293

Janes, Donald 270

Janes, Eva 292

Janes, Flora 293, 314

Janes, Iva Mae 29

Janes, Melvin 270

Jeckert, Vern 224

Jeffris, T. M. 99

Jellyman, Florence 30

Jenkins, Norman 252

Jenny, Beverly 270

Jensen, Agnes 29

Jensen, Gerald K. 84

Jensen, Wanda 30

Jenson, Marie 283

Jepson, Agnes 324

Jepson, Ann 324

Jepson, Clarence 324

John, Lena St. 142

Johns, Arlene 234

Johnson, Amy 28

Johnson, Anita 31

Johnson, Anton 156

Johnson, Bernice 178

Johnson, Esther 66

Johnson, Harold 130

Johnson, Ina 29

Johnson, Jenette 217

Johnson, Jimmy 316

Johnson, John 178

Johnson, Johnny 323

Johnson, Josephine 28

Johnson, Julius 131

Johnson, Kathryn 223-224

Johnson, Lucile 283

Johnson, Mabel 131

Johnson, Maggie 178

Johnson, Martha 38

Johnson, May 283

Johnson, Merrille 178

Johnson, Mildred 92

Johnson, Olga 323

Johnson, Orville 178

Johnson, Philip 287

Johnson, Sigurd 131

Johnson, Stanley 233, 235

Johnson, Ted 224

Johnson, Willie 204, 206

Johnston, Jeanette 27, 54

Johnston, Virginia 27

Jones, Ada 203

Kelsey, Edith 233

Kelsey, Lester 61

Kelsey, Margaret 233

Kelsey, Marie 61

Kemmerer, Walter 200

Kennedy, Elizabeth 60

Kennedy, Ellen E. 122

Kessler, Donald 92

Kettle, Dorothy 32

Kettle, Virginia 32

Kettlebone, F. 55

Kidder, Clark 1-2, 25, 210, 375

Kidder, Earl 8

Kidder, Joan 41

Kidder, Richard 43

Kilday, Kitty 178

Kilpatrick, Jennie 217

Kind, Arthur 215

Kinney, Miss 50, 53

Kirkpatrick, Betty 264

Kirkpatrick, Donna 264

Kitelinger, Alice 31

Kjelland, Carl 107

Klein, Nellie 233

Kleinsmith, Amber 283

Klick, Arnold 78

Klick, Jane Elizabeth 78

Klingburg, Mildred 31

Klitzman, Eldon 302

Klitzman, Mrs. Carl 284

Klitzman, Virgil 301

Kloften, Buelah Cole 283

Klug, Helen 294

Klusmeyer, Harold 271

Klusmeyer, Lois 270

Klusmeyer, Mabel 86, 97-98

Klusmeyer, William 107

Knauf, Ruth 66

Knight, Katherine 26

Knilans, Dr. A. J. 93

Knipp, Grace 91

Knoll, Dorothy 29

Knowles, Josephine 122

Knudson, Burnette 28

Knudson, Howard 155

Knueppel, Forrest D. 215

Knueppel, Julia 214

Knutson, Alice 28, 263

Knutson, Bertha 26

Knutson, Harold 29

Knutson, Jens 324

Knutson, John 324

Knutson, T. 124

Kohls, Alfred 233

Kohls, Janette Snyder 232

Kolberg, Alfred 78

Kolberg, Harlan 78

Kolman, Hylah 232

Kopp, Ernest 271

Kopp, Walter 301, 306

Kopp, Walter C. 270

Kopp., Walter C. 273

Kopplin, Harold 107

Korban, Edna 30

Lee, Barbara 123

Lee, Bennett 178

Lee, Carrie 28, 233, 263

Lee, Helen 178

Lee, Howard 123

Lee, Karoline 32

Lee, Marvin 178

Lee, Minnie 323

Lee, Mrs. Davey 123

Lee, Orville 123, 126

Leeder, Dale 294

Leeder, Dean 295

Leeder, Jack 290, 295

Leeder, Janice I. 294

Leeder, Lee 295

Leeder, Rodney 294

Leeport, Georgia 178

Lembrich, Alfred 83

Leng, Arice 111, 175

Leng, Elsie 178

Leng, Ethel 178

Leng, Harry 155

Leng, Lloyd 155

Leng, Marion 178

Leng, Oscar 178

Lewis, Achsah 232

Lewis, Edna 174

Lewis, Elizabeth 29

Lewis, Florence 141

Lhotok, Lillian 30

Libby, Jack 55

Libby, N. E. 292

Libby, Nath 314

Libby, Patricia 55

Libby, Roy 55

Libby, Shirley 55-56

Lichtfuss, Anne 99

Lien, Ella 26

Lincoln, Minnie 324

Linden, Mary 112-113

Linderud, Carol 32

Linney, Lorraine 30

Lipke, Josephine 31

Lippens, Andy 224

Lippens, Mildred 77, 213

Lippens, Ray 224

Liston, Bertha 27, 178

Liston, Conrad 178

Liston, Cora 178

Liston, Mabel 178

Liston, Oscar 178

Liston, Sofia 179

Liston, Stone 169, 181

Litch, Luella 31

Livingston, Alice 224

Lloyd, Raymond 84

Logan, Hazel 26

Logan, Nellie 27

Lokken, Serene 31

Long, Marion 32

Longbotham, G.T. 37

Longhenry, Susan 67, 78

Loofboro, Alice 26

Loofboro, Lewis 39

Nipple, Margaret 179

Nipple, Walter 156, 179

Nipple, Wayne 156, 159, 179

Nitz, William 87

Nodland, Charles 179

Nodland, Jesse 179

Nolan, Marie 66, 74, 83, 92

Nolan, Mary 155

Noonan, John 179

Norby, Leona 32

Norby, Martha Norum 282-283

Nordeng, Charles 156

Nordeng, George 156, 159

Nordeng, Pearl 155

Nordeng, Stanley 155

Nordrum, Esther 293

Northrup, Belle 203

Norum, Martha 26

Noss, LaVerne 87

Noss, Sidney 86

Nott, Albert F. 173

Noyes, Grant 179

Noyes, John 179

Noyes, Ralph 29

Noyes, Ruth 179

Noyes, Wesley 179

Nyberg, Irene 218

Nyman, Glen 181

Nyman, Marian 141-142, 149

Nyman, Mrs. William 181

Nyman, Orville 179

Nyman, Rona 142

Nyman, Shirley 179

Nyman, Thelma 29, 141, 179

O

O'Brien, Alfred 51, 53

O'Brien, Jean 301

O'Brien, Margaret 27

O'Leary, Charles 99

O'Leary, Eileen (Ryan) 86

O'Leary, Grace 293

O'Leary, Joe 84

O'Leary, John 84

O'Leary, Marie 29

O'Leary, Richard 83

O'Leary, Tom 83

Oberg, Clara 283

Ocher, Gladys 233

Odegaard, Alice 315

Odegaard, Bertha 283

Odegaard, David 316

Odegaard, Gerda 315

Odegaard, Gordon 316

Odegaard, Norman 317

Odegaard, Suzie 316

Odegaard, Suzy 316

Odegard, Bertha 29

Olin, Donald 179

Olin, Grant 73-74

Olin, Norman 142

Olin, Ramona 142

Olin, Thelma 123, 175

Oliver, J. B. 171, 181

Oliver, James 171, 181

Rehfeld, Rita 84

Reich, Anita 31

Reilly, Agnes 28

Reilly, Ann 29

Reimer, Billy 234

Reimer, Dorothy 234

Reimer, Gladys 233

Reimer, Harry Eugene 264

Reimer, Lulu 30

Reimer, Nellie 264

Reppen, Alice 31

Reuhlow, Albert 179

Reuhlow, Elsie 179

Reuhlow, Emma 179

Reuhlow, Minnie 179

Rhinehart, Pearl 156

Rhyner, Ada 141

Riaum, Herbert 132

Rice, Arlene 294

Rice, Blanche 38

Rice, Ella 124

Rice, Lucy 232

Richards, Beatrice 270

Richards, Emily 270

Richards, H.A. 36

Richards, Jane 174

Richards, Mrs. Bert 271

Richardson, Bernice 31

Richardson, Elver 67

Ridley, Marjorie 29

Riege, Cecelia 32

Riemer, Martha 264

Riemer, William L. 235

Riese, Pearl 142

Rindy, Alma 112-113

Rindy, Gehard 112-113

Rindy, Silva 112-113

Rindy, Sue 130

Ringhand, Roger 278

Risch, Mrs. Fred 61

Risch, Ronald 61

Risum, H. C. 126

Risum, Laura H. 155

Ritchart, Jill 60

Ritter, Fred F. 78

Robb, Harry 55

Robb, T. 55

Robbins, Judy 92

Roberts, Doris 288, 294

Roberts, Judd 252

Roberts, Lottie 293

Roberts, Ray 107

Robinson, Flora 26, 232

Robinson, Harold 295

Robinson, Luella 27

Robison, Lou B. 130, 134

Roeker, David 214

Roeker, Harold E. 215

Roen, Ella 27

Roen, Gladys 30

Roen, Lillian 28

Roen, Sylvia 29

Roenneburg, Louise Hintz 155

Rognstad, Mabel 31

Ulrich, Frank 224

Ulrich, Gertrude 224

Ulrich, Mary 224

Umland, Alice Mae 205

Umland, Billie 205

Umland, Fred 205

Umland, Margaret 205

Upson, Donald 37, 289

Upson, Donald E. 17, 37, 42-43, 73

Upson, Mr. 172

V

Valentine, Diane 271

Van Colter, Mansis 55

Van Colter, Ronnie 55

Van Galder, Nellie 213

Van Skike, Margaret 180

Van Skike, Robert 141, 145, 180

Van Skike, Roger 180

Vandervort, Bonnie 315

VanLandingham, Mrs. J. C. 218

Vaughan, Wilva 270

Veek, Myron 112-113

Veritatium, Q. W. 203

Vickerman, Alice 83

Vickerman, Loretta 28

Vickerman, Margaret 26

Vickerman, Marie 27

Vigdahl, Amanda 180

Vigdahl, Anna 180

Vigdahl, Bertina 180

Vigdahl, Charles 180

Vigdahl, Clifford 155, 180

Vigdahl, Ella 27, 98, 180

Vigdahl, Geneva 180, 189

Vigdahl, Isabelle 180

Vigdahl, Leona 180

Vigdahl, Lorraine 180

Vigdahl, Oscar 181

Vigdahl, Otto 180

Vigdahl, Viola 32, 175

Vigdahl, William 180, 189

Vigdal, Charles 156

Villella, Eleanor 301

Vobian, Maxine 66

Vogel, Betty 77

Vogel, Ethel 28

Vogel, Mabel 28

Vollhartd, Fred 180

Von Brocklin, Alice 94

Vorpagel, Yvonne 283

W

Wagner, Betty Jane 156

Waite, A. R. 52, 55

Waite, H. B. 293

Waite, Walter 200

Walker, Charles 218

Walker, Ethel 28

Walker, Jeanette 31

Walker, Margaret 293

Wall, Amy 283

Wall, Belle 180

Wall, Carol 324

Wall, Daisy 323

Wall, Floyd 324

Werle, Jeanene 278

Wesenberg, Robert 180

West, J. W. 36

West, Kittie 293

West, Orcelia 27

West, Wilva 31

Westby, Florence 27

Westby, Hazel 233

Whaley, Mildred 92

Wheeler, Anna 204

Wheeler, Beulah 29

Wheeler, Grace 263

White, Florence 28

White, Mae 27

Whitehead, Percy 113, 126

Whitford, A. C. 36

Whitmore, George 180

Whittier, John Greenleaf 18

Wichelt, Marie 130

Wieland, Katherine 28

Wieland, Margaret 27

Wierson, Delores 180

Wiggins, Gladys 30

Wilchelt, Anna 180

Wilchelt, August 180

Wilchelt, Bennie 180

Wilchelt, Bertha 180

Wilchelt, Jessa 180

Wilchelt, Ray 180

Wilchelt, Robert 180

Wilchelt, Willie 180

Wilder, Alice 26, 174

Wildermuch, Helen 219, 223

Wildermuth, Bob 234

Wildermuth, Ellen 213, 232

Wileman, Florence 28

Wilke, C. D. 142

Wilke, Claire 142

Wilke, Helen 31

Willard, Frances 65-66, 68, 91

Willard, Josiah 73-74

Williams, Darline 78

Williams, Eddie 180

Williams, Ella 174, 180

Williams, George 180

Williams, Julia 301

Williams, Marion 26

Williams, Nina 31

Williamson, Letha 31

Willing, Virginia 106

Willing, William 92

Willoughby, Claude 278

Wilson, Claria 316

Wilson, Clariece 317

Wilson, Janice 324

Wilson, Jerome 316

Wilson, Lucille 112

Winch, Madge 28

Winkley, Joyce 31

Winne, M. E. 232

Winsor, Charity 314

Wintlend, William 214

Witt, Christiane 214

Wobig, Alma 28

About the Author

Clark Kidder resides in Wisconsin. He is a freelance writer for international publications, and has authored several books, including Marilyn Monroe UnCovers (Quon Editions, 1994); Marilyn Monroe – Cover to Cover (Krause Publications, Inc., 1999); Marilyn Monroe Collectibles (Harper Collins, 1999); Orphan Trains and Their Precious Cargo (Willow Bend Books, 2001); Marilyn Monroe Memorabilia (Krause Publications, Inc., 2001); Marilyn Monroe – Cover to Cover, 2nd Ed. (Krause Publications, Inc., 2003), A Genealogy of the Wood Family, (Family Tree Publishers, 2003) and Emily's Story: The Brave Journey of an Orphan Train Rider (2007, 2014).

His magazine articles have appeared in The Wisconsin Magazine of History, and Family Tree Magazine.

Kidder was the recipient of the William Best Hesseltine Award in 2004 for his article titled West by Orphan Train, which appeared in the Winter 2003-2004 issue of the Wisconsin Magazine of History.

In 2013 Kidder co-wrote and co-produced the television documentary West by Orphan Train based on his book Emily's Story – The Brave Journey of an Orphan Train Rider.

Kidder has been interviewed by numerous reporters for articles in such newspapers as the Los Angeles Times, and the Chicago Tribune. His television appearances include MSNBC, PAX, WGN, Wisconsin Public Television and Iowa Public television. He has been interviewed on numerous radio shows around the nation, including Wisconsin Public Radio and Iowa Public Radio. Kidder was host of his own television show called Book Talk on JATV, in Janesville, Wisconsin. In addition, he has provided consultation and photographs for documentaries and television shows produced by CBS, and October Films in London, England.

He is past Vice President of the Milton Historical Society, which operates the Milton House Museum—a National Landmark located in Milton, Wisconsin. Kidder also does a book lecture on Orphan Train history around the Midwest, reading and showing photos via PowerPoint from his book Emily's Story: The Brave Journey of an orphan train rider. Details about booking Mr. Kidder for a lecture are given on his website listed below.

Contact Information:
Clark Kidder
E-mail: cokidder@hotmail.com
Website: www.clarkkidder.com

The Silent Bell

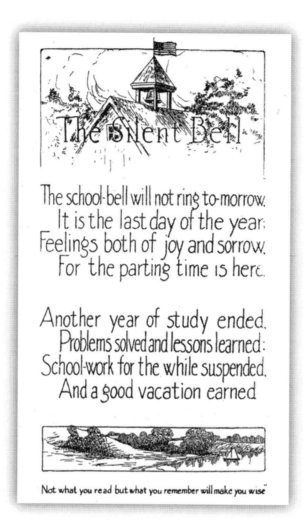

A page from the 1916 year-end souvenir booklet at Mary Miles School in Fulton Township.
Courtesy of the Rock County Historical Society.

The Builders

He wrought it with grace and skill,
Pillar and dome and arches all
He fashioned to work his will.
And the men said who saw its beauty,
"It shall never know decay,
Great is thy skill, Oh builder,
Thy fame shall live aye."

A teacher built a temple
With infinite love and care,
Planning each arch with patience
Laying each stone with prayer
None praised the unceasing efforts
None knew the wondrous plan
But the temple the teacher built
Was unseen by the eyes of man.

Gone is the builder's temple
Crumbled into the dust
Low lies each stately pillar
Food for the consuming rust.
But the temple the teacher built
Shall live while the ages roll
For the beautiful unseen temple
Was a child's immortal soul.

- Author unknown

22745875R00213

Made in the USA
San Bernardino, CA
20 July 2015